ACCESS TO JUSTICE AND INTERNATIONAL ORGANISATIONS

We live in a denial of justice age when it comes to the individual pursuit of justice against international organisations (IOs). Victims of institutional conduct are generally not provided reasonable means of dispute settlement at the international level. They also have been unable to seek justice at the national level due to IO immunities, which aim to secure institutional independence. Access to justice and IO independence are equally important values and realising them both has so far proven elusive. Private international law techniques can help allocate regulatory authority between the national and institutional orders in a nuanced manner by maintaining IO independence without sacrificing access to justice. As private international law rules can be adjusted nationally without the need for international action, the solution proposed can be readily implemented, thereby resolving a conundrum that public international law has not been able to address for decades.

Dr Rishi Gulati has a Bachelor of Laws (Hons) from the Australian National University, Advanced Masters in Public International Law from Leiden University and a PhD from King's College London. He has taught international law at leading universities, as Barrister, regularly appears before international courts and tribunals, and has acted as consultant for various international organisations.

Access to Justice and International Organisations

COORDINATING JURISDICTION BETWEEN THE NATIONAL AND INSTITUTIONAL LEGAL ORDERS

RISHI GULATI
Freie Universität Berlin

CAMBRIDGE
UNIVERSITY PRESS

CAMBRIDGE
UNIVERSITY PRESS

Shaftesbury Road, Cambridge CB2 8EA, United Kingdom

One Liberty Plaza, 20th Floor, New York, NY 10006, USA

477 Williamstown Road, Port Melbourne, VIC 3207, Australia

314–321, 3rd Floor, Plot 3, Splendor Forum, Jasola District Centre, New Delhi – 110025, India

103 Penang Road, #05–06/07, Visioncrest Commercial, Singapore 238467

Cambridge University Press is part of Cambridge University Press & Assessment, a department of the University of Cambridge.

We share the University's mission to contribute to society through the pursuit of education, learning and research at the highest international levels of excellence.

www.cambridge.org
Information on this title: www.cambridge.org/9781108931052

DOI: 10.1017/9781108946377

First published 2022
First paperback edition 2026

A catalogue record for this publication is available from the British Library

ISBN 978-1-108-83754-5 Hardback
ISBN 978-1-108-93105-2 Paperback

Contents

Acknowledgements

This book would not have been possible without the generous scholarship I received from King's College London that provided me the opportunity to research and prepare this manuscript. Work on this book was also carried out during my stay at the London School of Economics and Political Science during 2018–20. Thanks are reserved for all those who showed generosity with their time. The support that Professor Philippa Webb gave me throughout my time at King's College London and beyond is truly extraordinary. Professor Webb's outstanding support and friendship is something for which I am immensely grateful. I am also thankful for the very fruitful discussion with Professor Dapo Akande, University of Oxford, and Professor Alex Mills, University College London, who gave me very valuable feedback on my doctoral thesis that inspired this book project. There are numerous institutions at which I presented ideas connected to this book. They are too many to mention, but thanks to all those who engaged with me in all settings. One project I especially wish to note is the research project led by Professors Philippa Webb and Amal Clooney concerning the 'Right to a Fair Trial in International Law'. Being a part of this project proved especially valuable, for it significantly sharpened my understanding of the right to a fair trial, an understanding that has proven very important for key parts of this work. I thank Dr Dana Burchardt for the rich discussions that enhanced my thinking, especially relating to the theoretical parts of this book. I am also grateful to Ms Karolina Lewicka and Mr Matthew Nelson, who kindly assisted with what can often be a tedious editorial process at various stages. Finally, I thank the team at Cambridge University Press, whose expert guidance has proven most invaluable in the publication process.

Abbreviations

TREATIES AND INTERNATIONAL INSTRUMENTS

African Charter of Human Rights	African Charter on Human and Peoples' Rights (opened for signature 27 June 1981, entered into force 21 October 1986) 1520 UNTS 217
American Convention on Human Rights	American Convention on Human Rights, 'Pact of San Jose, Costa Rica' (opened for signature 22 November 1969, entered into force 18 July 1978) 1144 UNTS 123
Choice of Court Convention	Convention on Choice of Court Agreements (opened for signature 30 June 2005, entered into force 1 October 2015) 44 ILM 1294
DARIO	ILC, 'Draft Articles on the Responsibility of International Organizations' (26 April–3 June and 4 July–12 August 2011) (63rd session) UN Doc A/66/10, Yearbook of the International Law Commission (volume II, Part Two)
EUCFR	EU Charter of Fundamental Rights (26 October 2012) 2012/C 326/02
European Convention	Convention for the Protection of Human Rights and Fundamental Freedoms (opened for signature 4

	November 1950, entered into force 3 September 1953) 213 UNTS 221
General Convention	Convention on the Privileges and Immunities of the United Nations (opened for signature 13 February 1946, entered into force 17 September 1946) 1 UNTS 15
HCCH Judgments Convention	Convention of 2 July 2019 on the Recognition and Enforcement of Foreign Judgments in Civil or Commercial Matters
HCCH Judgments Convention	HCCH, Convention on the Recognition and Enforcement of Foreign Judgments in Civil or Commercial Matters (concluded 2 July 2019) <https://assets.hcch.net/docs/806e290e-bbd8-413d-b15e-8e3e1bf1496d.pdf>
ICCPR	International Covenant on Civil and Political Rights (adopted 16 December 1966, entered into force 23 March 1976) 999 UNTS 171, UNGA Res 2200 A (XXI)
ICJ Statute	Statute of the International Court of Justice, 33 UNTS 933
ICSID Convention	Convention on the Settlement of Investment Disputes between States and Nationals of Other States (1965) 575 UNTS 159
IFAD	International Fund for Agricultural Development
IFC Articles of Agreement	World Bank Group, International Finance Corporation Articles of Agreement (opened for signature 25 May 1955, amended as 27 June 2012) (Washington, DC)
ILOAT Statute	ILOAT Statute (International Labour Conference, 105th session) <www.ilo.org/global/about-the-ilo/how-the-ilo-works/departments-and-of

fices/jur/legal-instruments/WCMS_498369/lang–en/index.htm>

Recast Brussels I Regulation European Parliament and Council Regulation (EU) 1215/2012 of 12 December 2012 on Jurisdiction and the Recognition and Enforcement of Judgments in Civil and Commercial Matters

Specialized Agencies Convention Specialized Agencies Convention (opened for signature 21 November 1947, entered into force 2 December 1948) 33 UNTS 261

UDHR Universal Declaration of Human Rights (adopted 10 December 1948) UNGA Res 217 A(III)

UN Charter Charter of the United Nations (opened for signature 26 June 1945, entered into force 24 October 1945) 1 UNTS XVI

UN–US Headquarters Agreement United Nations and United States of America Agreement regarding the Headquarters of the United Nations (opened for signature 26 June 1947, entered into force 21 November 1947) No 147

Vienna Convention Vienna Convention of the Law of Treaties (opened for signature 23 May 1969, entered into force 27 January 1980) 1155 UNTS 331, 8 ILM 679

SOFT LAW AND OTHER

Article 6 Guide European Court of Human Rights, 'Guide on Article 6 of the European Convention of Human Rights – Right to a Fair Trial (Civil Limb)' (30 April 2020)

Bangalore Principles Bangalore Principles of Judicial Conduct 2002

Basic Principles	UN Basic Principles on the Independence of the Judiciary 1985
Burgh House Principles	Burgh House Principles on the Independence of the International Judiciary 2004
Code of Conduct	UNGA, 'Code of Conduct for the Judges of the United Nations Dispute Tribunal and the United Nations Appeals Tribunal' UN Doc A/RES/66/106
Commonwealth Principles	Commonwealth (Latimer House) Principles on the Three Branches of Government 2003
General Comment No 32	UN Human Rights Committee, 'General Comment No 32: Right to Equality before Courts and Tribunals and to a Fair Trial' (23 August 2007) UN Doc CCPR/C/GC/32
IAJC Guidelines	'Inter-American Juridical Committee Report. Immunities Of International Organizations' (16 August 2018) CJI/Doc 554/18 rev.2
IBA Standards	International Bar Association's Minimum Standards of Judicial Independence 1982
Montreal Declaration	Universal Declaration on the Independence of Justice 1983
Redesign Panel Report	'Report of the Redesign Panel on the United Nations System of Administration of Justice' (28 July 2006) (61st session) UN Doc A/61/205

GENERAL TERMS

ADB	Asian Development Bank
AfDB	African Development Bank
AMF	Arab Monetary Fund
CAO	Compliance Advisor Ombudsman
CCJE	Consultative Council of European Judges
CJEU	Court of Justice of the European Union
DRM	dispute resolution mechanism
EBRD	European Bank for Reconstruction and Development
EPO	European Patent Office
ESA	European Space Agency

European Court	European Court of Human Rights
HRC	United Nations Human Rights Committee
IAL	international administrative law
IAT	international administrative tribunal
ICA	international commercial arbitration
ICC	International Chamber of Commerce
ICJ	International Court of Justice
ICSID	International Centre for Settlement of Investment Disputes
IDB	Inter-American Development Bank
IFC	International Finance Corporation
IHL	international humanitarian law
IHRL	international human rights law
IJC	Internal Justice Council
ILO	International Labour Organisation
ILOAT	International Labour Organisation Administrative Tribunal
Inter-American Court	Inter American Court of Human Rights
IO	international organisation
ISA	investor-state arbitration
ITC	International Tin Council
MDBs	multilateral development banks
MIGA	Multilateral Investment Guarantee Agency
MINUSTAH	United Nations Stabilization Mission in Haiti
NATO	North Atlantic Treaty Organisation
OAJ	Office of the Administration of Justice
OSLA	Office of Staff Legal Assistance
PCA	Permanent Court of Arbitration
PIL	private international law
SOFAs	Status of Forces Agreements
UN	United Nations
UN tribunals	UNDT and UNAT collectively
UNAT	UN Appeals Tribunal
UNDT	UN Dispute Tribunal
UNESCO	United Nations Educational, Scientific and Cultural Organization
UNHCR	United Nations High Commission for Refugees
UNMIK	United Nations Mission in Kosovo
UNPROFOR	United Nations Protection Force
WBAT	World Bank Administrative Tribunal

Introduction

We live in a 'denial of justice age when it comes to the individual pursuit of justice against IOs.[1] The victims of the cholera epidemic introduced in Haiti by UN peacekeepers in 2010 are still awaiting justice. They have not yet had an opportunity to access a court to realise their rights.[2] The victims of the Srebrenica genocide for which the UN assumed moral responsibility have not received an effective remedy.[3] Vulnerable adults, young girls and boys, have been subjected to unspeakable sexual crimes by members of UN peacekeeping missions. Despite lofty rhetoric and promises of 'zero tolerance', justice for those victims continues to be unattainable.[4] Numerous communities and individuals have lost their lands and livelihoods as a result of projects financed by MDBs. Effective access to justice for such victims remains unrealisable.[5] In fact, IOs increasingly exercise administrative power over private persons adversely impacting their rights.[6] The most prominent

1 The concept of a 'denial of justice' is presently used to refer to circumstances where persons are denied the right to access a court and a fair trial provided for in international human rights law: C Focarelli, 'Denial of Justice' in R Wolfrum (ed), *Max Planck Encyclopedia of Public International Law* (Max Planck Institute for Comparative Public Law and International Law 2013), paras 2 and 35. The phrase 'denial of justice age' is borrowed from S Montt, *State Liability in Investment Treaty Arbitration: Global Constitutional and Administrative Law in the BIT Generation* (Hart 2012), 16.

2 See especially the discussion in Chapter 4.

3 Ibid.

4 See generally, JK Westendorf and L Searle, 'Sexual Exploitation and Abuse in Peace Operations: Trends, Policy Responses and Future Directions' (2017) 93 International Affairs 2, 365–87.

5 MDBs increasingly impact individual rights due to their development activity, which is an increasing aspect of their work: see G Fiti-Sinclair, *To Reform the World: International Organizations and the Making of Modern States* (Oxford University Press 2017), 202–35.

6 In this work, private persons include both natural and legal persons. Such persons are also referred to as 'third parties', being persons who are not a member state of an IO. As employees are not members of the IO as such, I include them in the broad category of private persons: see 'International Law Association Berlin Conference (2004) Accountability of International Organizations' (2004) 1 International Organizations Law Review 221.

example of the exercise of such power is perhaps the much discussed *Kadi* saga involving claims by an individual placed on the UN Security Council Sanctions Lists resulting in the freezing of assets and other interferences with human rights.[7]

An exponential rise in the number and types of disputes between IOs and private persons has been witnessed. Except for IATs that have been established to resolve employment claims between IOs and their staff members, efforts to deliver justice to the victims of IO conduct have been at best marginal and at worst completely non-existent.[8] In general, private actors impacted by IO conduct do not have access to fair trial compliant DRMs at the institutional level.[9] In the absence of institutional DRMs, victims of IO conduct end up approaching national courts. But most courts, in most countries, and in most cases, refuse to exercise jurisdiction in claims against IOs due to IO immunities. Such immunities are granted to ensure the functional independence of international institutions. As a result, the victims of IO conduct suffer denials of justice at multiple levels. Ensuring meaningful access to justice for victims of IO conduct has so far proven elusive.

The International Law Commission (ILC) adopted the Draft Articles on the Responsibility of International Organisations in 2011,[10] and did not address the issue of the rights of private persons vis-à-vis IOs.[11] The ILC left the 'individual in the cold'.[12] This book attempts to plug this gap by proposing a regulatory framework that can ensure access to justice for the victims of IO conduct, but without compromising on institutional independence. Both those values are equally important and the law must find a way to balance them, a balance that this work tries to realise. This book is divided into five

7 See *Kadi and Al Barakaat International Foundation v Council and Commission* [2008] Case C-402/05 P and C- 415/05; ECR I-6351. For an analysis of the Kadi litigation, see J Kokott and C Sobotta, 'The Kadi Case – Constitutional Core Values and International Law – Finding the Balance?' (2012) 23 European Journal of International Law 4.

8 See the discussion in Chapter 3.

9 As Chukwuemeke Okeke has noted, the only judicial protection created at the institutional level for private parties affected by IO conduct is 'administrative tribunals whose jurisdiction is limited to the adjudication of disputes between international organizations and their personnel': E Chukwuemeke Okeke, *Jurisdictional Immunities of States and International Organizations* (Oxford University Press 2018), 292.

10 ILC, 'Draft Articles on the Responsibility of International Organizations' (26 April–3 June and 4 July–12 August 2011) (63rd session) UN Doc A/66/10, Yearbook of the International Law Commission (volume II, Part Two) (DARIO).

11 See ibid, art 33(2).

12 See generally, A von Bogdandy and M Steinbruck Platise, 'ARIO and Human Rights Protection: Leaving the Individual in the Cold' (2012) 9 International Organisations Law Review 1, 67–76.

chapters, with each chapter forming a building block towards the proposed regulatory framework which can ensure access to justice without undermining institutional independence.

Chapter 1 explains what access to justice means as a value, and then goes on to show how that value has translated into legally enforceable rights in the form of the right to a fair trial found in all global and regional human rights treaties. The right to a fair trial provides that everyone has the right to approach an independent and impartial court or tribunal to resolve their legal claims fairly and justly. But how this right can be made realisable against IOs is a somewhat complex question. This is because IOs have not yet become party to human rights treaties. I show that IOs are required to provide access to justice to persons they harm under international law. Essentially, as IOs are granted jurisdictional immunities before national courts, they are placed under international legal obligations to provide for appropriate modes of dispute resolution to persons adversely impacted by IO conduct regardless of the type of claim pursued. Attempting to comply with their access to justice obligation, in some instances, IOs have indeed created DRMs which private persons can access. However, as later chapters show, these are deficient. What is more, relying on the jurisprudence of the ICJ, it is demonstrated that IOs must not only ensure that they provide a DRM to the victims of IO conduct, but also the delivery of justice at those DRMs must be consistent with fair trial standards found in IHRL.

Chapter 2 then goes on to specify what these fair trial standards founded in IHRL actually require. The discussion focuses on the three broad fair trial guarantees that an institutional DRM must incorporate if it is to be considered appropriate. These are: (1) independence, (2) impartiality and (3) fairness. Each of these criteria has various dimensions. First, for a DRM to be considered independent, it must possess institutional, decisional and personal/individual independence. Those three aspects will be explained succinctly. The discussion then focuses on the concept of judicial impartiality. For a fair trial to be provided, impartiality in its objective and subjective sense is critical. At institutional DRMs, the organisation will almost always be the respondent. Therefore, I argue that even a hint of favouritism shown towards an IO should be treated as suspect. Finally, the chapter demonstrates how the right to a fair trial also demands that a claimant be treated fairly. Fairness is a broad guarantee and is explored through seven subcomponent fair trial rights. Fairness cannot be achieved unless the right to equal access to the courts, the right to equality of arms, the right to an oral hearing, the right to appeal, the right to a reasoned judgment, the right to access justice without undue delay and the right to an effective remedy are provided for in the law, and importantly, practically realised. Each of the subcomponent fair trial rights will be explained so that there is a good basis to assess whether DRMs at IOs can be said to be appropriate, that is, fair trial compliant.

Chapter 3 assesses the compliance of institutional DRMs with the fair trial criteria developed. Three types of DRMs will be subjected to scrutiny. First, I assess permanent judicial mechanisms. As such mechanisms are principally established to resolve employment disputes, the focus is on the leading IATs, namely, the UN Dispute and Appeals Tribunals and the ILOAT. The chapter shows that even though IATs are relatively sophisticated, in varying degrees, both the regimes selected for scrutiny lack the structural safeguards necessary to deliver a fair trial. Second, the discussion focuses on the role international arbitration plays in resolving claims against IOs. In principle, international arbitration can provide for an appropriate DRM. But I show that based on the experience with arbitration so far, as of now, arbitration does not provide for a just and fair mode of dispute resolution. Amongst other things, arbitration is likely to prove simply unaffordable for most claimants. Moreover, little thought has been given to implement arbitration as a sustainable and viable option to resolve claims against IOs. I argue that unless a specialised arbitral regime is created that takes into account the particularities of disputes involving IOs, the chances of arbitration providing for an appropriate DRM are dim. Finally, the chapter makes a brief comment on non-judicialised DRMs, such as Ombudsman processes. I will argue that while such DRMs play an important complementing role, they cannot replace an independent and impartial forum empowered to render a binding judgment. Finally, the chapter highlights that alarmingly, in too many situations, private parties cannot access any DRM at the international level at all. Access to justice is thus comprehensively undermined. In the end, given that institutional DRMs are either completely absent or highly deficient, it is hardly surprising that an ever-increasing number of victims end up approaching national courts.

In Chapter 4, I will closely consider the approach national courts take when confronted with claims against IOs. Unfortunately, for the victims, an approach to national courts has generally not yielded access to justice either. I will show that even though IO immunities were always intended to be functional and limited, the term 'functional' has been made redundant when delimiting immunities. Whether it be the immunities of the UN, MDBs or any other IO, the term 'functional' is interpreted so broadly that IO immunities have become mostly absolute. Failing to limit IO immunities on a functional basis, victims have tried to argue that immunities ought to be contingent on the provision of appropriate modes of dispute resolution by the IO. The principle that IOs must provide reasonable alternative means of dispute resolution if immunity is to be retained is gaining acceptance. But I will demonstrate that most courts, in most countries, and in most cases, still deny claims against IOs without the merits ever being ventilated. Some courts refuse to make immunities contingent on the existence of an alternative mode of dispute resolution at all. Where a court is willing to do so, instead of checking whether the alternative forum is actually 'reasonable' and delivers justice consistently with fair trial standards, close scrutiny on the quality of justice provided is absent. Immunities are regularly upheld even where the quality of justice delivered is poor. So far, access to justice has not played a meaningful role in delimiting IO immunities. Ultimately, real or perceived concerns about IO independence, which justify the granting of jurisdictional immunities to international institutions, tend to trump the right to a fair trial.

Chapter 5 shows that it is possible to uphold IO independence and at the same time ensure access to justice if better coordination between the national and institutional legal orders can be achieved. I will show how private international law techniques can realise such coordination, and help balance the competing values of access to justice and institutional independence. The discussion commences by providing a theoretical justification for why private international law, which concerns itself with the rules on civil jurisdiction, applicable law and the recognition and enforcement of judgments, is best placed to mediate between the institutional and national orders. Overall, I will argue that access to justice should be used as a jurisdictional pivot that ultimately guides the decision whether or not a national court should take jurisdiction over an IO. In particular, institutional DRMs should be given the first opportunity to deliver justice to the victims of IO conduct. This provides IOs a ready opportunity to significantly reduce the risk of a national court taking jurisdiction over them. All IOs need to do is to create fair trial compliant modes of dispute resolution, which they are required to do by international law in any event. But if national courts are asked to exercise jurisdiction due to institutional failures, I argue that a modern private international law-based approach to adjudicative jurisdiction be taken. This approach requires that where a court is vested with civil jurisdiction due to the presence of well-recognised connecting factors, such as territoriality, the court must exercise its jurisdiction where doing so is necessary to realise access to justice. Taking such an approach would ensure that victims can access a fair trial at the national level where justice is denied at the international one, and IOs are not required to defend claims before distant forums. Where a national court takes jurisdiction over an IO in this circumscribed way, the rules on applicable law and the recognition and enforcement of judgments can further be calibrated to coordinate between the national and IO legal orders in such a nuanced way that the chance of intrusion into an IO's independence is eliminated.

In the end, this book proposes that a carefully crafted private international law-based framework allocates regulatory authority between the national and institutional orders so as to allow maintaining IO independence without sacrificing access to justice. The work concludes that the ideal approach to implement the proposed regime is through an international arrangement. Of course, international agreements can take time to negotiate. Given that private international law rules can be adjusted nationally without the need for action on the international plane, the proposed framework can be implemented even in the absence of immediate international action. It is submitted that private international law techniques can help bring to an end the denial of justice age for the victims of IO conduct. A conundrum that public international law has not been able to address for decades can readily be resolved using private international law.

1

International Organisations and Their Access to Justice Obligation

1.1 INTRODUCTION

This chapter explains the basis of the access to justice obligations placed on IOs under international law. Several key questions need addressing. One foundational issue is whether or not IOs are capable of being placed under international obligations in general. The answer to this question, as we will see, is most certainly in the affirmative. IOs are international legal persons or 'subjects' of international law that possess their own legal personality. This means that international law can bind IOs directly and impose obligations that ought to be implemented by the IO (Section 1.2). After showing how international law can directly place IOs under international obligations in general, the focus shifts to whether IOs can be placed under access to justice obligations in particular. I specifically discuss what is meant by access to justice as a value and how that value has translated into legal rights in the form of the right to a fair trial (Section 1.3). I then discuss how IOs specifically are put under access to justice obligations, including demonstrating the rationale behind doing so (Section 1.4). It is argued that IOs are required to provide justice consistently with fair trial guarantees to individuals and other private parties whenever IO actions adversely impact them.

1.2 IOS AS INTERNATIONAL LEGAL PERSONS

An international legal person, a classic example of which is the nation state, is a 'subject' of international law that is capable of directly possessing rights and bearing responsibilities on the international legal plane.[1] Now, not only states

[1] The 'subject' versus 'object' dichotomy in international law is a vexed one. According to the positivist view, states are the primary 'subjects' of international law, meaning that they are the central actors in the international legal system, enjoying rights and possessing responsibilities

but IOs have come to be seen as international legal persons and 'subjects' of international law.[2] Thus, while creations of their member states, IOs are independent legal persons with a status separate from their constituent members, constituting an independent actor at the international level who possess rights and obligations directly under international law. In this section, I explain the basis of an IO's international legal personality (Section 1.2.1) followed by the consequences of having such personality (Section 1.2.2).

1.2.1 *The International Legal Personality of IOs*

In the *Reparation case*,[3] the ICJ confirmed that IOs are international legal persons. That case involved the UN's attempt to seek compensation from Israel for the murder of the UN Mediator in the Middle East killed by terrorists in territory under the control of the provisional government of Israel.[4] Without international personality, the UN would have lacked the capacity to advance a claim against Israel in its own right.[5] Absent any express provision in the UN Charter[6] about its status in international law,[7] the question of the organisation's international personality became contentious.

With certain judges acknowledging the novelty of the situation observing that the ICJ was engaging in an exercise of law creation in light of the

directly on the international plane. On the other hand, individuals and other private persons are mere 'objects' of international law. This positivist view is well reflected in Article 34 of the Statute of the International Court of Justice, 33 UNTS 933 (ICJ Statute), which only gives states standing before that court: see AS Muller, D Raic and JM Thuranszky (eds), *The International Court of Justice: Its Future Role after Fifty Years* (Martinus Nijhoff 1997), 208. The 'subject' versus 'object' distinction is criticised by several prominent authors, see, for example, R Higgins, *Problems and Process: International Law and How We Use It* (Oxford University Press 1994), 50.

2 'International organizations are subjects of international law and, as such, are bound by any obligations incumbent upon them under general rules of international law, under their constitutions or under international agreements to which they are parties': *Interpretation of the Agreement of 25 March 1951 between the WHO and Egypt* (Advisory Opinion) [1980] ICJ Rep 73, 89–90, para 37.

3 *Reparation for Injuries Suffered in the Service of the United Nations* (Advisory Opinion) [1949] ICJ Rep 174 (*Reparation case*).

4 For a recent analysis and the facts that gave rise to the *Reparation case* (n 3), see RA Wessel, 'Reparation Case' in C Ryngaert, IF Dekker, RA Wessel and J Wouters (eds), *Judicial Decisions on the Law of International Organizations* (Oxford University Press 2016), 12.

5 *Reparation case* (n 3), 178.

6 Charter of the United Nations (opened for signature 26 June 1945, entered into force 24 October 1945) 1 UNTS XVI (UN Charter).

7 As Schermers and Blokker point out, most international organisations are not granted express international personality in their constituent instruments; HG Schermers and NM Blokker, *International Institutional Law* (5th edn, Brill 2011), section 1565.

exigencies of the times,[8] the Court was ready and willing to recognise the UN's international personality. In reaching its conclusion that the UN was an international legal person, the ICJ inferred the UN's international personality as an inescapable conclusion. The UN demonstrated a distinct existence in the domestic law of the member states; entered into treaties in its own right; was charged with tasks on the international plane; and the immunities accorded to the organisation through the Convention on the Privileges and Immunities of the United Nations 1946[9] (General Convention) created rights and duties between each member state and the UN which could only be explained based on the UN's international personality.[10] The ICJ concluded that '[i]n the opinion of the Court, the Organization was intended to exercise and enjoy, and is in fact exercising and enjoying, functions and rights which can only be explained on the basis of the possession of a large measure of international personality and the capacity to operate upon an international plane'.[11]

The practice of the UN, and the functions it was mandated to perform that presumed the existence of international status, sufficiently demonstrated that the UN was not only intended to but was already exercising the rights and capacities typically exercised by an international person.[12] The inference that the UN was an international legal person was thus logical and the only available conclusion that could possibly have been reached. Although the finding that the UN was an international person was pragmatic and no doubt correct, its theoretical foundations have remained contentious.

Some commentators suggest that international personality is grounded in the so-called will theory, meaning that it is the intention of the member states that results in international personality.[13] Others contend that 'as soon as an entity exists as a matter of law, (i.e., meets the requirements that international law attaches to its establishment) that entity possesses international legal

8 See the Separate Opinion of Judge Alvarez in *Reparation case* (n 3), 190.

9 Convention on the Privileges and Immunities of the United Nations (opened for signature 13 February 1946, entered into force 17 September 1946) 1 UNTS 15 (General Convention); also see R Gulati, 'Convention on the Privileges and Immunities of the United Nations, 13th February 1946' (1 UNTS 15, 1 UST 1418) OXIO 73 <http://opil.ouplaw.com/view/10.1093/law-oxio/e28.013.1/law-oxio-e28?rskey=4tJ2gf&result=9&prd=OXIO> accessed 28 May 2018.

10 *Reparation case* (n 3), 178.

11 Ibid, 178–9.

12 Ibid, 177; J Klabbers, *An Introduction to International Institutional Law* (2nd edn, Cambridge University Press 2009), 40.

13 For an analysis of the competing theories, see M Rama-Montaldo, 'International Legal Personality and Implied Powers of International Organizations' (1970) 44 British Yearbook of International Law 111, 112.

personality'.[14] According to the second school, personality is then 'objective', which is opposable against all other subjects of international law, including both member and non-member states. An objective view of personality, which now appears to have been endorsed in the commentaries to the International Law Commission's Draft Articles on the Responsibility of International Organisations 2011 (DARIO),[15] can be sourced in the *Reparation case*. In answering the question of whether the UN's personality was opposable against Israel, a non-member of the UN at the time, the ICJ said:

> [T]he Court's opinion is that fifty States, representing the vast majority of the members of the international community, had the power, in conformity with international law, to bring into being an entity possessing objective international personality, and not merely personality recognized by them alone.[16]

Universal organisations such as the UN clearly enjoy objective international personality based on the *Reparation case* rationale. Subsequent developments and practice also indicate that a liberal view on the acquisition of objective international personality by IOs now ought to be taken.[17] There is little evidence of any barriers in the acceptance of the international personality of IOs in practice,[18] although inconclusive academic debates about its basis continue. Overall, we may safely assume that IOs are international legal persons. With the definition provided by the DARIO expressly affirming that an IO possesses 'international legal personality',[19] without such personality an entity may even struggle to be characterised as an IO. For present purposes, the real issue is not whether IOs are international legal persons (which they are), but what particular consequences flow from this.

[14] See Klabbers (n 12), 47–9. Klabbers suggests a third approach demonstrated by practice, which he claims has 'shown a more pragmatic approach to questions of international legal personality, perhaps best captured by the phrase "presumptive personality": as soon as an organization performs acts which can only be explained on the basis of international legal personality, such an organization will be presumed to be in possession of international legal personality'.

[15] ILC, 'Draft Articles on the Responsibility of International Organizations' (26 April–3 June and 4 July–12 August 2011) (63rd session) UN Doc A/66/10, Yearbook of the International Law Commission (volume II, Part Two) (DARIO), para 87.

[16] *Reparation case* (n 3), 189.

[17] ILC, 'Report of the International Law Commission' (26 April–3 June and 4 July–12 August 2011) (63rd session) (ILC Report), para 10; also see, F Seyersted, *Common Law of International Organizations* (Martinus Nijhoff 2008), 43 and 51; Schermers and Blokker (n 7), section 1568; CF Amerasinghe, *Principles of the Institutional Law of International Organizations* (2nd edn, Cambridge University Press 2005), 84 and 87.

[18] Amerasinghe (n 17), 87.

[19] Article 2(a) of the DARIO (n 15) states '"international organization" means an organization established by a treaty or other instrument governed by international law and possessing its own international legal personality'.

1.2.2 *The Consequences of International Personality*

It is important to maintain a conceptual distinction between an IO's international legal personality and the consequences that flow from it,[20] although some of those consequences are intrinsically linked to personality. Of present concern are certain legal capacities that inexorably flow from the presence of personality. Kelsen has said that legal personality means 'the capacity of being a subject of legal duties and legal rights, of performing legal transactions and of suing and being sued at law'.[21] In other words, only if an entity possesses legal personality can it hold rights in its own name and be a party to a proceeding in its own right.[22] This proposition is equally true for IOs that are but one form of a legal person.

On the same lines, the ICJ also draws a close link between the existence of international personality and certain intrinsic capacities. In the *Reparation case*, it said:

> [T]he Organization is an international person. That is not the same thing as saying that it is a State, which it certainly is not, or that its legal personality and rights and duties are the same as those of a State. Still less is it the same thing as saying that it is 'a super State', whatever that expression may mean. It does not even imply that all its rights and duties must be upon the international plane, any more than all the rights and duties of a State must be upon that plane. What it does mean is that it is a subject of international law and capable of possessing international rights and duties, and that it has capacity to maintain its rights by bringing international claims.[23]

20 For a description of the terms 'functions', 'powers', 'rights', 'capacity' and 'competence', terms often used interchangeably, see G Verdirame, *The UN and Human Rights: Who Guards the Guardians?* (Cambridge University Press 2011), 68–9.

21 See H Kelsen, *The Law of the United Nations: A Critical Analysis of Its Fundamental Problems* (The Lawbook Exchange 1950), 329, cited in Rama-Montaldo (n 13), 135. An IO's other capacities include a circumscribed power to enter into treaties consistently with an organisation's constituent instruments: see Amerasinghe (n 17), 99; and other authors argue for a broad treaty power: see Klabbers (n 12), 40–1; and Finn Seyersted takes the broadest possible view stating that international organisations possess the 'inherent capacity to perform any act of international law which is in a practical position to perform, subject to such negative restrictions which are laid down in its constitution': Seyersted (n 17), 51. Although, strictly speaking, the capacity to enter into treaties does not logically follow from legal personality, the existence of personality means that the treaty-making capacity will be exercised in the name of the organisation: see R Higgins, P Webb, D Akande, S Sivakumaran and J Sloan, *Oppenheim's International Law – United Nations*, vol 1 (Oxford University Press 2017), 396.

22 Klabbers (n 12), 37–8.

23 *Reparation case* (n 3), 179.

That IOs are not analogous to states is self-evident.[24] And for different subjects of law to possess differing rights and legal capacities is not unusual. This is the case at the national level,[25] and is equally the case at the international one.[26] The status of an IO must then not be confused with the totality of its rights and capacities, which will differ from organisation to organisation. There is some confusion about whether the international personality of an IO can be possessed in degrees. This confusion is misplaced.

Although legal personality is intrinsically linked to some capacities, it does not follow that status should be equated with capacities. Legal status exists independently of the extent of an organisation's rights and capacities and does not exist in degrees. It should be recalled that in the *Reparation case*, when assessing the UN's status, the ICJ had remarked that the UN possessed a 'large measure of international personality'.[27] The use of that phrase causes much confusion. Either an entity is a legal person or not. As a leading treatise observes:

> In the *Reparation Advisory Opinion*, the Court stated that the UN was in possession of a 'large measure' of personality. This somewhat curious phrase is best understood as a statement concerning the substantive capacities of the organization, which are limited when compared to those of states and vary in degree considerably when compared with other international organizations, as opposed to international legal personality itself, which is not something that exists in degrees. Similarly, the term 'functional personality' that is sometimes used in this context reflects the way that the 'powers which fill, or give substance to, the organization's personality are limited and determined by the latter's purposes and functions'.[28]

IOs are thus to be understood as international legal persons even though their particular capacities may differ. That being said, some core capacities are so intrinsically linked to personality that they would be enjoyed by all IOs. As was stated earlier, these capacities are as follows. First, as international legal persons, IOs become capable of holding rights and assuming obligations directly under international law. The answer to the question whether IOs

24 See *Legality of the Use by a State of Nuclear Weapons in Armed Conflict* (Advisory Opinion) [1996] ICJ Rep 66 (*Nuclear Weapons Advisory Opinion*), 78, para 25.

25 For example, in *JH Rayner (Mincing Lane) Ltd v Department of Trade and Industry* [1989] 3 WLR 969, [1990] 81 ILR 670, 698–9; Lord Oliver clarified that status and capacity are distinct concepts (stating that minors possess status but may lack certain capacities), although status may be inferred from capacity.

26 As the ICJ noted in the *Reparation case* (n 3), 178, '[t]he subjects of law in any legal system are not necessarily identical in their nature or in the extent of their rights, and their nature depends on the needs of the community'.

27 *Reparation case* (n 3), 179.

28 Higgins, Webb, Akande, Sivakumaran and Sloan (n 21), 396.

can be placed under direct international legal obligations is most certainly in the affirmative. Second, the responsibility for any wrongful conduct that is attributable to an IO is that of its own, given its independent legal status. Whether or not an IO is responsible for its internationally wrongful acts need not be assessed through the nebulous exercise of determining the so-called measure of its personality as status does not exist in degrees. An IO cannot avoid its responsibility purporting that its impugned conduct does not fall within the scope of its personality. After all, as the DARIO state in its Article 3, IOs are responsible for their internationally wrongful acts.

Finally, it follows that if an IO wishes to raise a claim or be made answerable for conduct attributable to it, as an independent legal person, both of those things are to be done in the IO's own name. When a person is seeking a remedy concerning the breach of a legal obligation of an IO, it is the organisation, an international person, who is the proper respondent for it is the entity whose responsibility ought to be invoked.[29] Questions of which forum ought to determine a particular claim, who may approach such a forum,[30] what the applicable law relevant to the determination of a claim is, and the liability of other actors (such as states) for their own conduct, are altogether distinct matters considered in later chapters.[31]

[29] ILC Report (n 17), para 10; also see the cases of *Behrami v France* App no 71412/01 (ECtHR, 2 May 2007) and *Saramati v France, Germany and Norway* App no 78166/01 (ECtHR, 2 May 2007) where the Grand Chamber of the European Court held that the member states of the European Convention could not be impugned for alleged contraventions of the European Convention attributable to the UN, a separate legal person, see paras 133–44 and 152, especially para 144 – this, however, does not rule out the possibility of a state being responsible for its own contraventions (at para 151); also see, *Application of the Interim Accord of 13 September 1995 (The Former Yugoslav Republic of Macedonia v Greece)* [2011] ICJ Rep 644, paras 42 and 70. For an academic debate about shared responsibility in international law, and underdeveloped concept, see generally, A Nollkaemper and D Jacobs, 'Shared Responsibility in International Law: A Conceptual Framework' (SHARES 2011) Research Paper No 03, ACIL 2011-07 <www.sharesproject.nl> accessed 28 May 2018. For an excellent discussion about the DARIO (n 15) including on the problematic debate of 'attribution', see D Sarooshi, *Responsibility and Remedies for the Actions of International Organizations* (Martinus Nijhoff 2015); also see generally, I Brownlie and M Ragazzi, *Responsibility of International Organizations* (Brill 2013).

[30] 'Standing' means the right or ability of a party to be a party in a legal proceeding. In national law there is a distinction between the capacity to sue generally and the capacity to be a party to a specific proceeding, whereas before international courts, those two things are not always separated: see A Del Vecchio, 'International Courts and Tribunals, Standing' in R Wolfrum (ed), *Max Planck Encyclopedia of Public International Law* (Max Planck Institute for Comparative Public Law and International Law 2010), paras 1–3.

[31] Amerasinghe (n 17), 67–8. Even authors who submit that member states should be jointly held responsible for institutional conduct where they exercise relevant control over the decision-making (a debate that is in the nature of *de lege ferenda*) do not propose a direct cause of action against the member state: J d'Aspremont, 'Abuse of the Legal Personality of International

1.3 THE ACCESS TO JUSTICE OBLIGATION

The proposition that IOs are legal persons and distinct in law from their constituent member states, capable of holding rights and obligations in international law, and thus, responsible for their own conduct cannot be doubted. In other words, international law can directly place IOs under obligations on the international plane. However, the crucial question is what particular obligations can IOs be placed under? Presently, we are concerned with the obligations placed on IOs to ensure that they provide access to justice to private persons or third parties adversely affected by their conduct. Before explaining the basis of an IO's access to justice obligation, a preliminary but important question is what is meant by the phrase access to justice. For the purposes of this work, I consider access to justice as constituting a process value (Section 1.3.1) that translates into legally enforceable standards through the right to a fair trial (Section 1.3.2).

1.3.1 *Access to Justice as a Process Value*

Friedman states that according to its typical understanding, access to justice is a legal concept concerned with issues around a person's ability to pursue a legitimate claim or complaint, including a consideration of the underlying setting that facilitates this pursuit in a 'real and practical' way.[32] Highlighting the multiple process values the concept entails, Karayanni points to its three dimensions. The first value involves considering whether a party has adequate courses of action when their substantive rights have been compromised. The issues of relevance include the ability of parties to be able to bring proceedings against a defendant, such as states, including foreign state instrumentalities (one may safely add IOs to this list); or 'whether the system provides for class actions (or other forms of group litigation) for grievances that cannot be remedied through individual claims'.[33] The second value concerns 'making the legal process available to those with limited financial resources in light of the heavy burdens of modern day criminal and civil litigation'.[34] Here, issues

Organizations and the Responsibility of Member States' (2007) 4 International Organisations Law Review 91, 94.

32 LM Friedman, 'Access to Justice: Some Historical Comments' (2009) 37 Fordham Urban Law Journal 1, 3.

33 MM Karayanni, 'The Extraterritorial Application of Access to Justice Rights: On The Availability of Israeli Courts to Palestinian Plaintiffs' in HM Watt and DP Fernandez Arroyo (eds), *Private International Law and Global Governance* (Oxford University Press 2014), 217–18.

34 Ibid.

such as the availability of legal aid, contingency fee agreements, court fees, the existence of small claims courts and the ability to recover legal costs constitute the key areas of contention. Finally, the third value is concerned with the machinery employed to deliver justice, focusing on affording parties procedural mechanisms that make the legal process fair, such as 'guarantees for neutral adjudication, whether parties of weak standing possess sufficient procedural powers to conduct litigation against strong parties . . ., how efficient the process is as a whole in rendering judgment and having it executed within a reasonable time frame, and existing means of appeal and judicial review'.[35]

At its heart, 'access to justice' aims to create a fair and just environment for individuals to seek a remedy for the breach of their rights. It refers to the environmental factors that are critical to translate the pursuit of a substantive right or claim into practical reality. It is the typical process-based understanding of access to justice that this work is essentially concerned with. Those process-based 'access to justice' values acquire normative force through IHRL generally and the right to a fair trial specifically. As is discussed later, access to justice as a 'theoretical abstraction' has been translated into concrete reality via the right to a fair trial.[36]

1.3.2 *The Right to a Fair Trial Generally*

The fact that anyone seeking resolution of their legal claim has the right to access a fair trial is well entrenched in IHRL.[37] The right to a fair trial provides for the procedural safeguards in the administration of justice that

[35] Ibid.

[36] AA Cançado Trindade, *The Access of Individuals to International Justice* (Oxford University Press 2011), 60; see F Francioni, 'The Rights of Access to Justice under Customary International Law' in F Francioni (ed), *Access to Justice as a Human Right* (Oxford University Press 2007), 7–9; see also P Schmitt, *Access to Justice and International Organizations: The Case of Individual Victims of Human Rights Violations* (Edward Elgar 2017), 91–7 (where the author also draws a link between access to justice and the right to a fair trial).

[37] See Universal Declaration of Human Rights (adopted 10 December 1948) UNGA Res 217 A(III) (UDHR), art 10; International Covenant on Civil and Political Rights (adopted 16 December 1966, entered into force 23 March 1976) 999 UNTS 171 (ICCPR), art 14; Convention for the Protection of Human Rights and Fundamental Freedoms (opened for signature 4 November 1950, entered into force 3 September 1953) 213 UNTS 221 (European Convention), art 6; American Convention on Human Rights, 'Pact of San Jose, Costa Rica' (opened for signature 22 November 1969, entered into force 18 July 1978) 1144 UNTS 123 (American Convention on Human Rights), art 8; African Charter on Human and Peoples' Rights (opened for signature 27 June 1981, entered into force 21 October 1986) 1520 UNTS 217 (African Charter of Human Rights), art 7.

are essential to maintain the rule of law, both nationally[38] and internationally.[39] While the right to a fair trial is of a procedural nature, its significance to protect substantive rights is not to be underestimated.[40] The right is critical to ensure procedural justice but also bears significance for the just resolution of the merits. Given its significance to the administration of justice, fair trial guarantees should not only be formally provided for but must be fully and practically realised.[41]

Indeed, the right to a fair trial constitutes a fundamental human right and is a marked feature of all human rights instruments. Its acceptance as a fundamental principle of IHRL is evidenced by the near universal ratification of the International Covenant on Civil and Political Rights 1966 ('ICCPR')[42] which enshrines the right in Article 14. Article 14(1) states:

> All persons shall be equal before the courts and tribunals. In the determination of any criminal charge against him, or of his rights and

38 In his influential text, T Bingham, *The Rule of Law* (Penguin 2010), chapters 3–10, Bingham identified eight elements of a rule of law that state: 'The law must afford adequate protection of human rights; Means must be provided for resolving, without prohibitive cost or inordinate delay, bona fide civil disputes which the parties themselves are unable to resolve; judicial and other adjudicative procedures must be fair and independent; and there must be compliance by the state with its international law obligations': discussed in, R McCorquodale, 'Defining the International Rule of Law: Defying Gravity?' (2016) 65 International & Comparative Law Quarterly 2, 279–80.

39 See *Waite and Kennedy v Germany* App no 26083/94 (ECtHR, 18 February 1999) (*Waite and Kennedy*); IOs themselves are the principal proponents of the rule of law internationally: 'Report of the Secretary-General on the Rule of Law and Transitional Justice in Conflict and Post-Conflict Societies' (2004) UN Doc S/2004/616, para 6; after an exhaustive study of the subject, McCorquodale identified that the international rule of law requires 'measures to ensure adherence to the principles of supremacy of law, equality before the law, accountability to the law, fairness in the application of the law, separation of powers ... ': McCorquodale (n 38), 284; McCorquodale's definition has been critically commented at, Opinio Juris, 'Blog Archive Symposium: Defining the International Rule of Law-Defying Gravity?' (20 May 2016) <http://opiniojuris.org/2016/05/17/symposium-the-rule-of-law-thick-but-not-too-thick/> accessed 6 June 2016; it is however to be noted that the right to a fair trial and access to court is an uncontroversial aspect of the international rule of law.

40 The relationship between the right to an effective remedy and the right to a fair trial has been discussed at length in Cançado Trindade (n 36), 52, 64; also see the case of *Kudla v Poland* App no 30210/96 (ECtHR, 18 October 2000), paras 146–9 and 151–60, where the European Court drew a direct link between the fair trial rights in Article 6 and the right to an effective remedy in Article 13 of that convention; a similar relationship exists between Article 14 and Article 2 of the ICCPR (n 37); also see the discussion in Chapter 2.

41 UN Human Rights Committee, 'General Comment No 32: Right to Equality before Courts and Tribunals and to a Fair Trial' (23 August 2007) UN Doc CCPR/C/GC/32 (General Comment No 32); *Airey v Ireland* App no 6289/73 (ECtHR, 9 October 1979); *Golder v United Kingdom* App no 4451/70 (ECtHR, 21 February 1975); *Waite and Kennedy* (n 39).

42 ICCPR (n 37).

> obligations in a suit at law, everyone shall be entitled to a fair and public hearing by a competent, independent and impartial tribunal established by law. The press and the public may be excluded from all or part of a trial for reasons of morals, public order (ordre public) or national security in a democratic society, or when the interest of the private lives of the parties so requires, or to the extent strictly necessary in the opinion of the court in special circumstances where publicity would prejudice the interests of justice; but any judgement rendered in a criminal case or in a suit at law shall be made public except where the interest of juvenile persons otherwise requires or the proceedings concern matrimonial disputes or the guardianship of children.

Article 14 of the ICCPR is of a complex nature providing for a number of guarantees within the rubric of a fair trial. Key amongst them is the right to access an independent and impartial court or tribunal that renders justice equally and fairly.[43] All other human rights instruments replicate the guarantees provided for in Article 14 of the ICCPR, emphasising the aforementioned fair trial rights. Together with Article 14 of the European Convention on Human Rights (European Convention),[44] which provides for the non-discriminatory application of convention rights, Article 6 of the European Convention manifests the key component guarantees of the right to a fair trial. It provides in Article 6(1):

> In the determination of his civil rights and obligations or of any criminal charge against him, everyone is entitled to a *fair and public hearing within a reasonable time* by an *independent and impartial tribunal* established by law. (emphasis added)

Article 8(1) of the American Convention[45] and Article 7(1) of the African Charter[46] also enshrine the right to a fair trial in substantially similar terms. As to the scope of its application, the right applies throughout the life of a claim, that is, from its initiation to the enforcement stage.[47] Moreover, the right applies to the entire spectrum of criminal and civil cases, as well as in proceedings of an administrative law character. The HRC has clarified:

> [T]he concept of a 'suit at law' [in Article 14 of the ICCPR] . . . is based on the nature of the right in question rather than on the status of one of the

43 General Comment No 32 (n 41), para 27.

44 European Convention (n 37).

45 American Convention on Human Rights (n 37), art 8 (1).

46 African Charter of Human Rights (n 37), art 7(1).

47 This commences when the individual is impacted until the enforcement phase: European Court of Human Rights, 'Guide on Article 6 of the European Convention of Human Rights – Right to a Fair Trial (Civil Limb)' (30 April 2020) (Article 6 Guide), para 60.

> parties or the particular forum provided ... for the determination of particular rights. The concept encompasses (a) judicial procedures aimed at determining rights and obligations pertaining to the areas of contract, property and torts in the area of private law, as well as (b) equivalent notions in the area of administrative law such as the termination of employment of civil servants. ... In addition, it may (c) cover other procedures which, however, must be assessed on a case by case basis in the light of the nature of the right in question.[48]

While the specific application of the right to a fair trial has been well traversed in the criminal and private law spheres,[49] this is not the case for the administrative law context. It is important to note that the right equally applies in the administrative law sphere and is founded on the fair trial provisions in human rights treaties as well.[50] Not only the HRC and the European Court of Human Rights (European Court) have so held,[51] other regional human rights courts have also reached similar conclusions. For instance, the Inter-American Court of Human Rights (Inter-American Court) has stated that guarantees of a fair trial encompass situations where the acts or omissions of state agencies affect persons' subjective rights or legitimate interests.[52] Indeed, guaranteeing 'judicial review of administrative acts by a competent and independent court or tribunal that adheres to international and regional fair trial standards is fundamental to the protection of human rights and the rule of law'.[53]

Therefore, the right to a fair trial is of a broad scope applying when individuals seek to access justice alleging a contravention of their subjective legal interests regardless of the forum approached, the identity of the alleged wrongdoer or the specific cause of action pursued. Although the distinction between private and public administrative law claims is significant for the applicable law and the remedies available,[54] crucially, whenever privately held rights are contravened, the right to a fair trial is engaged

48 General Comment No 32 (n 41), para 16.

49 See, for example, A Clooney and P Webb, *The Right to a Fair Trial in International Law* (Oxford University Press 2021).

50 OSCE's Office for Democratic Institutions and Human Rights, 'Handbook for Monitoring Administrative Justice' (2013) (OSCE Handbook), 16 and 32–3.

51 See jurisprudence cited at Article 6 Guide (n 47), para 1.

52 *Baena Ricardo and Others v Panama* (IACHR, 2 February 2001) (Judgment on the merits); also see generally the discussion in OSCE Handbook (n 50); General Comment No 32 (n 41), section III; *Perterer v Austria*, 'HRC Communication 1015/2001' (20 July 2004) UN Doc CCPR/C/81/D/1015/2001, para 9.2.

53 OSCE Handbook (n 50), 13.

54 See Chapter 5 for a detailed discussion.

in principle. The various due process guarantees contained within the right to a fair trial ultimately form a constellation of rights which are the translation of the process-based access to justice values into legally enforceable human rights.

1.4 THE ACCESS TO JUSTICE OBLIGATION ON IOS

The applicability of fair trial rights in the national setting is beyond contention, with states required to ensure the practical realisation of this right to everyone located on its territory or within its jurisdiction.[55] However, as IOs are not parties to human rights treaties yet,[56] and the scope of the application of customary international law to IOs remains uncertain,[57] the bindingness of human rights-based fair trial standards to IOs is a somewhat contentious issue. There is a burgeoning view that as subjects of international law, IOs are bound by IHRL in general.[58] Leaving to one side that broader discussion, the present objective is a narrow one. It is to simply assess the obligation of IOs to provide access to justice to persons adversely affected by their conduct. This section traces the evolution of how IOs came to be put under access to justice obligations directly by international law through their constituent instruments. The discussion is carried out in four segments.

First, the discussion clarifies the rationale for ensuring that access to justice values are reflected in an IO's constituent instrument and apply whenever privately held rights are adversely impacted by IO conduct (Section 1.4.1). Second, internal justice systems created by IOs as an attempt to discharge their access to justice obligation are best explained via the language of human rights (Section 1.4.2). Third, fair trial standards are now fully incorporated into the delivery of justice at the institutional level and must be complied with (Section 1.4.3). Fourth, the scope of the access to justice obligation on IOs has expanded due to their increased activity (Section 1.4.4). I argue that the

55 General Comment No 32 (n 41), para 9.

56 Negotiations for the EU's accession to the European Convention on Human Rights are at an advanced stage, see: 'EU Accession to the ECHR' (2021) <coe.int/en/web/human-rights-intergovernmentalcooperation/accession-of-the-european-union-to-the-european-convention-on-human-rights> accessed 19 April 2021.

57 While the majority of commentators accept that IOs are in principle bound by customary international law, the precise obligations to which they are bound remain disputed: JE Alvarez, 'International Organizations: Then and Now' (2006) 100 American Journal of International Law 324–47; J von Bernstorff, 'Procedures of Decision-Making and the Role of Law in International Organizations' (2019) 9 German Law Journal 11, 1939–63, 1962.

58 von Bernstorff (n 57).

real question should not be whether IOs are required to provide fair trial compliant means of dispute resolution to affected persons, but whether they do so appropriately.

1.4.1 *Understanding the IO Access to Justice Obligation*

Initially, the principal way in which international law placed IOs directly under a basic access to justice obligation was through their constituent instruments. These constituent instruments stipulate that the IO is required to provide for appropriate modes of dispute settlement for private claimants alleging wrongful conduct by the IO.[59] As we will see, on its face, this type of provision requires that the IO ensures access to some form of 'appropriate' justice to private persons outside of national courts. The access to justice value that international law promotes here is to ensure the existence of an alternative forum where private claimants adversely impacted by IO action can raise claims against them.

The reason why IOs must provide appropriate modes or alternative means of dispute resolution outside of national legal systems warrants an explanation. To provide such an explanation, I primarily rely on the UN experience for two reasons. First, the UN is the supreme kind of international organisation that confronts claims against it more frequently than any other organisation. A study of the rules imposed on the UN vis-à-vis its access to justice obligations is thus crucial for purely practical reasons. Second, and perhaps more importantly, the General Convention (the treaty governing the UN's privileges and immunities) also forms a blueprint for the regulatory regimes of numerous other IOs, making this analysis broadly applicable.[60]

As the UN experience shows, the reason why IOs are placed under a basic form of access to justice obligation is to address the adverse impact of an IO's jurisdictional immunities before national courts. While the General Convention granted the UN immunities from the jurisdiction of domestic courts to preserve its functional independence (see Chapter 4), access to justice obligations were expressly imposed on the organisation upon its creation as a complement to its jurisdictional immunities. In other words, as jurisdictional immunities prevented claimants from approaching national courts to air their grievances against IOs, building a structural bias in the regulatory regime, access to appropriate modes of dispute resolution was

59 General Convention (n 9), section 29; and related provisions.

60 Specialized Agencies Convention (opened for signature 21 November 1947, entered into force 2 December 1948) 33 UNTS 261 (Specialized Agencies Convention).

imperative to address the adverse impact of this bias.[61] According to the organisation itself, such a provision would avoid impunity.[62]

In particular, Article VIII, Section 29, of the General Convention provides that the 'United Nations shall make provisions for appropriate modes of settlement of: Disputes arising out of contracts or other disputes of a private law character to which the United Nations is a party.'[63] Jenks identifies the inspiration behind this provision as Draft Article 18 of the so-called ILO Memorandum, which sought to create rules for the International Labour Office, which became the ILO immediately following the post-war period in 1945. The ILO Memorandum suggested that as a supplement to its immunities, the ILO establish a permanent tribunal that was vested with 'the jurisdiction to determine disputes arising out of contracts to which the Organisation is a party' and claims raised by staff members against the organisation.[64] At the time, these were presumably the types of claims that it was thought would arise against the organisation from time to time.

Although the ILO Memorandum motivated the inclusion of the access to justice obligation in respect of the UN, it did so in a modified form. The obligation to provide appropriate modes of dispute resolution was specified in Section 29 concerning disputes relating to contracts to which the organisation was a party, but also more generally to disputes of a 'private law character'. To understand the true import of this provision, it is necessary to gain a deeper understanding as to its meaning and scope. I show that both

61 While the preparatory discussions on the General Convention (n 9) simply assumed the human rights rationale behind Article VIII, Section 29, the preparatory documents to the Specialized Agencies Convention (n 60) expressly refer to the access to justice rationale behind placing the Specialized Agencies of the United Nations under obligations to provide alternative means. That obligation is assumed by, and imposed on, other IOs based on the same access to justice justification.

62 Notably, the UN considers that Section 29 of the General Convention (n 9) eliminates the possibility of impunity. In a memorandum of law in support of its motion to dismiss and to intervene in *Brzak v United Nations* (2d Cir 2010) 597 F.3d 107 (*Brzak v UN*), the UN stated: 'In civil cases, the uniform practice is to maintain immunity, while offering, in accord with section 29 of the General Convention, alternative means of dispute settlement [including negotiation, conciliation, mediation and/or arbitration]. . . . This practice achieves two fundamental goals: it ensures the independence of the United Nations and its officials from national court systems, but at the same time it eliminates the prospect of impunity'; see 'Memorandum of Law in Support of the Motion of the United Nations to Dismiss and to Intervene' (2 October 2007), https://www.brennancenter.org/sites/default/files/legal-work/New-York-et-al_v_Department_of_Commerce_Memorandum-of-Law-in-Support-of-Motion-to-Dismiss.pdf.

63 General Convention (n 9), art VIII, section 29, para (a).

64 Draft rule 18, ILO Memorandum, cited in CW Jenks, *International Immunities* (Stevens 1962), 17.

private law claims, such as in contract and tort (Section 1.4.1.1), and administrative law-based claims (Section 1.4.1.2) were intended to and are included within the scope of an IO's access to justice obligation.

1.4.1.1 Ensuring Access to Justice in Private Law Claims

According to its conventional meaning, a private law cause of action is where the parties to a dispute are on an equal footing given the nature of the action pursued.[65] Here, the status of either party to a dispute ought to be irrelevant for the purposes of characterising the claim. It is thus irrelevant whether one party to the dispute may be a public entity. This means that public authorities can in principle be sued when they have allegedly breached a contract or committed a tort. While the boundaries between the public and the private are increasingly becoming blurred, for the moment, it suffices to say that one set of private law claims clearly triggering an IO's access to justice obligation would involve disputes where the identity of the IO as a public international organisation is irrelevant to the determination of the claim at hand. In such instances, an IO behaves like any other private person with respect to the transaction or conduct at issue. In such cases, an IO's obligation to provide for appropriate modes of dispute settlement is therefore tailored towards disputes over rights and duties within the private law sphere, including classically private law claims in property, contracts, unjust enrichment and tort (i.e., personal injury, illness or death).[66]

Cases arising out of traffic accidents and routine contractual claims are unlikely to pose any issues as to their characterisation as private law claims.[67] However, the lack of a definition on what precisely claims of a 'private law character' mean is a matter that has given rise to recent controversy due to the increased instances of

65 Private law is generally understood as that 'part of the law that deals with such aspects of relationships between individuals that are of no direct concern to the state. It includes the law of property and of trusts, family law, the law of contract, mercantile law, and the law of tort': see 'private law' in J Law (ed) *A Dictionary of Law* (OUP, 9th ed, 2018); in comparison, public law is that part of the law that 'deals with the constitution and functions of the organs of central and local government, the relationship between individuals and the state, and relationships between individuals that are of direct concern to the state. It includes constitutional law, administrative law, tax law, and criminal law': see 'public law' in J Law (ed) A Dictionary of Law (OUP, 9th ed, 2018).

66 K Schmalenbach, 'Dispute Settlement (Article VIII Sections 29–30 General Convention)' in A Reinisch and P Bachmayer (eds), *The Conventions on the Privileges and Immunities of the United Nations and Its Specialized Agencies: A Commentary* (Oxford University Press 2016), 529–31.

67 A Reinisch, 'Convention on the Privileges and Immunities of the Specialized Agencies New York, 21 November 1947' (*Introductory Note*, United Nations Audiovisual Library of International Law) (2009) <http://legal.un.org/avl/ha/cpiun-cpisa/cpiun-cpisa.html> accessed 20 June 2018.

mass tort cases against several IOs.[68] Instances of such cases include the *Srebrenica case* against the UN,[69] the lead poisoning case against UNMIK,[70] the Haiti cholera cases against the UN,[71] and the *Jam* case against the International Finance Corporation.[72] These are hard cases and the same set of facts can be characterised in multiple ways.[73] But this does not mean that such claims stop being of a private law character. Such cases clearly trigger an IO's obligation to provide appropriate modes of dispute resolution to harmed persons as well.

1.4.1.2 Ensuring Access to Justice in Disputes of an Administrative Law Character

In addition to private law-based causes of action, the obligation on IOs to provide for appropriate modes of dispute settlement was also included to require and ensure access to justice in disputes of an administrative law character. Administrative law claims belong to that branch of public law where affected individuals challenge the administrative acts of public authorities.[74] At the domestic level, administrative acts are best understood as 'legal and physical acts taken in the exercise of public authority that may affect the rights, liberties or interests of natural or legal persons. This includes the refusal to act, an omission to act (in cases where the administrative authority is under an obligation to act), and regulatory acts'.[75]

Administrative power is now regularly exercised by IOs at the international level. This is an example of the exercise of international public authority. Bogdandy and others define international public authority as 'any authority exercised on the basis of a competence instituted by a common international act

68 For a discussion on the private–public distinction in international dispute resolution, see generally, B Hess, *The Private-Public Divide in International Dispute Resolution: The 2017 Hague Lecture*, vol 388 (Recueil des Cours 2018), 49–266.

69 *Stichting Mothers of Srebrenica v The Netherlands* App no 65542/12 (ECtHR, 11 June 2013) (*Srebrenica case*).

70 *NM and Others v UNMIK* (Human Rights Advisory Panel, 26 February 2016) Case no 26/08.

71 'Cholera Litigation' (*Institute for Justice and Democracy in Haiti*) <www.ijdh.org/cholera/cholera-litigation/> (2018) accessed 3 June 2016.

72 *Jam et al. v International Finance Corporation* (D.D.C. 2016) no 15-612 (this case has been subject to various appeals and is further considered in Chapter 4).

73 See Chapter 5.

74 Administrative law is the 'branch of public law governing the exercise of powers and duties by public authorities. ... It is particularly concerned with the control of public power by judicial review and by non-judicial mechanisms. ... There is no universally accepted demarcation of the area of administrative law, but it conventionally includes the exercise of power' by public authorities: see Oxford Quick Reference, 'Administrative Law' in A Dictionary of Law <www.oxfordreference.com/view/10.1093/oi/authority.20110803095351924> (2018) accessed 25 April 2021.

75 OSCE Handbook (n 50), 20.

of public authorities, mostly states, to further a goal which they define, and are authorized to define, as a public interest'.[76] They go on to observe that in numerous cases 'public authority under international law is vested in an institution that qualifies as an international organization with international legal personality'.[77] IOs exercise considerable authority over private actors for the former possess the 'legal capacity to determine [the latter's] and to reduce their freedom, i.e. to unilaterally shape their legal or factual situation'.[78] And as Goldmann observes, more than ever before, IOs execute international administrative acts directly or indirectly impacting on the subjective interests of private actors.[79]

That IOs exercise ever-increasing forms of international public authority impacting on private rights is a matter subjected to much academic scrutiny (more on this in Section 1.4.4). It is worth remembering that IOs have always exercised administrative power over private persons in one form or another since their inception. A typical situation is the IO's exercise of administrative power over its staff members, giving rise to countless claims in this sphere. As was said, the motivation behind the Section 29 obligation in the General Convention was also to facilitate justice for IO staff members, with the UN required to create an appropriate forum to resolve international administrative or international civil service disputes (employment disputes between IOs and their staff members).[80] The rationale is again the same. IO staff were barred access to national courts due to IO immunities, so an alternative forum was needed to ensure access to justice for such individuals.

While the General Convention did not make mention of claims by staff members, the omission is unexceptional. This is because the drafting committee to the General Convention recommended the establishment of an administrative tribunal to deal with staff disputes between the UN and its employees. Consistent with this recommendation, the UN went on to establish the UN Administrative Tribunal,[81] and now there exist numerous other

76 A von Bogdandy, M Goldmann and I Venzke, 'From Public International to International Public Law: Translating World Public Opinion into International Public Authority (2016) Research Paper No 2016-02, Max Planck Institute for Comparative Public Law & International Law (MPIL) <https://ssrn.com/abstract=2770639> accessed on 25 April 2021, 1381–3.

77 Ibid.

78 Ibid.

79 M Goldmann, 'Inside Relative Normativity: From Sources to Standard Instruments for the Exercise of International Public Authority' (2008) 9 German Law Journal 1.

80 *Effect of Awards of Compensation Made by the United Nations Administrative Tribunal* (Advisory Opinion) [1954] ICJ Rep 47 (*Effect of Awards Advisory Opinion*).

81 See generally, A Megzari, *The Internal Justice of the United Nations: A Critical History 1945–2015* (Brill 2015).

tribunals based on the same rationale.[82] The point being that the obligation to provide appropriate modes of dispute settlement was always intended to apply to claims by any private actor who otherwise would be denied justice due to the jurisdictional immunities of an IO.

The basic access to justice obligation requiring IOs to create appropriate modes of dispute resolution for private parties adversely impacted by IO conduct was never meant to be limited to conventional private law claims such as in contract or tort. If this was the case, claims by staff members, which are considered to be claims of an administrative law nature, would not have formed the type of claim that fall within the scope of the Section 29 obligation of the General Convention, which they do. Thus, the obligation on the UN, and for that matter other IOs, to create appropriate or alternative modes of dispute settlement for private persons seeking to raise claims against them applies to any claim alleging wrongdoing by the latter causing harm to the former. This is irrespective of whether a claim may be in contract, tort or administrative law. Such a reading is consistent with the language of a Section 29 type obligation; squarely in line with its object and purpose; and consistent with the rationale behind such obligations in the first place.

Overall, the obligation on IOs to provide for appropriate modes of dispute settlement ultimately requires that whenever IO immunity prevents access to national courts for a claimant whose subjective rights or interests are impacted by an IO, that person should be granted access to an appropriate mode of dispute settlement. This must be done to address or remove the possibility of a denial of justice to a private party due to the application of jurisdictional immunities in favour of an IO.[83] That IOs must provide appropriate modes of dispute resolution to private persons is of course a compelling proposition. However, a crucial question is what is meant by the term 'appropriate'? As I show in the next two sections, the word 'appropriate' must be given content or substance by referring to human rights and fair trial considerations.

1.4.2 *From the IO's Access to Justice Obligation to the Individual Right to Access Justice*

As was shown in the previous section, the constituent instruments of IOs create an access to justice obligation on them. This obligation provides that IOs have to provide appropriate modes of dispute settlement. The word 'appropriate' is

[82] See the discussion in Chapter 3.

[83] K Wellens, *Remedies against International Organisations* (Cambridge University Press 2002), 22.

left undefined and it is necessary to give it meaning. To give substance to the word 'appropriate', we must take the fair trial notion from IHRL into account. The right to a fair trial helps give real content to the word 'appropriate' and aids in interpreting the substance of an IO's access to justice obligation. In other words, human rights considerations make it possible to operationalise an IO's access to justice obligation. What has historically been a basic treaty-based obligation on IOs to provide for appropriate modes of dispute resolution now squarely corresponds to the individual right to a fair trial.

Individuals now possess rights directly on the international plane enforceable against other international legal persons.[84] The legal infrastructure to protect human rights is relatively well developed.[85] This is the case both at the international and regional level.[86] The legal relationship and infrastructure to guarantee access to justice for private persons impacted by IO conduct is not immune to the aforementioned reality. The access to justice obligation on IOs is now perceived, understood and given substance through IHRL in general, and the right to a fair trial in particular. So much so that an 'appropriate' mode of dispute settlement can now be equated to a system of dispute resolution that provides for the constellation of fair trial guarantees mentioned earlier (see Section 1.3).

Indeed, in the preceding decades, attempting to comply with their access to justice obligation, IOs have sought to create appropriate DRMs within their institutional structures based on a human rights and fair trial rationale. What is more, the modes of dispute settlement are becoming judicialised, replicating domestic courts and tribunals. Important practice is provided by the relatively recent reformed internal justice system at the UN set up to resolve international administrative disputes. Following decades of criticism of the old UN internal justice system, which lacked independence and impartiality, was bogged by undue delays in the resolution of disputes, and was generally lacking in fairness,[87] a brand new system of internal justice was implemented approximately ten years ago.[88] In advocating a new system of internal justice,

84 See generally, K Parlett, *The Individual in the International Legal System: Continuity and Change in International Law* (Cambridge University Press 2011).

85 Even though the human rights framework faces considerable pressures, it is relatively well developed.

86 For a list of international regional human rights courts and monitoring mechanisms, see International Justice Resource Center, 'Courts & Monitoring Bodies' <https://ijrcenter.org/courts-monitoring-bodies/> accessed 25 April 2021.

87 R Gulati, 'The International Dispute Resolution Mechanism of the United Nations' (2011) 15 Max Planck Yearbook of United Nations Law.

88 Ibid.

a high-profile group of experts (the Redesign Panel) advising the UN on its internal justice system had observed:

> [E]stablishing a professional system of internal justice is essential if the United Nations is to avoid the double standard – which currently exists – where the standards of justice that are now generally recognized internationally and that the Organization pursues in its programmatic activities are not met within the Secretariat or the funds and programmes themselves. These international standards include the right to a competent, independent and impartial tribunal in the determination of a person's rights, the right to appeal and the right to legal representation.[89]

Due to the Redesign Panel's recommendations, a much reformed UN internal justice system now exists.[90] This new system comprises of a two-tier formal justice mechanism that highly resembles domestic judiciaries, consisting of judicial officers who can render binding decisions.[91] A similar rationale had also inspired internal justice systems at other IOs in the context of resolving employment disputes. For example, Amerasinghe, a leading authority in the field, when speaking about the creation of the WBAT, remarked:

> [W]here administrative power was exercised, there should be available machinery, in the event of disputes, to accord a fair hearing and due process to the aggrieved party. Hence, there was a need for an independent judicial body to decide complaints relating to the exercise of administrative power.[92]

A human rights and fair trial rationale is not limited to IOs creating internal justice systems to resolve employment disputes, but has also led to increased judicialisation in differing contexts. De Chazournes and Fromageau have said:

> [i]n the short time-span since the establishment of [mechanisms to provide for] remedies [at IOs], their profiles and structure have evolved, indicating a path towards due process, not to mention a preference for judicial procedure. This exemplifies the fact that due process requirements have played, and continue to play, an important role in the shaping and the evolution of the structure and function of remedies established by international organizations. Protection of the rights of non-state actors requires the setting up of

89 'Report of the Redesign Panel on the United Nations System of Administration of Justice' (28 July 2006) (61st session) UN Doc A/61/205 (Redesign Panel Report), para 9.

90 Gulati (n 87).

91 Ibid.

92 Amerasinghe (n 17), 319.

remedies with judicial features. Remedies are thus becoming more and more judicial in nature.[93]

It may be concluded that a fair trial rationale has inspired the creation of numerous DRMs at several prominent IOs. Importantly, any IO practice to create, or attempt to create, appropriate modes of dispute resolution or internal justice systems compliant with fair trial standards should not be seen as optional. In discharging their access to justice obligation, IOs must in fact take into account how they may do so appropriately, that is, by referring to standards consistent with the individual right to access a fair trial. Therefore, what is 'appropriate' in terms of the quality of justice required ought to be informed by the requirements of a fair trial. This much is borne out by the applicable jurisprudence in this field.

1.4.3 *The Incorporation of the Right to a Fair Trial at IOs through the Principle of the 'Good Administration of Justice'*

Whereas the nuanced development of fair trial norms as they apply in the national setting has largely happened in the civil and criminal law context, for IOs, this has happened in the international civil service or employment sphere. This should not come as a surprise for IOs have conventionally tended to establish internal justice systems only with respect to employment disputes. As Shihata observed, 'review mechanisms of the actions and omissions of international organizations have traditionally been limited to the review of staff appeals in personnel matters through an administrative tribunal'.[94]

Indeed, the ICJ has rendered important judgments clarifying the key structural guarantees that must accompany the delivery of justice at an IO's internal justice system. This, the ICJ has primarily done in the context of its now-abolished review function concerning the two major international administrative regimes. These are the UN Administrative Tribunal (the ICJ's advisory role was abolished in 1995)[95] and the ILOAT (the ICJ's advisory

93 L Boisson de Chazournes and E Fromageau, 'Balancing the Scales: The World Bank Sanctions Process and Access to Remedies' (2012) 21(4) European Journal of International Law 963, 966.

94 IFI Shihata, *The World Bank Inspection Panel* (2nd edn, Oxford University Press 2000), 234–6.

95 In respect of the now-abolished ICJ review mechanism pertaining to the UN Administrative Tribunal, between 1956 and 1995, Article 9 of the then applicable UN Administrative Tribunal's Statute provided the possibility for the ICJ to render an Advisory Opinion (binding on the parties), to determine the question whether the UN Administrative Tribunal had made a 'fundamental error in procedure having occasioned a failure of justice'.

role was abolished in 2016).[96] The ICJ's review function concerning the decisions of the UN Administrative Tribunal and ILOAT permitted it to render binding judgments effectively overruling those tribunals where it could be shown that the tribunal seized had failed to comply with fundamental rules of procedure, being rules consisting of key fair trial guarantees. If these fundamental rules of procedure were absent, a 'failure of justice' would ensue. Accordingly, ICJ jurisprudence hones in on the key structural and fundamental fair trial guarantees without which justice can simply not be delivered.

Significantly, in its *Effect of Awards Advisory Opinion*, the ICJ said that judicial organs within IOs must be independent and impartial (Section 1.4.2.1), and in the *UNESCO Advisory Opinion*, it properly separated law from politics.[97] It said that judicial organs at IOs must not be deterred from performing their judicial function when adjudicating disputes even in sensitive political contexts (Section 1.4.2.2); and in its more recent jurisprudence, the ICJ ultimately incorporated the core fair trial guarantees into the delivery of justice at the institutional level (Section 1.4.2.3). All of this goes to show that an appropriate mode of dispute settlement must be consistent with fair trial standards.

1.4.3.1 The *Effect of Awards Advisory Opinion*

The basic obligation to provide for appropriate modes of dispute resolution to private parties was imposed on IOs through their constituent instruments to address or remove the possibility of a denial of justice due to the application of jurisdictional immunities. It was precisely such a rationale that led the ICJ in its *Effect of Awards Advisory Opinion*[98] to conclude that despite the absence of an express power in the UN Charter, the UN General Assembly had the power to create a judicial organ vested with the jurisdiction to resolve employment disputes between the UN and its employees. Importantly, the creation of such an independent judicial body was actually needed to ensure access to justice for private actors, in this case, the organisation's staff members.

96 Megzari (n 81), 10, chapter 17. Regarding the Article XII regime, see the Amendments to the Statute of the ILOAT adopted at its 105th Session (June 2016), which repealed Article XII of the ILOAT Statute (International Labour Conference, 105th session) <www.ilo.org/global/about-the-ilo/how-the-ilo-works/departments-and-offices/jur/legal-instruments/WCMS_498369/lang–en/index.htm> accessed 20 June 2018.

97 *Effect of Awards Advisory Opinion* (n 80); *Judgements of the Administrative Tribunal of the International Labour Organisation upon Complaints Made against the United Nations Educational Scientific and Cultural Organization* (Advisory Opinion) [1956] ICJ Rep 77 (*UNESCO Advisory Opinion*).

98 *Effect of Awards Advisory Opinion* (n 80).

The facts giving rise to the request for the Advisory Opinion in *Effect of Awards* is perhaps one of the darkest periods in UN staff affairs, questioning the functional independence of the UN generally, and that of the international civil service specifically.[99] Following a secret agreement between the first UN Secretary-General and the US Government regarding the 'US Loyalty Program', during 1952–1953, several UN staff members possessing US nationality were terminated from their employment at the UN for suspected links to the American Communist Party, within the broader context of the 'witch-hunt' of the McCarthy era.[100] All of the affected staff filed claims before the then UN Administrative Tribunal, the predecessor to the UNDT and the UNAT regimes. Ten out of the eleven claims filed by the permanent staff succeeded for their termination was contrary to the relevant staff regulations and staff rules.[101]

Attempting to defy the UN Administrative Tribunal's decisions, the General Assembly issued a request for an Advisory Opinion to the ICJ, asking whether the UN could refuse to implement a decision of that tribunal.[102] The United States, supported by several other member states, submitted that the General Assembly could refuse to comply with the decisions of the UN Administrative Tribunal for it was the General Assembly that created the tribunal, and the latter could thus not bind the former.[103] The ICJ not only said that the UN had validly created a judicial body empowered to render final and binding decisions,[104] but it also laid down the human rights and access to justice-based rationale behind the creation of an appropriate judicial body in the form of the UN Administrative Tribunal. The *Effect of Awards Advisory Opinion* explained the very need for judicial mechanisms to resolve employment disputes between the UN and its employees to protect the latter's right to access justice at a forum that was independent of the executive or political organs. The ICJ highlighted that the UN as an organisation charged with the promotion of human rights generally could not possibly deny the right of its own employees to access a judicial or arbitral mechanism when their employment rights were allegedly breached.[105]

99 See, for example, UN Charter (n 6), art 100, enshrining the requirement of the independence of the international civil service.

100 For a background of those cases, see Megzari (n 81), 130–52, citing amongst others, *Glaser* (21 August 1953) UN Administrative Tribunal Judgement No 38; *Crawford* (21 August 1953) UN Administrative Tribunal Judgement No 18.

101 See ibid.

102 'Supplementary Estimates for the Financial Year 1953' UNGA Res 785 (VIII) (9 December 1953) UN Doc A/RES/785 (VIII).

103 *Effect of Awards Advisory Opinion* (n 80), 13.

104 Ibid, 53.

105 Ibid, 57.

The views of the ICJ in the *Effect of Awards Advisory Opinion* form the earliest exposition of the principle that private persons having claims against IOs (including IO staff) ought to have access to an independent tribunal or arbitral process based on what may only be described as a human rights rationale. Critically, the ICJ left no doubt as to the independence of the UN Administrative Tribunal as a judicial body, saying that its decisions were final and binding on the other organs of the UN.[106] Judicial DRMs at IOs are then to be understood as wholly independent from the political or executive organs of an IO, with the concept of the separation of powers applying within the context of institutional dispute resolution.[107] Further support for this proposition can be garnered from another important ruling of the ICJ involving yet another case that concerned the impact of the US Loyalty Program.

1.4.3.2 The *UNESCO Advisory Opinion*

This time, it was UNESCO that had terminated the employment of certain US nationals within its employment following an agreement between the US Government and UNESCO's Director-General.[108] On this occasion, the ILOAT went a step further than the UN Administrative Tribunal, not only determining that the termination was contrary to the relevant staff regulations and staff rules, but also questioned the very propriety of the agreement between the Director-General and the US Government concerning the US Loyalty Program.[109]

Similar to the UN's reaction in the *Effect of Awards Advisory Opinion*, unhappy with the ILOAT's findings, UNESCO triggered the mechanism seeking the ICJ's Advisory Opinion regarding its obligations to comply with certain decisions of the ILOAT which it considered to be beyond its competence because they concerned political questions.[110] The ICJ held that the

106 Ibid, 53.

107 The principle of the separation of powers was endorsed in the context of the delivery of international administrative justice by the Internal Justice Council of the UN charged with monitoring the administration of justice in the reformed UN's internal justice system: see 'Report of the Internal Justice Council – Administration of Justice' UNGA Res 72/210 (24 July 2017) UN Doc A/72/210 (IJC 2017 Report), para 3.

108 *UNESCO Advisory Opinion* (n 97).

109 See *Re Duberg (Judgment No 17)* (1955) ILOAT; *Re Leff (Judgment No 18)* (1955) ILOAT; *Re Wilcox (Judgment No 19)* (1955) ILOAT; *Re Bernstein (Judgment No 21)* (1955) ILOAT; *Re Froma (Judgment No 22)* (1955) ILOAT; *Re Pankey (Judgment No 23)* (1955) ILOAT; *Re Van Gelder (Judgment No 24)* (1955) ILOAT. For analysis, see Megzari (n 81), 181–2. In each of the cases, the ILOAT said the decision to dismiss the officials was unfounded and impinged on the independence of the international civil service.

110 *UNESCO Advisory Opinion* (n 97), 17.

ILOAT was empowered to hear and determine the relevant cases, issue final and binding decisions,[111] and its judicial character must be fully respected.[112] The ICJ thus dismissed UNESCO's argument that questions about the permissibility of the US Loyalty Program constituted a political question and that it was allegedly non-justiciable. Political or executive organs of an IO, including member states, must not then interfere in the administration of justice by wrongly colouring legal disputes as political ones. Thus, the judicialisation of internal justice systems at IOs (discussed in Section 1.4.2) should not just be seen as a matter of institutional preference, but is in fact supported by ICJ jurisprudence, clarifying what an 'appropriate' mode of dispute settlement at IOs should look like.

1.4.3.3 Incorporation of the Entire Constellation of Fair Trial Rights into the Institutional Legal Order and the Principle of the 'Good Administration of Justice'

In its subsequent jurisprudence, the ICJ has expressly incorporated the key component fair trial rights as applying to the delivery of justice at internal justice systems. In its Advisory Opinion in the *Application for Review of Judgement No 158 of the United Nations Administrative Tribunal*,[113] the ICJ stated that if internal justice systems fail to comply with fundamental rules of procedure, a failure of justice occurs:

> [C]ertain elements of the right to a fair hearing are well recognized and provide criteria helpful in identifying fundamental errors in procedure which have occasioned a failure of justice: for instance, the right to an independent and impartial tribunal established by law; the right to have the case heard and determined within a reasonable time; the right to a reasonable opportunity to present the case to the tribunal and to comment upon the opponent's case; the right to equality in the proceedings vis-à-vis the opponent; and the right to a reasoned decision.[114]

Indeed, the fair trial guarantees identified by the ICJ as forming fundamental rules of procedure, that is, judicial independence and impartiality,[115] and the various subcomponent rights to fairness and equality,[116] form core fair trial rights under IHRL. While certain judges of the ICJ have shown a willingness

[111] Ibid, 65.

[112] Ibid.

[113] *Application for Review of Judgment No 158 of the United Nations Administrative Tribunal* (Advisory Opinion) [1973] ICJ Rep 166 (*Review of Judgment No 158*).

[114] Ibid, para 92.

[115] General Comment No 32 (n 41), para 19.

[116] See ICCPR (n 37), arts 2, 14(1) and 26 (enshrining the right to equality in the administration of justice) for a discussion of the right to a fair hearing without undue delay (see General Comment No 32 (n 41), para 27), and for a discussion of the right to be present at one's trial,

to presume the application of fair trial provisions contained in human rights treaties as directly applicable to IOs,[117] overall, the ICJ prefers to translate fair trial rights into the international institutional context through the concept of the 'good administration of justice'.[118] The principle of the 'good administration of justice' was specifically devised to ensure that the right to a fair trial could be operationalised within IOs. The principle was first used to address the manifest equality deficit in the ILOAT Statute (as it read prior to 2016).

Article XII of the ILOAT Statute empowered a respondent IO (but not the complainant before the ILOAT) to invoke the jurisdiction of the ICJ to issue a binding judgment where it found that a decision of the ILOAT was 'vitiated by a fundamental fault in the procedure followed'.[119] Two distinct intrusions into the right to equal access to justice prevailed in the Article XII regime. First, it only allowed the defendant organisation to seek the ICJ's Advisory Opinion where the very employee who initiated the litigation at the ILOAT had no ability to do so. Second, as individuals do not have standing before the ICJ,[120] the complainant before the ILOAT could not exercise his or her fair trial rights on an equal basis with the organisation. Such a scheme is demonstrably contrary to the right to a fair trial, breaching the right to equality of arms. Equality of arms, also a fundamental rule of 'fairness',[121] requires that all parties to the proceedings are given an equal opportunity to present their case. As the HRC has said 'there is no equality of arms if, for instance only [one party] is allowed to appeal a certain decision. The principle of equality … demands, inter alia, that each side be given the opportunity to contest all the arguments and evidence adduced by the other party'.[122]

On numerous occasions, the ICJ itself observed that the inability of the very individual who initiated the litigation at the ILOAT to approach the ICJ, and put their case forward in their own right, raised grave issues of equality in

and other rights of defence (including the ability of communicating with counsel of one's choosing) (see ibid (n 41), paras 36–7).

117 Seperate opinion Judge Cancado Trindade, Judgment No 2867 of the Administrative Tribunal of the International Labour Organization upon a Complaint Filed against the International Fund for Agricultural Development (Advisory Opinion) [2012] ICJ 10 (IFAD Advisory Opinion), 51; dissenting opinion in *South West Africa (Ethiopia v South Africa) (Second Phase)* [1966] ICJ Rep 6, 250 (per Judge Tanaka).

118 *Judgment No 2867 of the Administrative Tribunal of the International Labour Organization upon a Complaint Filed against the International Fund for Agricultural Development* (Advisory Opinion) [2012] ICJ 10 (*IFAD Advisory Opinion*).

119 ILOAT Statute (n 96), art XII.

120 For limitations as to standing, see ICJ Statute (n 1), art 66.

121 General Comment No 32 (n 41), paras 15–29.

122 Ibid, para 14.

proceedings that effectively constituted a contentious dispute,[123] resulting in a binding judgment.[124] When first confronted by the equality deficit in the Article XII regime, in its *UNESCO Advisory Opinion* rendered in 1954,[125] the ICJ allowed the employee to make submissions through the organisation, and dispensed with oral hearings altogether to bring about so-called actual equality.[126] Crucially, the Court justified creating 'actual equality' by stating that the right to access justice on an equal basis follows from the requirements of 'good administration of justice'.[127] The principle of the 'good administration of justice' is best understood through the lens of a general principle of law operational at IOs.[128] The ICJ has invoked general principles of law most frequently in respect of procedural matters, even if that label is not used.[129] The concept of 'good administration of justice', clearly of a procedural character, may be thus best classified as an overarching general principle derived from the right to a fair trial helping embed the rule of law at IOs.[130]

The ICJ has gone on to confirm that the concept of 'good administration of justice' is motivated by considerations of a fair trial. It is worth noting the views of Judge Greenwood in the *IFAD Advisory Opinion*,[131] which perhaps had some role in causing a much awaited repeal of Article XII of the ILOAT Statute. In his declaration in the *IFAD Advisory Opinion*, Judge Greenwood said

> there is a marked inequality of access to justice in that the employer, but not the employee, may challenge a decision of the Tribunal. While that inequality might have been acceptable fifty years ago (although for some judges it aroused concerns even then), I do not believe that it is acceptable today ... [this] procedure ... is at odds with contemporary concepts of due process and the integrity of the judicial function.[132]

123 *IFAD Advisory Opinion* (n 117), para 5, Judge Greenwood said: 'the reality of such proceedings as a confrontation between a staff member and the organisation'.

124 Ibid, para 4; also see the separate Opinion of Judge Antonio Augusto Cançado Trindad in the *IFAD Advisory Opinion* (n 117), paras 28, 92 and 101.

125 *UNESCO Advisory Opinion* (n 97), 86.

126 Ibid.

127 Ibid.

128 For a brief discussion of general principles of law in the institutional context, see generally, R Gulati, Acquired Rights in International Administrative Law (March 2021). *Max Planck Yearbook of United Nations Law*, Vol. 24, Forthcoming, Available at SSRN: https://ssrn.com/abstract=3813411.

129 See generally, R Yotova, 'Challenges in the Identification of the "General Principles of Law Recognised by Civilized Nations": The Approach of the International Court' (University of Cambridge, August 2017) Research Paper No 38/2017.

130 A von Bogdandy, 'General Principles of International Public Authority: Sketching a Research Field' (2008) 9 German Law Journal 11, 18–19.

131 *IFAD Advisory Opinion* (n 117).

132 Ibid, para 3.

Thus, for a mode of dispute resolution to be considered as 'appropriate', it must comply with the principle of the 'good administration of justice', which is essentially derived from, and is synonymous with, the right to a fair trial as found in IHRL. Whether the right to a fair trial is translated into the institutional context based on the application of fair trial provisions directly on IOs,[133] through the principle of the 'good administration of justice', or perhaps even customary international law, the point is that fair trial guarantees constitute binding procedural standards that must accompany the delivery of justice within an IO's internal justice system.

The very creation and existence of DRMs and internal justice systems at IOs can be explained by the demands of human rights generally, and access to justice specifically. The access to justice and human rights imperative behind the creation of internal justice systems can now be said to be accepted wisdom.[134] IOs create internal justice systems not just as a matter of policy preference, but to implement an organisation's obligation to provide appropriate modes of dispute settlement to private parties affected by their conduct. The word 'appropriate' in this context is now given meaning and content through the various component fair trial rights that apply at internal justice systems. Such appropriate modes must be created to ensure that private persons allegedly harmed by IO conduct can access a fair trial. In the end, if the mode of dispute resolution is not 'appropriate', a failure of justice is the consequence.

1.4.4 *The Broadening of the Access to Justice Obligation on IOs*

As a result of the increased exercise of international public and administrative power by IOs, new types of administrative disputes against IOs arise frequently. Due to this increased exercise of public power, where an IO unilaterally shapes an individual's 'legal and factual situation',[135] access to justice obligations placed on IOs have been brought into sharp focus.[136] As Kingsbury and Donaldson observe:

> [M]any international organizations also engage in administration that more directly affects entities and individuals outside the organization. … Perhaps the most prominent examples of administration of this kind are the various

[133] EU Charter of Fundamental Rights (26 October 2012) 2012/C 326/02 (EUCFR), art 47.

[134] Wellens (n 83), 14.

[135] See generally, A von Bogdandy, P Dann and M Goldmann, *The Exercise of Public Authority by International Institutions: Advancing International Institutional Law* (Springer 2010); also see A von Bogdandy, P Dann and M Goldmann, Developing the Publicness of Public International Law: Towards a Legal Framework for Global Governance Activities (2008) 9 German Law Journal 11.

[136] See generally, Goldmann (n 79).

> activities of the UN Security Council and its committees, taking binding decisions applicable to particular States (for example, the imposition of sanctions), and even to particular individuals (for example, the listing of persons linked to particular terrorist organizations, and thereby rendered subject to asset-freezing and restrictions on movement). The UN High Commissioner for Refugees … is similarly acting in an administrative capacity when conducting refugee status determinations and administering refugee camps. The World Health Organization … assesses global health risks and issues warnings, and the World Bank sets standards for good governance for specific developing countries as a condition for financial aid. At least some aspects of all of these activities may be understood as administrative.[137]

The increased administrative activity by IOs has of course meant that the type and number of disputes of an administrative law character beyond the employment context have witnessed a marked rise. As is evident, global administrative disputes may arise in several contexts and raise particularly challenging accountability issues. Kingsbury and Stewart point out that international organisations

> more and more find themselves confronting the question of their accountability to non-employee and non-state third parties whom they may allegedly have harmed. … More often the issues relate to specific regulatory actions directly affecting individual third parties: refugee status determinations, day-to-day administration of camps and, indeed, of entire territories (as in both Kosovo and East Timor in the first decade of the 21st century), as well as military and peacekeeping operations.[138]

The access to justice obligation on IOs, and the corresponding right to a fair trial held by individuals, would be equally applicable to administrative law claims beyond the employment context.[139] Jurisdictional immunities bar private actors impacted by increased IO administrative activity from approaching national courts in general. There is no principled reason as to why the access to justice obligation on IOs should or does not apply in respect of global

[137] B Kingsbury and M Donaldson, 'Global Administrative Law' in R Wolfrum (ed), *Max Planck Encyclopedia of Public International Law* ((Max Planck Institute for Comparative Public Law and International Law 2011) para 15.

[138] B Kingsbury and RB Stewart, 'Legitimacy and Accountability in Global Regulatory Governance: The Emerging Global Administrative Law and the Design and Operation of Administrative Tribunals of International Organizations' in K Papanikolaou and M Hiskaki (eds), *International Administrative Tribunals in a Changing World* (Esperia 2008), 193–220.

[139] See B Kingsbury, N Krisch and RB Stewart, 'The Emergence of Global Administrative Law' (2005) 68 Law and Contemporary Problems 16, 17.

administrative claims more broadly. Ultimately, as Schmalenbach has said, the access to justice obligation 'cushions' the adverse effects of jurisdictional immunities.[140] Thus, what is relevant to the existence of the access to justice obligation is not how a claim may be characterised, but the need to ensure justice whenever IO conduct affects the rights of private parties.[141] Clearly, the access to justice obligation on IOs now has much more work to do. The debate is not whether IOs are required to provide for appropriate modes of dispute resolution (which they must do) whenever privately held rights are allegedly breached, but whether such modes of dispute resolution are 'appropriate'.

Attempting to provide for such appropriate modes of dispute settlement, IOs have sought to create sector-specific mechanisms to provide private actors redress due to alleged excesses in the exercise of IO public/administrative power. Such mechanisms include various types of ombudsman processes, including the mechanism in place to hear complaints from persons subject to certain UN Security Council terrorism sanctions,[142] redress mechanisms for persons adversely impacted by development projects funded by MDBs,[143] mechanisms for persons/entities accused of corruption in relation to MDB-funded projects to contest debarment decisions,[144] appellant mechanisms for individuals dissatisfied with refugee status determinations by the UNHCR,[145] complaint mechanisms at INTERPOL for individuals subject to INTERPOL Red Notices,[146] to name just a few.

140 See Schmalenbach (n 66), 529.

141 Such an understanding is also reflected in treaty arrangements. See, for example, Article 24(1) of the Headquarters Agreement between France and INTERPOL (entered into force 1 September 2009), which provides that 'unless the parties to the dispute decide otherwise, any dispute between the organization and a private party shall be settled in accordance with the Optional Rules for Arbitration between International Organizations and Private Parties of the Permanent Court of Arbitration'.

142 See N Schrijver, 'Beyond Srebrenica and Haiti, Exploring Alternative Remedies against the United Nations' (2013) 10 International Organizations Law Review 2, 588–600, 596–7.

143 See A Riga Sureda, 'Process Integrity and Institutional Independence in International Organizations: The Inspection Panel and the Sanctions Committee of the World Bank' in L Boisson de Chazournes, CPR Romano and R Mackenzie (eds), *International Organizations and International Dispute Settlement: Trends and Prospects* (Brill 2002), 184.

144 Ibid, 186.

145 BS Chimni, 'Co-option and Resistance: Two Faces of Global Administrative Law' (Global Administrative Law Series, 2015) IILJ Working Paper No 2015/16, 18, where the author highlights the refugee determination role of the UNHCR and points to the fair trial deficits in the appeal process respecting adverse determinations; also see M Smrkolj, 'Public Authority & International Institutions and Individualized Decision Making: An Example of UNHCR's Refugee Status Determination' (2008) 9 German Law Journal 1.

146 For an excellent background, see M Savino, 'Global Administrative Law Meets "Soft" Powers: The Uncomfortable Case of Interpol Red Notices' (2011) 43 New York University Journal of International Law and Politics 263, 311–12.

The redress mechanisms in place for private persons to access justice in the varied types of global administrative disputes against IOs are rising significantly. Providing such legal recourse is crucial to deliver justice to the countless individuals who are impacted by IO conduct. As Von Bernstorff points out,

> [i]n case of unlawful exercise of power by public officials affected persons and entities [must] have legal recourse to an independent court or tribunal. If formalized procedural constraints for the exercise of public authority are important at the national level they are all the more so at the international level since conflicts over substantive legal standards and disagreement over community values are usually more acute[147]

In the final analysis, the real question is not whether IOs ought to provide fair trial compliant means of dispute settlement to any private actor whose subjective interests they impact, which they must do. The issue of critical significance is whether IOs do so 'appropriately'.

1.5 CONCLUSION

IOs impact the rights of private parties more than ever before. As a result, they increasingly confront class actions in tort, complex contractual claims, and an assortment of claims of an administrative law nature given the ever-increasing exercise of international public authority. All such claims are equally impacted by IO immunities in terms of access to national courts, and thereby trigger the operation of the access to justice obligation on IOs. What is relevant to the existence of the access to justice obligation is not how a claim is framed (may it be in tort, contract, administrative law, etc.), but the need to ensure justice whenever IO conduct affects the rights of private parties. As was discussed in this chapter, IOs have indeed developed internal justice systems and provided review mechanisms seeking to comply with their access to justice obligation. The real question is whether such mechanisms are 'appropriate', that is, are they compliant with fair trial standards? To answer this crucial question, we need to understand what the component fair trial rights require with much more specificity. Only once detailed standards to assess internal justice systems with the right to a fair trial are developed can the 'appropriateness' of a particular mode of dispute settlement be properly assessed. In the next chapter, I consider what these standards entail.

[147] Von Bernstorff (n 57), 1939.

2

The Criteria for Assessing the Appropriateness of Dispute Resolution Mechanisms at International Organisations

2.1 INTRODUCTION

In Chapter 1, we saw that for an IO's internal justice system to be considered as an 'appropriate' mode of dispute settlement, it must deliver justice consistently with fair trial standards. Without knowing what the component fair trial rights specifically require, the task of assessing a DRM established at an IO cannot be undertaken. In this chapter, I develop precise criteria relevant to assess a DRM's compliance with fair trial standards. The right to a fair trial is a complex one, incorporating several component rights within its rubric.[1] It is presently impractical and unnecessary to discuss each and every component fair trial right. The aim is to focus on those guarantees that form a precondition to the 'good administration of justice'. Those key structural guarantees concern the right of private actors impacted by IO conduct to have access to an independent and impartial DRM that delivers justice fairly. These three things are interrelated and structurally significant to ensure access to justice. Of course, it is trite to say that courts and tribunals should be independent, impartial and fair. Indeed, the word 'fair' appears in the very name of the right. In addition, the right to access an independent and impartial court is the most critical fair trial guarantee.[2] The HRC states that the requirement of 'independence and impartiality ... is an absolute right that is not subject to any exception'.[3] The CJEU has explained that the qualities of independence and impartiality, for their part, are 'inherent in the task of adjudication'.[4] Overall, if a DRM lacks the basic tenets of independence, impartiality and fairness, then

[1] See Chapter 1.

[2] HRC, 'General Comment No 32: Right to Equality before Courts and Tribunals and to a Fair Trial' (23 August 2007) UN Doc CCPR/C/GC/32 (General Comment No 32), para 3.

[3] Ibid, para 19.

[4] CJEU Opinion 1/17 (Full Court, 30 April 2019), paras 202–3.

it cannot be considered to constitute a judicial body in the first place.[5] Accordingly, these three guarantees are the focus of the present analysis.

In determining the content of independence, impartiality and fairness, guidance is drawn from judicial decisions, especially those of human rights courts and monitoring mechanisms. Increasingly, soft law instruments are becoming more and more prominent[6] and will be referred to as well. These soft law instruments are of much significance, for they have been created following detailed and lengthy deliberations, reflect basic concepts of a fair trial and mutually reinforce each other. These standards are primarily contained in the International Bar Association's Minimum Standards of Judicial Independence 1982 (IBA Standards),[7] UN Basic Principles on the Independence of the Judiciary 1985 (Basic Principles),[8] the Bangalore Principles of Judicial Conduct 2002 (Bangalore Principles),[9] Commonwealth (Latimer House) Principles on the Three Branches of Government 2003 (Commonwealth Principles),[10] and the Burgh House Principles on the Independence of the International Judiciary 2004 (Burgh House Principles).[11] The Burgh House Principles have been developed in the context of international courts and tribunals, as well as in respect of

5 *Bahrain, Egypt, Saudi Arabia and United Arab Emirates v Qatar* (Appeal Relating to the Jurisdiction of the ICAO Council under Article 84 of the Convention on International Civil Aviation) (14 July 2020) ICJ General List No 173 (ICAO Case).

6 For the role soft law plays in the sphere of human rights, see generally Stéphanie Lagoutte, Thomas Gammeltoft-Hansen and John Cerone (eds), Tracing the Roles of Soft Law in Human Rights (Oxford University Press 2016); for the potential legal impact of soft law on international law generally, see, Andreas Zimmermann and Nora Jauer, Possible Indirect Legal Effects under International Law of Non-Legally Binding Instruments (May 2021) *KFG Working Paper Series*, No. 48, May 2021, Berlin Potsdam Research Group 'The International Rule of Law – Rise or Decline?' <https://ssrn.com/abstract=3840767>, pp 8, 10.

7 International Bar Association, 'IBA Minimum Standards of Judicial Independence' (1982) <www.ibanet.org/Document/Default.aspx?DocumentUid=10917543-8F09-4A68-8324-9228BB6237A1> accessed 3 June 2018 (IBA Standards).

8 Seventh United Nations Congress on the Prevention of Crime and the Treatment of Offenders UNGA Res 40/32 (6 September 1985, adopted 29 November 1985) (40th session, 96th meeting) UN Doc A/RES/40/32 (Basic Principles).

9 Judicial Group on Strengthening Judicial Integrity, 'The Bangalore Draft Code of Judicial Conduct' (2002) <www.unodc.org/pdf/crime/corruption/judicial_group/Bangalore_principles.pdf> accessed 4 June 2018 (Bangalore Principles).

10 The Commonwealth, 'Latimer House Principles: Practitioner's Handbook' (2017) <http://thecommonwealth.org/sites/default/files/news-items/documents/LatimerHousePrinciplesPH7Jul17.pdf> accessed 4 June 2018 (Commonwealth Principles).

11 Study Group of the International Law Association on Practice and Procedure of International Courts and Tribunals, and the Project on International Courts and Tribunals, 'The Burgh House Principles on the Independence of the International Judiciary' (2004) <www.ucl.ac.uk/international-courts/sites/international-courts/files/burgh_final_21204.pdf> accessed 4 June 2018 (Burgh House Principles).

mechanisms and individuals performing roles of a judicial character (including arbitrators).[12] The Burgh House Principles thus have direct relevance to the work of internal justice systems at IOs.[13] However, as was clarified in the Universal Declaration on the Independence of Justice 1983 (Montreal Declaration),[14] the principles of independence, impartiality and fairness, applicable in the national context generally, apply internationally too.[15] Therefore, all the aforementioned sources are relevant to develop the fair trial criteria against which DRMs at IOs should be assessed.

2.2 THE MEANING OF INDEPENDENCE, IMPARTIALITY AND FAIRNESS

Independence, impartiality and fairness have overlaps and are interrelated. However, they are discussed separately as they emphasise different aspects of a fair trial. In particular, the concept of independence requires that judges make decisions free from undue extraneous pressures, especially from the executive and legislative arms of government. For IO's internal justice systems, this would amount to a DRM's independence from comparable IO organs.[16] Impartiality requires that the judge maintains an equal distance from either party to a case and does not favour one party over another.[17] In other words, the court should be independent from the parties to a given case as well.[18] As they are somewhat different things, independence (Section 2.2.1) and impartiality (Section 2.2.2) are discussed in distinct subsections. The concept of 'fairness', which consists of several further subcomponent fair trial rights, is discussed in Section 2.2.3. These guarantees include the right to equality in the administration of justice (Section 2.2.3.1), the right to

12 Ibid, Preamble.

13 See ibid, which states that the 'Principles which shall apply primarily to standing international courts and tribunals [shall apply] to full-time judges. The Principles should also be applied as appropriate to judges ad hoc, judges ad litem and part-time judges, to international arbitral proceedings and to other exercises of international judicial power'. Burgh House Principles (n 11), para 1.2, establishes their applicability to IATs and similar judicial bodies.

14 Montreal Declaration: Universal Declaration on the Independence of Justice (adopted on 10 June 1983) <www.icj.org/wp-content/uploads/2016/02/Montreal-Declaration.pdf> accessed 4 June 2018 (Montreal Declaration).

15 Ibid, paras 1.06–.07.

16 N Blokker, 'The Governance of International Courts and Tribunals: Organizing and Guaranteeing Independence and Accountability' in A Follesdal and G Ulfstein (eds), *The Judicialization of International Law: A Mixed Blessing?* (Oxford University Press 2018) 37-8.

17 CJEU Opinion 1/17 (n 4), paras 202–3.

18 G Robertson, 'Judicial Independence: Some Recent Problems' (International Bar Association's Human Rights Institute, June 2014) Thematic Paper No 4, 3.

equality of arms (Section 2.2.3.2), the right to an oral hearing (Section 2.2.3.3), the right to appeal (Section 2.2.3.4), the right to a reasoned judgment (Section 2.2.3.5), the right to a fair trial without undue delay (Section 2.2.3.6) and the right to an effective remedy and fair trial (Section 2.2.3.7).

2.2.1 *Independence*

The concept of judicial independence triggers considerations around the judiciary's structural design, with the central demand being that the executive and the legislature must not interfere in the performance of the judicial function.[19] This concept, referred to as the 'separation of powers', is fundamental to the rule of law.[20] It is as much applicable to the administration of justice in national systems as it is in the IO setting.[21] Clearly, if an IO's executive or legislative organ, or for that matter any other external entity or person, interferes in the work of a judicial organ, then it can hardly be said that the judicial branch can render justice independently and fairly. As has been said in the context of the UN's internal justice system:

> In a formal setting, independence of the judiciary is directly related to the separation of powers in respect of the arms of the governance structures of the United Nations. If there is no separation of power properly recognized and supported, not only do the necessary checks and balances not function properly in respect of the matters within the jurisdiction of the Dispute Tribunal and the Appeals Tribunal, but there can be no proper assertion of the rule of law or provision of justice[22]

To embed the separation of powers within a given legal order, being a necessary precondition to the existence of an independent judiciary, various structural guarantees need to be provided for. It is necessary to secure the institutional, decisional and individual independence of a court and its judges.[23] Institutional independence requires that a court is operationally

19 See Burgh House Principles (n 11), paras 1.1–.2; Montreal Declaration (n 14), paras 1.02–.03 and 1.07; Basic Principles (n 8), para 1.

20 See, for example, Commonwealth Principles (n 10), Principle 1; as pointed out in A Nollkaemper, *National Courts and the International Rule of Law* (Oxford University Press 2011), 54.

21 Burgh House Principles (n 11), para 1.2: 'Where a court is established as an organ or under the auspices of an international organisation, the court and judges shall exercise their judicial functions free from interference from other organs or authorities of that organisation'; also see Montreal Declaration (n 14), para 1.7.

22 'Report of the Internal Justice Council – Administration of Justice' UNGA Res 72/210 (24 July 2017) UN Doc A/72/210 (IJC 2017 Report), para 27.

23 Bangalore Principles (n 9), Value 1; Commonwealth Principles (n 10), Principle IV.

independent from the executive and legislative organs and has a distinct presence within the structures of an IO (Section 2.2.1.1). To guarantee the decisional independence of a court or tribunal, the judiciary must be able to conclusively decide on its own jurisdiction, and decide cases based on the relevant law and facts, without external interference or pressures (Section 2.2.1.2). To secure the individual independence of judges, security of tenure must be provided for and the method of judicial appointment must be transparent, with merit being the primary criteria based on which judicial appointments are made (Section 2.2.1.3).

2.2.1.1 Institutional Independence

Institutional independence requires that a DRM created by an IO be operationally independent from the legislative/policymaking organs, executive organs or any member state/s of an IO. It specifically requires that courts and tribunals possess administrative and financial autonomy.[24] Principle 1.2 of the Burgh House Principles states:

> Where a court is established as an organ or under the auspices of an international organisation, the court and judges shall exercise their judicial functions free from interference from other organs or authorities of that organisation. This freedom shall apply both to the judicial process in pending cases, including the assignment of cases to particular judges, and to the operation of the court and its registry.

And Principle 1.3 goes on to state:

> The court shall be free to determine the conditions for its internal administration, including staff recruitment policy, information systems and allocation of budgetary expenditure.

The principle that a court must enjoy administrative and financial independence vis-à-vis its operations is now well accepted. How this may be achieved requires further explanation. First, if administrative and financial independence is to be achieved, then justice machinery must be adequately funded so that it can operate without external interference.[25] The CCJE explains that '[a]lthough

24 IBA Standards (n 7), para 7; Montreal Declaration (n 14), para 2.40; Burgh House Principles (n 11), paras 1.2 and 1.3.

25 Especially note Burgh House Principles (n 11) para 6 that states: 'State parties and international organisations shall provide adequate resources, including facilities and levels of staffing, to enable courts and the judges to perform their functions effectively'; also see IBA Standards (n 7), para 7; Basic Principles (n 8), para 7; Commonwealth Principles (n 10), Principle IV(c); Montreal Declaration (n 14), para 2.41.

the level of funding [an IO] can afford for its courts is a political decision, care must always be taken, in a system based on the separation of powers, to ensure that neither the executive nor the legislative authorities are able to exert any pressure on the judiciary when setting its budget'.[26]

Second, ensuring that a court's registry is not susceptible to impermissible pressures is a crucial aspect of maintaining a court's operational independence. Registries play a significant role in organising and directing a court's operations generally. They recruit staff, liaise with parties and are generally charged with a court's administrative working. Any undue interference in the work of the registry can undermine trust as well as the institutional independence of a court.[27] Cartier and Hoss have noted:

> [A]ll Registries and Legal Secretariats (RLS), as organs of the judicial institutions, play an indispensable role in inspiring trust in their institution by interacting with the parties in a fair and effective manner, in the midst of conflicting views and interests. Parties are more likely to accept adverse findings if they believe that their case was handled with utmost care, not only by individual judges, but also by those with whom they are in regular contact at [Registries]. This is true in any international judicial institution, such as inter-state courts, international criminal courts, and human rights courts. A fair, strictly neutral, and discrete [Registry] greatly contributes to generating trust in any judicial institution.[28]

Third, to secure operational independence, an internal justice system in general, and DRM in particular, must have a distinct presence within the institutional structure of an IO. If such a distinct presence is not achieved, then the occurrence or risk of occurrence of impermissible interference in a court or tribunal's operations is obviously high. The manner in which a court or tribunal's separate presence may be secured is by creating a distinct judicial organ within the relevant IO's institutional structures.[29] Failing such a step,

[26] Consultative Council of European Judges, Opinion No 2 (2001) on the Funding and Management of Courts, para 5.

[27] See generally, R Gulati, 'Judicial Independence at International Courts and Tribunals: Lessons Drawn from the Experiences of the International Court of Justice and the Appellate Body of the World Trade Organisation' in Berlin Potsdam Research Group, *The International Rule of Law – Rise or Decline?* (2020) KFG Working Paper Series, No 41.

[28] S Cartier and C Hoss, 'The Role of Registries and Legal Secretariats in International Judicial Institutions' in CPR Romano, Y Shany and K Alter (eds), *The Oxford Handbook of International Adjudication* (Oxford University Press 2014), 712.

[29] As Blokker points out, international courts can be set up under three models: 'from almost pure ad hoc meetings having hardly any pre-established rules to fully fledged international [organisations] that may either be a self-standing treaty organ or an organ of an international

a dispute resolution forum could simply amount to an extension or arm of the administration as opposed to constituting an independent judicial body.[30]

Accordingly, express guarantees concerning the operational independence of a DRM must be provided for,[31] and the forum should ideally be established as a distinct organ of an IO. At the very least, a judicial body must be strictly separated from any other organ of an IO. Only with such a degree of autonomy present can a court or tribunal's institutional independence be guaranteed.

2.2.1.2 Decisional Independence

Decisional independence requires that, first, a court should be able to autonomously and conclusively determine its own jurisdiction.[32] Second, the court or tribunal must decide cases based on the law and facts of a case and not any extraneous considerations.

On the first dimension, Principle 3 of the Basic Principles relevantly states that the 'judiciary shall have jurisdiction over all issues of a judicial nature and shall have exclusive authority to decide whether an issue submitted for its decision is within its competence as defined by law'. It is important to briefly explain what 'jurisdiction' in the present sense means. International courts and tribunals, including those created at IOs, are established by agreement amongst states and do not possess plenary jurisdiction. The adjudicative jurisdiction of a DRM found in an IO's internal justice system is only triggered if it has been specifically endowed with powers to exercise its adjudicative powers over a particular person (jurisdiction *ratione personae* or personal jurisdiction), subject matter (jurisdiction *ratione materiae* or subject-matter jurisdiction), the dispute in light of its temporality (jurisdiction *ratione temporis*) or the events in question (jurisdiction *ratione loci*).[33] If these jurisdictional criteria are not established, a DRM's jurisdiction will not exist.

organization (of which in most cases the relevant international court or tribunal is also an organ)': Blokker (n 16), 35.

30 ICAO Case (n 5), para 60.

31 The Basic Principles (n 8) provide for the independence of the judiciary to be 'guaranteed by the State and enshrined in the Constitution or the law of the country'.

32 See Basic Principles (n 8) para 3 that states: 'The judiciary shall have jurisdiction over all issues of a judicial nature and shall have exclusive authority to decide whether an issue submitted for its decision is within its competence as defined by law'; also see Montreal Declaration (n 14), para 2.5.

33 For an excellent analysis of grounds of jurisdiction (including issues around admissibility), see generally, Y Shany, 'Jurisdiction and Admissibility' in CPR Romano, Y Shany and K Alter (eds), *The Oxford Handbook of International Adjudication* (Oxford University Press 2014), 781.

Thus, when assessing the decisional independence of DRMs created at IOs, it is important to bear in mind that the autonomy such mechanisms have regarding the cases they can hear and determine is fairly limited. Although where a forum has been established to resolve claims advanced by individuals or other private persons seeking to access justice, jurisdiction may be liberally interpreted.[34] Overly restrictive reading of jurisdictional provisions can result in denials of justice, thereby defeating the very purpose of creating such courts and tribunals in the first place, that is, to protect the individual.[35] In the end, for a court or tribunal to be considered decisionally independent, it must have the ability to autonomously and independently determine jurisdictional matters. In other words, the court must possess the jurisdiction to determine its own jurisdiction (*compétence de la compétence*).[36] As long as a court can autonomously determine questions about its own jurisdiction, decisional independence would exist.

Second, decisional independence requires the ability of a court to conclusively determine its own jurisdiction, but also that it can make decisions based on the law and facts of a case without any undue external interference. Basic Principle 2 relevantly states that the 'judiciary shall decide matters before them … on the basis of facts and in accordance with the law, without any restrictions, improper influences, inducements, pressures, threats or interferences, direct or indirect, from any quarter or for any reason'. The Burgh House Principles state in their preamble:

> [T]o ensure the independence of the judiciary, judges must enjoy independence from the parties to cases before them, their own states of nationality or

34 In *Judgments of the Administrative Tribunal of the ILO upon complaints made against the United Nations Educational Scientific and Cultural Organization* (Advisory Opinion) [1956] ICJ Rep 77, 23, the ICJ commented: 'The Court has not lost sight of the fact that both before the Administrative Tribunal and in the statements submitted to the Court it has been contended, on the one hand, that the Administrative Tribunal was an international tribunal and, on the other hand, that it was a Tribunal of limited jurisdiction ("juridiction d'attribution") and not of general jurisdiction ("juridiction de droit commun"). That contention has been put forward with a view to achieving a restrictive interpretation of the provisions governing the jurisdiction of the Tribunal. The Court does not deny that the Administrative Tribunal is an international tribunal. However, the question submitted to the Tribunal was not a dispute between States. It was a controversy between UNESCO and one of its officials. The arguments, deduced from the sovereignty of States, which might have been invoked in favour of a restrictive interpretation of provisions governing the jurisdiction of a tribunal adjudicating between States are not relevant to a situation in which a tribunal is called upon to adjudicate upon a complaint of an official against an international organization.'

35 Ibid. Human rights courts and monitoring mechanisms are other typical adjudicative mechanisms established to protect the individual.

36 For a useful exposition of the *compétence de la compétence* principle, see *Prosecutor v Dusko Tadić* (Decision on the Defence Motion for Interlocutory Appeal on Jurisdiction) Case no IT-94-1-AR72 (1996) 35 ILM 32, paras 9–64.

> residence, the host countries in which they serve, and the international organisations under the auspices of which the court or tribunal is established.

To maintain decisional independence, impermissible interference by external actors in its work is strictly prohibited, and a judge must not be put under undue pressure by other members of the court itself. As the CCJE clarifies:

> a judge is in the performance of his or her functions no-one's employee; he or she is holder of a State office. He or she is thus servant of, and answerable only to, the law. It is axiomatic that a judge deciding a case does not act on any order or instruction of a third party inside or outside the judiciary.[37]

While any undue interference into the judiciary will undermine the independence of a court, a careful balance nevertheless needs to be struck between 'the need to protect the judicial process against distortion and pressure, whether from political, press or other sources, and the interests of open discussion of matters of public interest in public life and in a free press'.[38] Of course, open and genuine debate ought not to be stifled, but where interference in the judiciary subjectively or objectively pressurises a court or its judges to decide a case on anything other than the facts and the law, independence would be undermined.

2.2.1.3 Individual/Personal Independence

Only if each individual judge's personal independence is guaranteed can they render substantively independent justice without fear or favour. Substantive independence requires that individual judges 'have a right and a duty to decide cases before them according to law, free from outside interference including the threat of reprisals and personal criticism'.[39] Obviously, if the substantive independence of a judge(s) is lacking, the court as an institution cannot be decisionally independent either, showing how personal and decisional independence interact. Given its significance to the concept of independence generally, it is critical to secure the personal independence of judges.

Maintaining personal independence requires that 'the terms and conditions of judicial service are adequately secured to guarantee that individual judges

37 CCJE, Opinion No 1 (2001) on standards concerning the independence of the judiciary and the irremovability of judges, para 64.

38 Ibid, para 63.

39 International Bar Association, 'Human Rights in the Administration of Justice: A Manual on Human Rights for Judges, Prosecutors and Lawyers' (OHCHR, 2003) (OHCHR Report), para 4.5.8.

are not subject to executive [or other undue] control'.[40] In General Comment No 32, the HRC clarified that 'to safeguard their independence, the status of judges, including their term of office, their independence, security, adequate remuneration, conditions of service, pensions and the age of retirement shall be adequately secured by law'.[41] To ensure individual independence, the relevant criteria thus focus on matters concerning (1) judicial appointment and (2) the security of tenure.

(1) JUDICIAL APPOINTMENT Transparency in the judicial appointment process is crucial, and judges must be appointed based on merit as the primary consideration. Who appoints judges and how and on what basis judges are appointed constitute the central matters of concern.[42] It is increasingly considered that the executive or legislature (or comparable organs at IOs charged with appointing international judges) ought to have a minimal role in the selection and appointment of judges, and that only appropriately qualified persons be appointed to judicial office. On the former, if the executive, for example, has undue influence on the appointment process, then serious questions about the motives behind the appointment could be raised.[43] Principle 10 of the Basic Principles states:

> Persons selected for judicial office shall be individuals of integrity and ability with appropriate training or qualifications in law. Any method of judicial selection shall safeguard against judicial appointments for improper motives.

Judicial appointments made by the executive alone may not automatically cause the breach of the principle of individual independence.[44] However, the greater its role, the more scrutiny ought to be given when issues of

[40] Ibid, para 1(b); Basic Principles (n 8), para 11; Bangalore Principles (n 9), Value 1.1; Montreal Declaration (n 14), para 2.2.

[41] General Comment No 32 (n 2), para 19.

[42] Traditionally, there are no strict criteria regarding the method of appointments or qualifications for appointment required. For method of appointment, see IBA Standards (n 7), para 3 (appointments should preferably be done by bodies comprising members of the judiciary); Montreal Declaration (n 14), para 2.12 states that judicial appointments should be non-discriminatory but allowing for nationality to be a criterion for appointments to international courts. For requirements on qualifications, see IBA Standards (n 7), para 26 (only appointments based on merit are permissible); Basic Principles (n 8), para 10 (requires that 'Persons selected for judicial office shall be individuals of integrity and ability with appropriate training or qualifications in law. Any method of judicial selection shall safeguard against judicial appointments for improper motives').

[43] See, for example, HRC, 'Views: Communication No 486/1991' (10 November 1993) (49th session) UN Doc CCPR/C/49/D/468/1991 (*Ol Bahamonde v Equatorial Guinea*), para 5.1.

[44] E Cannon and I Warlam, 'The Judicial Independence of the International Labour Organization Administrative Tribunal: Potential For Reform' (Report, Amsterdam

independence and impartiality are engaged. In such cases, other safeguards that help mitigate the independence deficit caused by the appointment process should be enacted, such as by providing for strong guarantees regarding the security of tenure.[45] This would be especially the case where the executive appears regularly before a court or tribunal whose judges the former appoints. As one of the parties to any case before a DRM created by an IO is always likely to be the IO itself, any significant role by an executive organ in the appointment of judges should be treated as suspect. To address this suspicion, transparency is critical.

Principle IV(a) of the Commonwealth Principles provides that to achieve judicial independence 'appointments should be made on the basis of clearly defined criteria and by a publicly declared process', where 'merit and proven integrity' are the criteria of eligibility for appointment to public office.[46] Similarly, Principle 2.3 of the Burgh House Principles states that '[i]nformation regarding the nomination, election and appointment process and information about candidates for judicial office should be made public, in due time and in an effective manner, by the international organisation or other body responsible for the nomination, election and appointment process'.[47] Emphasising the need for transparency and independence in the selection process, it has been noted that it is 'now relatively uncommon for judicial appointments to be in the hands of the executive alone, without the involvement of any other public body in selecting or shortlisting candidates'.[48] Transparent processes that are independent of the executive or legislature in the appointment of judges are required to ensure that the executive does not make appointments based on ulterior motives, as well as to guarantee that the best possible candidates are identified and appointed to judicial office. Establishing independent and appropriately constituted bodies playing a key role in the judicial selection process, with

International Law Clinic, 2007) (Amsterdam Report), 3435: 'In sum, the jurisprudence confirms that while appointment by the executive is not in itself cause to question the independence of a tribunal, such a circumstance should be counter-balanced with guarantees that insure the independence of the tribunal at hand.'

45 Human Rights Committee, 'Consideration of Reports Submitted by States Parties under Article 40 of the Covenant – Concluding Observations of the Human Rights Committee – Slovakia' (4 August 1997) (79th session) UN Doc CCPR/C/79/Add.79, para 18. In *Lauko v Slovakia* App no 26138/95 (ECtHR, 19 October 1995) the combination of appointment by the executive and the 'lack of any guarantees against outside pressures and any appearance of independence' led the Court to conclude that the bodies in question could not be considered to be independent of the executive.

46 Commonwealth Principles (n 10), Principle V(a).

47 Burgh House Principles (n 11), Principle 2.3.

48 Ibid, para 2.22.

a well-defined mandate, would thus be a key factor in ensuring the individual independence of a judge.[49]

Moreover, judicial appointments must be made on merit and based on legal qualifications as the primary consideration.[50] Without relevant experience and minimum qualifications required before an individual may be considered for a judicial role, it is hard to imagine how a judge can discharge their function in a substantively independent way. As the Burgh House Principles provide in Principle 2.1:

> [J]udges shall be chosen from among persons of high moral character, integrity and conscientiousness who possess the appropriate professional qualifications, competence and experience required for the court concerned. While procedures for nomination, election and appointment should consider fair representation of different geographic regions and the principal legal systems, as appropriate, as well as of female and male judges, appropriate personal and professional qualifications must be the overriding consideration in the nomination, election and appointment of judges.

In the context of courts or tribunals created by an IO, in addition to requirements of diversity of nationality, criteria typical to international judicial appointments, proven experience in the relevant subject matter, or related fields, must be a pre-condition for judicial selection.[51] An inexperienced candidate lacking in minimum qualifications cannot deliver justice competently, independently or fairly.

(2) SECURITY OF TENURE Once meritorious individuals are appointed to judicial office, to secure their personal independence, security of tenure must

[49] Commonwealth Principles (n 10) do not specify the mechanism by which judges should be appointed. However, the Parliamentary Supremacy, Judicial Independence: Latimer House Guidelines for the Commonwealth (19 June 1998) (Commonwealth Principles (n 10)) indicate that an 'independent process' should be used and recommend that a genuinely independent judicial appointments commission be established where no such mechanism exists.

[50] The HRC has said that judges should be selected primarily on the grounds of their legal qualifications: HRC, 'Consideration of Reports Submitted by States Parties under Article 40 of the Covenant – Concluding Observations of the Human Rights Committee – Sudan' (19 November 1997) (79th session) UN Doc CCPR/C/79/Add.85, para 21.

[51] The UN regime is discussed in Chapter 3. Another example is provided by the Statute of the World Bank Administrative Tribunal, art IV (1), providing that the 'Tribunal shall be composed of seven members, all of whom shall be nationals of Member States of the Bank, but no two of whom shall be nationals of the same State. The members of the Tribunal shall be persons of high moral character and must possess the qualifications required for appointment to high judicial office or be jurisconsults of recognized competence in relevant fields such as employment relations, international civil service and international organisation administration…'.

be provided for. Important considerations relate to the length of a judge's tenure, financial security and method of judicial dismissal. Each of these aspects is discussed next.

First, the length of the term of a judge is key to assessing individual independence. Short renewable terms tend to decrease independence, and relatively longer non-renewable terms enhance it.[52] The assumption that a judge would wish for their term to be renewed is an obvious one. That being the case, subconsciously or sometimes even consciously, a judge's decision-making may be compromised. Instead of basing the decision on the law and facts of a given case, the decision may be driven by ulterior motives, jeopardising the individual independence of a judge.[53] Following an extensive analysis that included interviews with several judges from various international courts and tribunals, Dunoff and Pollack reach the conclusion that longer terms that cannot be renewed maximise judicial independence.[54] Implementing relatively lengthy tenures with limited to no possibilities for renewal (if at all) ought to then be the standard for judicial appointments. An example of good practice is provided by the UN's internal justice system which has created seven-year non-renewable terms for UNDT judges. Further, a matter especially relevant for DRMs at IOs is that of the contract judge, with IOs often securing the services of a judge based on short-term contracts. The position of a judge on temporary contracts is akin to the situation of a judge whose tenure is short and renewable. Where the renewing person or organ is almost always a respondent before the judge (as will be the case at DRMs at IOs), there is little doubt that structural independence is seriously and adversely affected.[55] In such circumstances, a court or tribunal cannot be said to be independent.[56]

Second, providing financial security to judges is also necessary to maintain individual independence. Generally, judicial salaries and pension rights

[52] See generally JL Dunoff and MA Pollack, 'The Judicial Trilemma' (2017) 111 American Journal of International Law 2, 225–76.

[53] See especially Burgh House Principles (n 11), paras 3.1–.2. Para 3.2 provides that: 'The governing instruments of each court should provide for judges to be appointed for a minimum term to enable them to exercise their judicial functions in an independent manner.'

[54] See generally Dunoff and Pollack (n 52), 225–76.

[55] Robertson (n 18). Also note that international instruments state that temporary appointments must be avoided: see IBA Standards (n 7), para 22(b).

[56] See especially Bangalore Principles (n 9), Values 1.2 and 1.3, which state that '[a] judge shall be independent in relation to society in general and in relation to the particular parties to a dispute which the judge has to adjudicate' and '[a] judge shall not only be free from inappropriate connections with, and influence by, the executive and legislative branches of government, but must also appear to a reasonable observer to be free therefrom'.

ought not to be subject to reduction by other organs of an IO. Such a threat of action or its carrying out may compromise the financial security of judges, creating a risk that decisions adverse to the IO are not made for fear of retaliation.[57] A recent commentary to the Commonwealth Principles explains 'appropriate security of tenure and protection of levels of remuneration must be in place in relation to the judiciary. Such guarantees serve to shield judges from external pressures and conflicts of interest when they hold powerful individuals or government bodies legally to account'.[58] Finally, one way in which non-judicial organs of an IO may intrude into the independence of the judiciary is through the process of dismissal. It is now well accepted that dismissal is only permissible for the most exceptional reasons, such as in cases of proven misbehaviour or where a judge is of unsound mind.[59] Should a judge be dismissed, they must be accorded due process.[60]

2.2.1.4 The Importance of Securing Judicial Independence

As has been shown, for a justice machinery to be considered independent, it must enjoy institutional, decisional and individual independence. All those aspects are interlinked. When assessing a justice system, the criteria for judicial independence should be considered holistically. The task of assessing a justice system is not always straightforward. Where judges are comprised of members of the executive,[61] such as civil servants,[62] or where the executive manifestly controls the judiciary,[63] the breach of the standards of independence can be readily established. On one view, once independence is impaired, 'the whole functioning of the courts is prejudiced', and fair trial standards have thus been breached.[64] In other cases, structural deficiencies on their own may not justify holding a trial or a proceeding unfair. It may become difficult to establish that justice has not been administered appropriately based on

57 See Burgh House Principles (n 11), para 4.2; IBA Standards (n 7), para 15(b); Commonwealth Principles (n 10), Principle IV(b); Montreal Declaration (n 14), para 1.14.

58 J van Zyl Smit, The Appointment, Tenure and Removal of Judges under Commonwealth Principles: A Compendium and Analysis of Best Practice' (British Institute of International and Comparative Law, 2015), 19–20.

59 Burgh House Principles (n 11), para 17.1–.4; IBA Standards (n 7), para 4(a)- (b) and 30; Basic Principles (n 8), para 12; Commonwealth Principles (n 10), Principle IV(d).

60 Burgh House Principles (n 11), para 17.2; Basic Principles (n 8), para 17; Montreal Declaration (n 14), paras 2.30 and 2.33.

61 *Belilos v Switzerland* App no 10328/83 (ECtHR, 29 April 1988).

62 Ibid.

63 See ibid; also see *Sramek v Austria* App no 8790/79 (ECtHR, 22 October 1984).

64 See for example, *Grieves v The United Kingdom* App no 57067/00 (ECtHR, 16 December 2003).

structural deficiencies alone, such as the length of a judge's tenure.[65] In such situations, it becomes even more important to conduct a heightened scrutiny of whether or not a court can be said to be impartial in a particular case.

2.2.2 *Impartiality*

Whereas judicial independence requires that a judge(s) must not be subjected to undue outside pressures, impartiality demands that the judges hearing a case maintain an equal distance from all parties in that case, without favouring one party over another. As Robertson puts it, '[i]ndependence means putting judges in a position to act according to their conscience and the justice of the case, free from [external] pressures. Impartiality, on the other hand, is the judicial characteristic of disinterest towards parties and their causes in litigation'.[66]

Even though independence and impartiality are different things, they do overlap. This is the case especially where an IO would be a respondent before a DRM that it establishes and funds. Indeed, IOs would almost always be the respondent to a case pursued by a private claimant against an IO at a DRM created by the latter. Clearly, if a DRM lacks independence from other organs of an IO, it can hardly be concluded that the forum can be objectively impartial. As has been said, '[j]udges who are not independent of the state [or organisation] will be perceived (and may actually become) partial to the state [or organisation] when it is a party to litigation in their court'.[67] The need for enshrining norms guaranteeing impartiality at a DRM are thus necessary to ensure a fair trial. Specifically, in so far as the de jure guarantees pertaining to impartiality are concerned, well-accepted standards require that the judiciary does not promote the interests of one party over the other.[68] A judge should be free from objective and subjective bias. The HRC has said:

> The requirement of impartiality has two aspects. First, judges must not allow their judgement to be influenced by personal bias or prejudice, nor harbour preconceptions about the particular case before them, nor act in ways that improperly promote the interests of one of the parties to the detriment of the

65 See Amsterdam Report (n 44), 38, citing, *Siglfirdingur Ehf v Iceland* App no 34142/96 (ECtHR, 30 May 2000); also see jurisprudence considered in the Amsterdam Report (n 44), section 5.2.1.

66 Robertson (n 18), 3.

67 Ibid.

68 See HRC, 'Communication No 802/1998' (3 April 2002) (7th session) UN Doc CCPR/C/74/D/802/1998 (*Rogerson v Australia*), para 7.4, the HRC held that the '[i]mpartiality of the court implies that judges must not harbour preconceptions about the matter before them, and they must not act in ways that promote the interests of one of the parties'.

other. Second, the tribunal must also appear to a reasonable observer to be impartial.[69]

Instances where a judge's conduct, such as demonstrable hostility towards a particular party, or corrupt conduct, is proved, subjective bias may readily be established. Most cases concern objective bias as it can be difficult to produce compelling evidence regarding the personal conduct of a judge. Objective bias, also known as apparent or apprehended bias, requires an assessment from the perspective of the reasonable person. The question asked is whether the court or the tribunal can reasonably bring an impartial mind to the case before it: if not, the judge must be disqualified from hearing the case.[70] It is trite to say that justice should not only be done, but justice must be seen to be done.[71] Therefore, any conflict of interest, such as previous involvement in a case, personal knowledge of the facts or economic interest in the outcome, ought to disqualify a judge from hearing it.[72]

There are several other circumstances where a judge's behaviour and conduct would demand a recusal. Value II of the Bangalore Principles states that '[i]mpartiality is essential to the proper discharge of the judicial office. It applies not only to the decision itself but also to the process by which the decision is made'.[73] Applying this value, Principle II of the Bangalore Principles encapsulates the applicable standards.[74] First, a 'judge shall ensure that his or her conduct, both in and out of court, maintains and enhances the confidence of the public, the legal profession and litigants in the impartiality of the judge and of the judiciary'.[75] Second, a 'judge shall, so far as is reasonable, so conduct himself or herself as to minimise the occasions on which it will be necessary for the judge to be disqualified from hearing or deciding cases'.[76] Third, judges are expressly prohibited from showing hostility to a party to litigation, indicating the presence of bias.[77]

69 See General Comment No 32 (n 2), para 21; also see, *Findlay v The United Kingdom* App no 22107/93 (ECtHR, 25 February 1997) (*Findlay v The United Kingdom*), para 73. In deciding whether there is a legitimate reason to fear that a particular court lacked independence or impartiality, the standpoint of the accused is important without being decisive. What is decisive is whether his doubts can be held to be objectively justified (see *Findlay v The United Kingdom*, para 76).

70 See, for example, Burgh House Principles (n 11), paras 9.1–.2 and 11.1–.2; IBA Standards (n 7), para 44; Bangalore Principles (n 9), Value 2.5; Montreal Declaration (n 14), para 2.27.

71 Bangalore Principles (n 9), Value 3.2.

72 Burgh House Principles (n 11), paras 9.1–.2 and 11.1–.2; Bangalore Principles (n 9), Value 2.5.

73 Bangalore Principles (n 9).

74 See, for example, IBA Standards (n 7), paras 40 and 45.

75 Bangalore Principles (n 9), Value 2.2.

76 Ibid, Value 2.3.

77 Ibid, Value 2.4: 'A judge shall not knowingly, while a proceeding is before, or could come before, the judge, make any comment that might reasonably be expected to affect the outcome

Unsurprisingly, in practice, impartiality may be difficult to establish.[78] (1) A party to a proceeding may not wish to raise it fearing adverse consequences. Parties may be reluctant to make challenges to what effectively can amount to the credibility of a judge. (2) In cases of alleged subjective bias, unless a party can produce evidence of personal conduct, which is obviously difficult to do, impartiality is virtually impossible to establish. (3) Where a judge does not recuse themselves of their own accord, the very judge accused of bias often may determine an application for recusal. This matter becomes of special concern where appellate mechanisms are absent. Because a party may hesitate to raise issues of impartiality, it is even more important that a compliant regime protecting and promoting judicial independence and impartiality is enacted. Particularly, the statutes of courts and tribunals must provide for a judge's disqualification to guard against conflicts of interest. The opportunity to seek recusal of an allegedly biased judge is a must. The right to appeal also assumes much significance. The presence of a judicial code of conduct and the creation of a judicial complaint mechanism are also important tools that can go a long way in ensuring that impartiality can be secured.

Guarding against judicial bias at an institutional forum is absolutely critical as one of the parties to litigation, the IO, is always the person exercising a degree of control over the justice system. In such situations, the rules on impartiality become highly relevant, especially in its objective sense. The examination of the court's treatment of the parties in general, and that of the complainant in particular, will be especially important. Where even a hint of favouritism towards an IO is present, the independence and impartiality of a DRM is undermined, making it an inappropriate forum to access justice. In such circumstances, serious questions about 'fairness' also arise.

2.2.3 *Fairness*

For justice to be appropriately rendered, it must be delivered fairly.[79] 'Fairness' is a broad concept that is closely linked to the principle of 'equality' in the administration of justice. It incorporates within its domain several subcomponent fair trial guarantees. These guarantees operate throughout the lifecycle of a legal claim. In this section, I identify the key guarantees of 'fairness' and 'equality' that must accompany the delivery of justice at an IO's

of such proceeding or impair the manifest fairness of the process. Nor shall the judge make any comment in public or otherwise that might affect the fair trial of any person or issue.'

78 Unless impartiality is readily apparent.

79 For a discussion, see OHCHR Report (n 39), para 4.5.8.

internal justice system. These are the right to equal access to the courts (Section 2.2.3.1), equality of arms (Section 2.2.3.2), right to an oral hearing (Section 2.2.3.3), right to appeal (Section 2.2.3.4), right to a reasoned judgment (Section 2.2.3.5), right to justice without undue delay (Section 2.2.3.6) and right to an effective remedy (Section 2.2.3.7).

2.2.3.1 The Right to Equal Access to the Courts

Access to a DRM created at an IO must be consistent with the right to equality in the administration of justice. The right is a fundamental guarantee. The HRC has explained:

> The right of access to courts and tribunals and equality before them ... must ... be available to all individuals. ... A situation in which an individual's attempts to access the competent courts or tribunals are systematically frustrated de jure or de facto runs counter to the guarantee of article 14, paragraph 1, first sentence. This guarantee also prohibits any distinctions regarding access to courts and tribunals that are not based on law and cannot be justified on objective and reasonable grounds.[80]

Ultimately, the right to equality before the courts is a manifestation of the substantive right to equality and non-discrimination contained in all international and regional human rights instruments,[81] with certain ICJ judges even characterising it as a norm of jus cogens.[82] Equality in the administration of justice is central to the realisation of a fair trial given that the principle of equality, which is inexorably linked to human dignity, is one of the foundations on which the international human rights system is based.[83]

At its core, the right requires that similarly situated persons should be treated comparably unless there are justifiable reasons not to do so (formal equality), and differently placed persons may require distinct treatment to ensure substantive equality.[84] Distinctions in treatment are manifestly impermissible when they are based on a person's protected characteristic, such as

80 General Comment No 32 (n 2), para 9.

81 HRC, 'General Comment No 18: Non-Discrimination' (10 November 1989) (37th session) (General Comment No 18).

82 See Ahmadou Sadio Diallo (*Republic of Guinea v Democratic Republic of the Congo*) (Merits) [2010] ICJ Rep 639, Separate Opinion of Judge Cançado Trindade, para 163. It is also a general principle of international administrative law, see *De Merode v World Bank (Decision No 1)* (5 June 1981) 1 WBAT Rep 734.

83 See General Comment No 32 (n 2), para 65.

84 General Comment No 18 (n 81).

their race, religion, gender and so on,[85] or the difference in treatment is otherwise unreasonable or arbitrary.[86] Where a DRM at an IO limits access to a person based on a protected characteristic or in an arbitrary manner, discriminatory treatment will be the result. Therefore, equality requires that those adversely impacted by IO conduct are granted access to its internal justice system with full equality and in a non-discriminatory manner. This means that 'similar cases are dealt with in similar proceedings'.[87] At the very least, where access to an internal justice system is absent for a person(s), they must be granted access to another 'appropriate' mode of dispute resolution.

2.2.3.2 The Equality of Arms

Another dimension of the right to equality, also constituting a fundamental rule of 'fairness', is the right to equality of arms. Equality of arms requires that the parties to a case be treated equally by a court or tribunal. The HRC has explained:

> [T]he same procedural rights are to be provided to all the parties unless distinctions are based on law and can be justified on objective and reasonable grounds, not entailing actual disadvantage or other unfairness to the defendant. . . . The principle of equality between parties applies also to civil proceedings, and demands, inter alia, that each side be given the opportunity to contest all the arguments and evidence adduced by the other party. In exceptional cases, it also might require that the free assistance of an interpreter be provided where otherwise an indigent party could not participate in the proceedings on equal terms or witnesses produced by it be examined.[88]

Similarly, as the European Court has clarified, equality of arms requires that there be a fair balance between the opportunities afforded to the parties involved in litigation.[89] For instance, each party should be able to call witnesses and cross-examine the witnesses called by the other party; if one party is entitled to appeal a particular decision, the other party to litigation should also be given such an appeal right, and so on.[90] Indeed, it was the

85 International Covenant on Civil and Political Rights, opened for signature on 16 December 1966, 999 UNTS 171 (entered into force 23 March 1976), art 26.

86 General Comment No 18 (n 81), para 13.

87 General Comment No 32 (n 2), para 14.

88 Ibid, para 13.

89 European Court of Human Rights, 'Guide on Article 6 of the European Convention of Human Rights – Right to a Fair Trial (Civil Limb)' (30 April 2020) (Article 6 Guide), paras 346–8.

90 Ibid.

equality deficit in the internal justice systems of IOs subscribing to the jurisdiction of the ILOAT and the old UN Administrative Tribunal that triggered severe criticism by the ICJ, leading up to the demise of its review function of the judgments of those two tribunals (see Chapter 1). Where the right to equality of arms is systematically contravened in favour of the respondent organisation, the independence and impartiality of the tribunal may also be seriously questioned.

Of course, equality of arms does not require that a justice system ensures factual equality between the parties as this is an impossible undertaking. It nevertheless demands that legal equality be maintained and provided for. While the right to equality of arms can manifest in several contexts, it is especially relevant in terms of (1) the right to legal representation, and (2) the allocation of costs associated with legal proceedings.

(1) THE RIGHT TO COUNSEL To make the equality of arms realisable, the right to legal representation, which is also an autonomous fair trial guarantee, must be fulfilled. As the Redesign Panel had said, to guarantee equality before courts and tribunals, access to lawyers and legal services is crucial.[91] Such access should not be merely theoretical, but real. The starting point is that the right to counsel of one's own choosing is an express fair trial guarantee and must not be contravened. This much is uncontroversial. If an IO does not permit a claimant before a DRM to be represented by a lawyer, the right to counsel is adversely impacted.

A significant issue concerns the plight of indigent claimants, or claimants who are otherwise in a weaker position vis-à-vis the organisation (such as IO employees). The HRC has explained that the 'availability or absence of legal assistance often determines whether or not a person can access the relevant proceedings or participate in them in a meaningful way … free legal aid [should be provided] for individuals who do not have sufficient means to pay for it'.[92] Thus, an IO ought to be placed under an obligation to provide some form of legal aid to indigent or otherwise disadvantaged categories of litigants.[93]

In fact, private persons raising claims against IOs are almost always disadvantaged. Unlike the IO itself who can approach a national court to seek a remedy, private actors cannot do so due to an IO's jurisdictional immunities

91 'Report of the Redesign Panel on the United Nations System of Administration of Justice' (28 July 2006) (61st session) UN Doc A/61/205 (Redesign Panel Report), para 14.

92 General Comment No 32 (n 2), para 10; also see, Article 6 Guide (n 89), para 133.

93 *Airey v Ireland* App no 6289/73 (ECtHR, 1981), 1.

(see Chapter 4). Already, structural inequality is built into the international regulatory regimes governing IOs. Therefore, the most viable option for private persons to seek justice against IOs is to approach an international forum. But pursuing claims before an international court or tribunal involves navigating difficult issues of procedure and substance, requiring significant legal expertise. To add to that, IOs would tend to possess far greater human and financial resources when compared to the victims of IO conduct. Factual inequality between the IO and a victim is therefore generally present. Where structural inequality is built into the system, private parties are expected to navigate often complex and difficult legal issues, and where IOs have vastly superior financial and human resources compared to most private litigants, it would be unfair and inequitable not to provide some form of legal aid to indigent or otherwise disadvantaged claimants.

In the end, without affordable legal representation, it is unlikely that a vast category of private persons would be able to exercise their right to a fair trial before an IO's internal justice system in a fair and equitable manner. Moreover, unrepresented litigants can clog up the justice machinery because cases take longer to resolve, resulting in undue delays in the administration of justice (see Section 2.2.3.6). The fulfilment of the right to legal representation thus plays a critical role in ensuring a fair trial for the person availing of the right, but also for other users of the justice system.

(2) ALLOCATION OF COSTS Ensuring that the costs associated with advancing claims against IOs does not constitute a barrier to access judicial protection is necessary to the realisation of a fair trial as well. Such matters tend to involve (1) the payments of court or arbitrator fees and (2) the recovery of costs of legal representation. Prohibitive cost rules can undermine the right to a fair trial.

If court or arbitrator fees are high, indigent and disadvantaged claimants are unlikely to even file a claim in the first place, breaching the right to effective access to the courts.[94] And if a claimant fears being made liable to reimburse the costs of a respondent IO in case their claim does not succeed, access to justice is undermined. Any costs regime must guard against the use or threat of use of financial muscle to quell what would otherwise constitute a justified claim. As the HRC has explained, 'a rigid duty under law to award costs to

[94] General Comment No 32 (n 2), para 11; also see *R (on the application of UNISON) v Lord Chancellor* [2017] UKSC 51, para 104, where the UK Supreme Court stated that if the court fees imposed 'has the practical effect of making it unaffordable for persons to exercise rights conferred ... or of rendering the bringing of claims to enforce such rights a futile or irrational exercise, it must be regarded as rendering those rights nugatory'.

a winning party without consideration of the implications thereof or without providing legal aid may have a deterrent effect on the ability of persons to pursue the vindication of their rights'.[95] A DRM would be clearly inappropriate if the applicable costs rules prevent victims from accessing judicial protection concerning their justified claims.[96]

What type of costs rules can ensure a DRM's appropriateness is a complex question. Admittedly, designing a costs regime involves a difficult balancing exercise between fairness to a particular claimant and ensuring the efficient administration of justice.[97] Ultimately, it is the court or tribunal approached that possesses, or must possess, a discretion to allocate costs. If such allocations are to be fair, a court must take into account the disadvantaged position of claimants pursuing a remedy against IOs. Moreover, to ensure access to justice, the discretion to allocate costs should focus on the amount of costs imposed,[98] the financial means of the party,[99] the stage at which the costs are imposed,[100] and the conduct of the parties.[101] Where costs of the proceedings are excessive or prohibitive, may it be due to the prevalence of high court or arbitrator fees, or the imposition or potential imposition of adverse costs orders, a claimant is likely to desist from pursuing their claim at all.

An appropriate costs regime must therefore ensure that any court or arbitrator fees do not constitute a barrier to access justice. As it is the IO who benefits from jurisdictional immunities before national courts, and it is the IO who is

95 Ibid.

96 It has been held that 'a rigid duty under law to award costs to a winning party may have a deterrent effect on the ability of persons who allege their rights ... have been violated to pursue a remedy before the courts ... the imposition by [a court] of substantial costs award, without the discretion to consider its implications for the particular authors, or its effect on access to court of other similarly situated claimants, constitutes a violation' of the right to a fair trial and effective remedy: see *Aarela and Nakkalajarvi v Finland* (24 October 2001) Communication No 779/97, para 7.2; also see jurisprudence contained in Article 6 Guide (n 89), para 97.

97 *Weissman and Others v Romania* App no 63945/00 (ECtHR, 2 December 2011), para 35; *Stankov v Bulgaria* App no 68490/01 (ECtHR, 12 July 2007), para 57.

98 *Kreuz v Poland* App no 28249/95 (ECtHR, 19 June 2001), paras 60–7; and as the European Court clarified, where the amount of court fee imposed was roughly equal to the average yearly salary in the state party, the costs were substantial and breached the right to a fair trial (at para 62); where the amount of court fee was roughly equal to the compensation claimed, the right to a fair trial was also contravened for the costs were disproportionate: see *Stankov v Bulgaria* (n 97), para 58.

99 *Podbielski and PPU Polpure v Poland* App no 39199/98 (ECtHR, 26 July 2005), paras 64–6.

100 Ibid. If the costs are prohibitive at first instance, the impact on fair trial rights is especially grave: *Weissman and Others v Romania* (n 97), para 42; also see, *Tolstoy Miloslavsky v United Kingdom* App no 18139/91 (ECtHR, 13 July 1995), paras 61–4.

101 *Cernius and Rinkevicius v Lithuania* App no 73579/17 and App no 14620/18 (ECtHR, 18 June 2020), paras 68–9 and 74.

responsible for providing appropriate modes of dispute resolution, it is the IO's responsibility to ensure that the costs rules in place do not inhibit a fair trial. Moreover, indigent claimants should be granted legal aid and should not be subjected to adverse costs implications should their otherwise justified claim not succeed. Claimants who are not typically indigent but are otherwise in a demonstrably weak position vis-à-vis the IO, such as employees, should be provided the opportunity to avail of some form of legal assistance, and not be subjected to prohibitive adverse costs orders. If these conditions are not met at a DRM, then access to justice cannot be practically realised.

2.2.3.3 Right to an Oral Hearing

The right to an oral hearing is a significant component fair trial guarantee.[102] Cases at an IO's internal justice system are too often determined based on written submissions only (see Chapter 3). This can be highly suspect. Written submissions on their own may not provide a full opportunity to present one's case. Where disputes on the facts exist, issues of credibility are at stake or complex points of law are to be determined, oral hearings should be provided as a matter of right. It would be unfair if a person lacks the opportunity to put forward their case through an oral hearing, at least before a first instance mechanism. As has been said, 'written submissions do not afford the flexibility of oral presentations; they do not permit the recipient to mould his argument to the issues the decisionmaker appears to regard as important. Particularly where credibility and veracity are at issue, . . . written submissions are a wholly unsatisfactory basis for decision'.[103] In *R (H) v Secretary of State for Justice*,[104] Cranston J summarised the importance of oral hearings, stating:

> There can be greater confidence with an oral hearing that the relevant standards have been properly applied and that the facts on which the decision is based are accurate. The oral hearing also gives the person affected by the decision the opportunity to tailor the arguments to the concerns of the decision maker.[105]

102 Redesign Panel Report (n 91), paras 10 and 92.

103 See *Smith v Parole Board* [2005] UKHL 1, (per Lord Bingham), citing, *Goldberg v Kelly* (1970) 397 US 254, 269.

104 *H, R (On the Application of) v Secretary of State for Justice* [2008] EWHC 2590 (Admin).

105 Ibid, para 1. For other jurisprudence demonstrating the importance of oral hearings, see the short analysis of A Mackenzie, 'Oral Hearings – Who Needs Them?' (9 April 2020) <https://insights.doughtystreet.co.uk/post/102g4es/oral-hearings-who-needs-them> accessed 25 April 2021.

Equally, in the international institutional context, the importance of an oral hearing was emphasised by the Redesign Panel in the following terms:

> Hearings ... are a clear requirement in international standards whenever there are disputed issues of fact. To guarantee due process and to facilitate decisions, oral hearings should be promoted and accepted.[106]

The conduct of an oral hearing can be transformative for the outcome of a case. In *Sengupta v Holmes*, Laws LJ said 'oral argument is perhaps the most powerful force there is ... to promote a change of mind by a judge. That judges in fact change their minds under the influence of oral argument is not an arcane feature of the system; it is at the centre of it'.[107] It can hardly be contested that the right to an oral hearing can be significant for ensuring the fairness of proceedings and the good administration of justice. Moreover, if the right to an oral hearing is realised, then other important subcomponent fair trial rights, including the right to be present,[108] also become achievable. While the provision of an oral hearing can be crucial to ensure a fair trial, how it can be practically implemented at internal justice systems deserves brief reflection.

International courts and tribunals can be geographically based at significant distances from the location of one or more parties to a case. How to conduct oral hearings is said to present a logistical challenge. This challenge can be readily met. Oral hearings can be routinely conducted using audiovisual means, as is common practice in the sphere of international arbitration.[109] Moreover, the COVID-19 pandemic that the world is witnessing has caused serious disruptions to the day-to-day operation of courts and tribunals around the world. This has provided an opportunity to turbocharge the migration of oral hearings to audiovisual means generally, with technological innovation making electronic hearings demonstrably viable and perhaps even preferable in many instances. Where the tyranny of distance makes it difficult for litigants

106 Redesign Panel Report (n 91), para 10.

107 *Sengupta v Holmes and Others* [2002] EWCA Civ 1104, para 38.

108 See General Comment No 32 (n 2), paras 25 and 33–6.

109 See, for example, Korean Commercial Arbitration Board, 'The Seoul Protocol on Video Conferencing in International Arbitration' (2020) <https://globalarbitrationreview.com/virtual-hearings/seoul-protocol-video-conferencing-unveiled> accessed 20 April 2021. See also, Maxi Scherer and Franz Schwarz, In a 'First' Worldwide, Austrian Supreme Court Confirms Arbitral Tribunal's Power to Hold Remote Hearings Over One Party's Objection and Rejects Due Process Concerns, *Kluwer Arbitration Blog* (24 October 2020) <available at, http://arbitrationblog.kluwerarbitration.com/2020/10/24/in-a-first-worldwide-austrian-supreme-court-confirms-arbitral-tribunals-power-to-hold-remote-hearings-over-one-partys-objection-and-rejects-due-process-concerns/>, accessed 24 September 2021.

and their lawyers to appear in person, audiovisual means of conducting proceedings not only can help secure the right to an oral hearing in particular, but also make access to justice more affordable and viable. Thus, any real or perceived logistical challenges to the conduct of oral hearings at an IO's internal justice system must not be used as an excuse to deny the right to an oral hearing.

2.2.3.4 Right to Appeal

The provision of a first instance judicial mechanism to pursue a legal claim is a recognised fair trial guarantee that must form a feature of internal justice systems at IOs.[110] Moreover, where appellate mechanisms exist, equality of arms would of course require that both parties have access to such procedures on an equal basis.[111] Failing this, a fundamental rule of procedure is contravened, resulting in a failure of justice.[112]

However, where appellate courts do not exist, it remains somewhat uncertain whether the right to a fair trial requires creating such courts in civil cases.[113] In the context of dispute resolution at IOs, it is suggested that for an internal justice system to be fair-trial compliant, the right to appeal must be accorded. Concerning the pre-2009 UN's internal justice system, where only one layer of judicial review existed, the Redesign Panel had said that:

> [E]stablishing a professional system of internal justice is essential if the United Nations is to avoid the double standard ... where the standards of justice that are now generally recognized internationally and that the Organization pursues in its programmatic activities are not met within the Secretariat or the funds and programmes themselves. These international standards include the right to a competent, independent and impartial tribunal in the determination of a person's rights, *the right to appeal* and the right to legal representation (emphasis added).[114]

The Redesign Panel went on to say:

> When 'in the determination of ... his rights and obligations in a suit at law' an individual is deprived of the right to appeal, this severely weakens the fairness of the procedure. International standards establish the right to 'an effective

[110] ICCPR, art 14(1).
[111] *Sholam Weiss v Austria* CCPR/C/77/D/1086/2002 (HRC, 8 May 2003).
[112] See especially Chapters 3 and 5.
[113] ICCPR, art 14(3). The right to appeal in civil cases has not attracted as much jurisprudence as it has in criminal cases.
[114] Redesign Panel Report (n 91), para 9.

> remedy', 'the right to simple and prompt recourse, or any other effective recourse, to a competent court or tribunal' and 'the right to an appeal'.[115]

The right to an appeal should now be seen as a fundamental rule of fairness. In fact, the UNAT (the second instance court at the UN's internal justice system operational since 2009) considers the right to appeal so fundamental that it has decided that where there has been no neutral first instance judicial process, it cannot exercise its appellate jurisdiction.[116] The practical implementation of the right to appeal is crucial for several reasons. It provides an opportunity to correct any errors made at first instance, enhancing the overall fairness of a justice system. Moreover, appellate courts can advance a consistent interpretation of the law, ensuring that it is developed in a coherent way. As a result, as much as possible, comparable cases are then decided similarly. Consequently, the right to appeal promotes both fairness and equality in the administration of justice.

2.2.3.5 The Provision of a Reasoned Judgment

If a court or tribunal does not provide a properly reasoned decision, then the fairness of proceedings is undermined.[117] A reasoned judgment serves several purposes. It shows that the parties' submissions and arguments have actually been listened to.[118] This then becomes an aspect of the right to be heard. Reasoned judgments avoid arbitrary decision-making for a judge must set out the law and facts on which their decision is based, demonstrating independence and impartiality.[119] A reasoned judgment helps realise the right to a public hearing,[120] promoting fairness for the party concerned specifically, and transparency in proceedings generally.[121] And where a person wishes to appeal a first instance decision, the provision of reasons is necessary. Without such reasons, the appellant would not know the basis on which an appeal may be advanced.[122]

115 Ibid, para 10.
116 'Report of the Internal Justice Council – Administration of Justice' UNGA Res 75/154 (10 July 2020) UN Doc A/75/154 (IJC 2020 Report), paras 40–3.
117 S Trechsel, *The General Right to a Fair Trial in The Collected Courses of the Academy of European Law* (Oxford University Press 2006), 103.
118 Ibid, 106.
119 Ibid, 104.
120 Ibid, 104.
121 In *Hadjianastassiou v Greece* App no 69/1991/321/393 (ECtHR, 23 November 1992), it was explained that this was so that 'the public in a democratic society may know the reasons for judicial decisions, and to enable (the individual affected) to decide whether to appeal'.
122 Trechsel (n 117), 104.

A court must therefore render a fully reasoned decision that conducts a proper examination of the submissions, arguments and evidence adduced by the parties.[123] Reasons must address each and every important aspect of a case. A detailed answer to every argument may not be required,[124] but reasons must be given in answer to every argument put forward by the party which could be relevant for the decision; in other words, those reasons 'which would, if accepted, be decisive for the outcome of the case'.[125]

At first instance, if a court fails to address the arguments and submissions of a party that could have been determinative, fails to explain as to why it did not hear from a witness or otherwise consider evidence that can relevantly bear on a fact in issue,[126] and ignores relevant points of law, a fair trial will be denied. Similarly, at the appellate level, any decision must be accompanied by reasons. A properly reasoned judgment requires something more 'than a formulaic response ... the Court should indicate ... the main reasons why the Court' reached the decision it did.[127] Where an oral hearing has not been granted at first instance, an appellate court should respond to any new arguments put forward by a party.[128]

Whether at first instance or on appeal, a judgment must explain the rationale and basis on which findings of fact or law are made. If it fails to do so, then the decision could appear to rubberstamp one side's argument over another. This would most obviously breach the right to a fair trial. In the end, the right to a reasoned judgment is a critical due process guarantee that assists in the realisation of numerous key fair trial guarantees, and is a fundamental rule of procedure. If this right is breached, justice is not appropriately rendered.

2.2.3.6 The Right to a Fair Trial without Undue Delay

The adage 'justice delayed is justice denied' is not to be treated as an empty slogan but must be given substance to. The right is a key fair trial guarantee that is a precondition to the 'good administration of justice'. The HRC has

123 *Kraska v Switzerland* App no 90/1991/342/415 (ECtHR, 19 April 1993), para 30; *Van der Hurk v the Netherlands* App no 16034/90 (ECtHR, 19 April 1994), para 59.

124 *Van der Hurk v the Netherlands* (n 123), para 61; *Garcia Ruiz v Spain* App no 30544/96 (ECtHR, 21 January 1999), para 26; *Helle v Finland* App no 20772/92 (ECtHR, 19 December 1997), para 55.

125 *Ruiz Torija v Spain* App no 18390/91 (ECtHR, 9 December 1994).

126 *Bricmont v Belgium* App no 10857/84 (ECtHR, 1989); Article 6 Guide (n 89), paras 151–3.

127 *Aboushanif v Norway* (2 September 2008) Communication No 1542/2007, CCPR/C/93/D/1542/2007, para 7.2.

128 *Helle v Finland* (n 124), para 60.

provided guidance on the factors that can assist in determining whether a delay in the conduct of proceedings is 'undue'. It has said:

> [D]elays in civil proceedings that cannot be justified by the complexity of the case or the behaviour of the parties detract from the principle of a fair hearing. . . . Where such delays are caused by a lack of resources and chronic under-funding, to the extent possible supplementary budgetary resources should be allocated for the administration of justice.[129]

Where delays are systemic and structural, including due to chronic under-funding of the justice machinery, access to justice is undermined. Assuming that the judiciary is appropriately resourced, what ultimately constitutes undue delay in the completion of a legal proceeding is a fact-specific inquiry, requiring an analysis of the complexity of a case, the parties' behaviour and what is at stake for the claimant.[130] It is difficult to state in the abstract whether a claim has been determined in a timely manner. However, in general, if a relatively straightforward claim against an IO (such as an employment case) takes more than a few months to be determined (see further Chapter 3), the right to a fair trial without undue delay will be contravened. If an IO builds an internal justice system which looks robust on paper but fails to provide timely justice, the right to a fair trial is breached. Undue delay in the conduct of a case also contravenes the right to an effective remedy, an autonomous right that closely interacts with the right to a fair trial.

2.2.3.7 The Right to an Effective Remedy and Fair Trial

The right to an effective remedy is an autonomous right provided for in all global and regional human rights treaties.[131] It requires that where a person's rights are breached, an effective remedy must be provided to remediate any such breach.[132] Remedies can take the form of compensation, restitution, non-monetary remedies, or even require changes to the law to address systemic violations.[133] As such, an effective remedy may be realised through judicial, administrative or any other means,[134] as long as the entity granting the remedy

129 General Comment No 32 (n 2), para 27.

130 See jurisprudence discussed at Article 6 Guide (n 89), para 427.

131 See for example, ICCPR, art 2(3).

132 Ibid.

133 D Shelton, 'Human Rights, Remedies' (July 2006) in *Max Planck Encyclopedia of International Law*.

134 ICCPR, art 2(3)(b).

is independent of the person/entity responsible for the violation.[135] This right interacts and overlaps with the right to a fair trial in at least three ways.

First, as a set of procedural guarantees, the right to a fair trial plays an important role in the ultimate implementation of substantive rights that a party seeks to enforce through a judicial process.[136] The right to an effective remedy and fair trial thus overlap given that they both aim to secure a remedy for breaches of substantive rights – the former does this in a general way, and the latter in the context of a suit at law. For a fair trial to be effective or meaningful, the court or tribunal approached must be empowered to grant a remedy that is 'effective' in light of the claims pursued. Therefore, if a court's jurisdictional scheme is so restrictive that it cannot in any meaningful way decide the substance of the complaint advanced, or it lacks the power to grant appropriate relief that fully compensates the victim for the harm suffered, then the right to a fair trial in conjunction with the right to an effective remedy is undermined.

Second, the right to an effective remedy requires that a remedy must be enforceable to be characterised as 'effective'.[137] Similarly, for a court or tribunal to amount to an independent and impartial decision-maker, it is well accepted that its decisions should be final, binding and respected.[138] As has already been said, without the power of making binding decisions, a forum charged with resolving legal disputes cannot even be characterised as a judicial mechanism. Any interference into the execution of a judgment directed at nullifying it manifestly breaches the right to a fair trial.[139] Therefore, where a DRM's decision(s) is not enforceable in law, or is not enforced in a timely way, the right to a fair trial and effective remedy are independently and cumulatively contravened.[140]

Finally, in principle, an effective remedy may be accessed through judicial or any other means, although judicial means are preferable.[141] On the other hand, the right to a fair trial enshrines a right to access a remedy through an independent and impartial judicial mechanism that must deliver justice consistently with all fair trial guarantees. This is a much higher procedural

135 Shelton (n 133).

136 General Comment No 32 (n 2), para 58. For instance, if legal aid to disadvantaged litigants is not provided, then a fair trial cannot be accessed, meaning that an effective remedy cannot be realised by such individuals through the judicial process: General Comment No 32 (n 2) para 10.

137 ICCPR, art 2(3)(c).

138 OHCHR Report (n 39).

139 See especially jurisprudence discussed in Article 6 Guide (n 89), paras 198–200.

140 Ibid, para 171.

141 Shelton (n 133), para 16.

threshold to meet. The right to a fair trial is ultimately to be considered as a lex specialis to the right to an effective remedy.[142] Accordingly, where an individual seeks to vindicate a right through a suit at law, the right to an effective remedy must be made realisable through the provision of a fair trial before a judicial body, or a forum that is functionally equal to it. In the final analysis, to ensure meaningful access to justice, only a judicialised DRM can be classified as an appropriate mode of dispute resolution for private actors pursuing legal claims against IOs.

2.3 CONCLUSION

The discussion in this chapter sets out the core fair trial rights that must be realised at a DRM created or resorted to by an IO to provide justice to private persons if it is to be considered appropriate. There are three broad fair trial guarantees that a DRM must incorporate: (1) independence, (2) impartiality and (3) fairness. Each of these criteria have clear interlinkages and they should be considered holistically when assessing a DRM. Further, each of these criteria has various dimensions. First, for a DRM to be considered independent, it must possess institutional, decisional and personal/individual independence. Institutional independence requires that a court must be operationally autonomous. This requires that a court possesses financial and administrative independence. A court or tribunal's registry must be sufficiently independent from any non-judicial organ or body of an IO. And a DRM should enjoy a distinct presence within the structures of an IO. Second, a court must also be decisionally independent. A DRM should have the jurisdiction to conclusively determine its own jurisdiction. This does not mean that a DRM's jurisdictional scheme cannot be limited through its constituent instruments. All that decisional independence requires is that, within the scope of its jurisdictional scheme, the DRM can finally decide questions of its own competence. Of course, decisional independence also requires that every case must be determined on its merits alone as opposed to impermissible external or internal pressures. Finally, individual/personal independence is necessary to ensure that every judge can act independently and impartially. Overall, the judicial appointment process must be transparent and based on merit. Moreover, all aspects of the security of tenure must be guaranteed. A relatively lengthy non-renewable term secures judicial independence. Financial security of judges is necessary. And a judge should only be dismissed

142 General Comment No 32 (n 2), para 58.

in extreme circumstances, that is, where proven misbehaviour can be established.

Second, for a fair trial to be provided, judicial impartiality in its objective and subjective sense is critical. At institutional DRMs, the organisation will almost always be the respondent. Therefore, independence and impartiality can interact closely. Even a hint of favouritism shown towards an IO in a given case should be treated as suspect. If a DRM's statute or rules do not contain standards guarding against conflict of interest, impartiality cannot be ensured. If a party cannot seek a judge's recusal for alleged subjective or objective bias, the rules on judicial impartiality are mostly rendered meaningless. Enacting a judicial code of conduct and a judicial complaints mechanism can also give greater confidence to parties that a DRM is impartial. Finally, implementing the right to appeal can go a long way in ensuring judicial impartiality. Doing so allows a party to seek review of a decision allegedly tainted with bias. Finally, the right to a fair trial requires that a claimant is treated equally and fairly. Indeed, the term 'fair' appears in the very name of the right. This chapter divided fairness into seven sub-criteria or rights. Each of those rights also constitutes an autonomous fair trial guarantee. A DRM cannot be considered as an appropriate mode of dispute resolution unless the right to equal access to the courts, the right to equality of arms, the right to an oral hearing, the right to appeal, the right to a reasoned judgment, the right to access justice without undue delay and the right to an effective remedy are provided for in the law, and importantly, practically realised.

3

Assessing Dispute Resolution Mechanisms at International Organisations

3.1 INTRODUCTION

This chapter assesses the compliance of DRMs set up by IOs with the fair trial criteria developed in Chapter 2. Such DRMs, where they exist, come in various forms, and it is presently not feasible to assess every single DRM created at every IO.[1] However, by selecting the most prominent DRMs that impact a significant number of private actors affected by IO conduct, a highly representative sample is considered. I divide the discussion into three sections. First, I analyse permanent judicial mechanisms set up at IOs to resolve claims raised against them (Section 3.2). A judicial body is normally considered to be a permanent institution that consists of independent and impartial judges capable of rendering binding decisions.[2] The courts and tribunals created at IOs that fit this description are largely confined to the sphere of international administrative or international civil service disputes,[3] although some international financial institutions have started to create bodies resembling courts to resolve certain other types of claims. A good example is provided by the World Bank's Sanctions Board that hears and determines claims brought by private actors facing debarment

[1] Case studies on the varied accountability mechanisms IOs establish are slowly emerging: see, for example, Stian Øby Johansen, *The Human Rights Accountability Mechanisms of International Organizations* (Cambridge University Press 2020). The author considers mechanisms established to provide redress to individuals impacted by the conduct of EU peacekeeping and peacebuilding missions, review mechanisms for individuals impacted by their detention at the ICC detention centre and accountability mechanisms that are applicable to situations where individuals are the victim of violations of rights by UNHCR.

[2] See Section 3.2.

[3] IATs are set up to resolve employment disputes between international organisations and their staff members. For a background, see A Riddell, 'Administrative Boards, Commissions and Tribunals in International Organizations' in *Max Planck Encyclopedia of Public International Law* (Oxford University Press 2012), 66.

action.[4] In this study, however, I assess the two most influential international administrative regimes. The first concerns the UN's internal justice system, consisting of the UNDT and UNAT (collectively referred to as the UN tribunals) (Section 3.2.1), and the ILOAT (Section 3.2.2). By selecting the principal justice regimes that together exercise jurisdiction over more than sixty IOs and well in excess of 100,000 international civil servants operating around the world,[5] this chapter identifies the fair trial deficits for a significant proportion of private persons affected by IO conduct. To the extent that DRMs not presently considered possess similarities with the regimes included within the scope of this work, analogies may be drawn.[6]

Second, I also consider the role of international arbitration in resolving disputes against IOs, and assess whether it provides for an 'appropriate' mode of dispute resolution (Section 3.3). International arbitration involves a neutral third party chosen by the disputing parties that is empowered to determine the dispute at hand in a final and binding way. It is now generally carried out within the auspices of permanent institutions, such as the International Centre for Settlement of Investment Disputes (ICSID), the PCA and the ICC, and has become highly proceduralised.[7] When rendering their

4 For a study of the review mechanisms created by international financial institutions in the context of sanctions, see J Madir, *Sanctions Regimes of Multilateral Development Banks* (Brill Nijhoff, 2020).

5 According to the available information, 39,651 people were employed by, and thus had access to, the UN Tribunals: Report of the Secretariat, 'Composition of the Secretariat: Staff Demographics' (11 July 2017) (72nd session, Agenda Item 142) UN Doc A/72/123. The UNDT is also open to, amongst others, staff working at UN Offices away from the headquarters, and UN Funds and Programmes, so its personal jurisdiction would be significantly higher. See <www.un.org/en/oaj/dispute/jurisdiction.shtml> accessed 2 June 2018. According to its website, the ILOAT is open to well in excess of 58,000 international civil servants from fifty-eight IOs: see ILO, 'ILO Administrative Tribunal' < https://www.ilo.org/tribunal/about-us/lang--en/index.htm > accessed 25 September 2021.

6 Other international administrative regimes do undergo periodic reforms. Those matters are outside the scope of this work. See, for example, the reforms carried out within the internal justice system of NATO: H Dijkstra, 'Functionalism, Multiple Principals and the Reform of the NATO Secretariat after the Cold War' (2014) 50(1) *Cooperation and Conflict* (2015), 128; for a rating of various justice systems in terms of compliance with fair trial standards, brief observations are made in R Dhinakaran and AP Haines, 'Internal Justice Systems of International Organisations Legitimacy Index 2017' <www.ialcoe.org/wp_site/wp-content/uploads/2017/10/6190BWL_CoE_Legitimacy_Index_2017.pdf> accessed 3 June 2018.

7 Arbitral houses exist in every major commercial centre. Notably, while the PCA traditionally is engaged in interstate dispute resolution, it has opened up its facilities to resolving disputes between IOs and private parties adopting specialised arbitral rules. Some IOs have chosen to seek its services. INTERPOL agreed as a default mechanism that any dispute should be settled in accordance with the CPA, 'Optional Rules for Arbitration between International Organizations and Private Parties' (1996) <https://docs.pca-cpa.org/2016/01/Optional-Rules-for-Arbitration-Between-International-Organizations-and-Private-Parties-1996.pdf> accessed 15 April 2021, by a Tribunal composed either of one or three members to be appointed by the Secretary-General

decisions, international arbitral tribunals frequently rely on previous judicial decisions and arbitral awards, just like courts do. Whether one talks about international investment arbitration or international commercial arbitration, arbitral awards are more or less final and binding due to the application of the ICSID and the New York Conventions.[8] While I discuss international arbitration separately from the section on permanent judicial mechanisms, this is more for reasons of convenience. International arbitration should be considered as a judicialised mode of dispute resolution.

Finally, I will consider commonly used non-judicialised mechanisms created at IOs, such as ombudsman processes (Section 3.4). Even though non-judicialised DRMs would instinctively seem to fall short of a fair-trial-compliant justice system, given their prevalence at IOs, it is important to briefly consider them. What is more, it does not really matter as to what a DRM may be called. If a forum is comprised of independent and impartial decision-makers empowered to determine a legal dispute in a final and binding way, then regardless of its name, a DRM could provide an 'appropriate' mode of dispute resolution.[9] Overall, the analysis in this chapter will show that, by and large, private actors raising claims against IOs do not have access to an 'appropriate' mode of dispute resolution (Section 3.5).

3.2 PERMANENT JUDICIAL MECHANISMS

IATs are perhaps the only true full-fledged judicial DRMs created at IOs.[10] They are set up with the intention to provide access to justice to IO employees to resolve employment claims. Some commentators have even suggested that the subject matter jurisdiction of IATs could be expanded so that they may determine non-employment claims too.[11] The potential of IATs resolving a broader category of cases may be instinctively appealing as a simplistic response to

of the PCA. This was enacted in the revised Headquarters Agreement (concluded between France and INTERPOL, entered into force on 1 September 2009), art 24(1).

8 ICSID Convention, Regulation and Rules (entered into force 14 October 1966) <https://icsid.worldbank.org/sites/default/files/ICSID%20Convention%20English.pdf> accessed 15 April 2021 (ICSID Convention); New York Convention on the Recognition and Enforcement of Foreign Arbitral Awards (New York, entered into force on 7 June 1959) <www.newyorkconvention.org/english> accessed 15 April 2021 (New York Convention).

9 See the jurisprudence discussed in the European Court of Human Rights, 'Guide on Article 6 of the European Convention of Human Rights – Right to a Fair Trial (Civil Limb)' (30 April 2020) (Article 6 Guide), para 148.

10 An exception is provided by the judicial mechanisms created at the EU.

11 See N Schrijver, 'Beyond Srebrenica and Haiti, Exploring Alternative Remedies against the United Nations' (2013) 10 *International Organizations Law Review* 2, 588–600, 597.

a difficult problem. However, before any such step is seriously contemplated or considered, we must assess whether IATs are appropriately fulfilling their current role in terms of administering justice independently, impartially and fairly. To answer this question, I consider the two most prominent IAT regimes: the UN tribunals (Section 3.2.1) and the ILOAT (Section 3.2.2).

3.2.1 *An Assessment of the UN Tribunals*

The UN's internal justice system arguably provides for the most sophisticated justice regime concerning the resolution of international administrative disputes. These disputes can involve a range of employment-related grievances, including unlawful dismissal, claims of bullying and harassment, disciplinary cases and breaches of employee entitlements.

To address employment claims at the UN, a significant informal dispute resolution regime exists. The UN Ombudsman plays an important role to help resolve disputes without the need for formal litigation. If informal means fail to resolve a dispute, aggrieved staff members can access formal means. They are first required to seek administrative review through a process known as Management Evaluation.[12] The Management Evaluation process gives an opportunity for UN Management to correct any breach of staff rights.[13] However, if a Management Evaluation does not resolve the dispute, a staff member can access the UN tribunals which sit atop of the UN's internal justice system.[14] The UN tribunals provide for a two-tier justice mechanism. The UNDT is the first-instance judicial mechanism.[15] It presently consists of three full-time and six half-time judges,[16] exercising their functions at three registries, located in New York, Geneva and Nairobi.[17] The UNAT is the second instance appellate tribunal hearing appeals from the UNDT.[18] It presently consists of seven judges and its registry is based in New York.[19]

12 Management evaluation is required in most cases: see UNDT, 'The Management Evaluation. What Is Management?' <www.un.org/en/internaljustice/undt/the-management-evaluation.shtml> accessed 22 April 2021.

13 Ibid.

14 See UNAT, 'What Is the United Nations Appeals Tribunal?' <www.un.org/en/internaljustice/unat/> accessed 22 April 2021.

15 Statute of the United Nations Dispute Tribunal (24 December 2008) UNGA Res A/RES/63/253 (last amended 22 December 2018 by UNGA Res 73/276) (UNDT Statute), art 1.

16 Ibid, art 4(1).

17 Ibid, art 5.

18 See Statute of the United Nations Appeals Tribunal (24 December 2008) UNGA Res A/RES/63/253 (last amended 23 December 2016 by UNGA Res 71/266) (UNAT Statute), arts 1 and 2.

19 Ibid, arts 4(1) and 5(2).

The two-tier justice regime prevailing at the UN supposedly constituting an independent, professionalised, expedient, transparent and Decentralised justice system has been operational for around ten years now.[20] The UN tribunals were established in 2009 following decades of reform efforts,[21] with the old UN internal justice system receiving severe criticism for its manifest lack of independence and a myriad of other due process deficiencies.[22] Whether or not this relatively new justice regime can be said to provide for a fair-trial-compliant DRM is, however, an open question requiring close scrutiny. Given that the UN's so-called reformed internal justice system was specifically designed to be compliant with the right to a fair trial, it is even more pressing to consider if that intention has been fulfilled. In the following sections, I consider whether the UN tribunals are rendering justice independently (Section 3.2.1.1), impartially (Section 3.2.1.2) and fairly (Section 3.2.1.3).

3.2.1.1 Judicial Independence at the UN Tribunals

As was discussed in Chapter 2, for a court to be independent, it must possess (a) institutional; (b) decisional; and (c)individual independence. Each of these factors is discussed next in respect of the UN tribunals.

(A) INSTITUTIONAL INDEPENDENCE AT THE UN TRIBUNALS To be considered institutionally independent, the UN tribunals must enjoy operational independence. This requires that those DRMs must possess administrative and financial independence, their registries must function free from impermissible pressures, and the tribunals must enjoy a distinct presence at the UN. All those dimensions overlap and are closely interlinked. As such, the UNDT and the UNAT are empowered to enact their own rules of procedure concerning the organisation of their work, functions of the Registries, evidentiary procedure or any other matters relevant to their functioning.[23] However, on

20 See GA, 'Administration of justice at the United Nations' UNGA Res A/RES/61/261 (30 April 2007) UN Doc A/RES/61/261 <https://undocs.org/en/A/RES/61/261> accessed 15 April 2021 (UNGA Res 61/261), para 4.

21 See generally R Gulati, 'The International Dispute Resolution Mechanism of the United Nations' (2011) 15 Max Planck Yearbook of United Nations Law 489–538.

22 Ibid.

23 UNDT Statute (n 15), art 7(1); also see United Nations Dispute Tribunal Rules of Procedure (16 December 2009) UNGA Res A/RES/64/454 (UNDT Rules of Procedure), art 18 (evidentiary requirements); art 19 (case management powers); art 21 (rules concerning support from the Registry). Note, however, the UNDT's ability to determine the number of judges that should hear a case is limited. While the UNDT Statute gives the UNDT the ability to institute

closer scrutiny, it becomes apparent that the UN tribunals' operational independence is significantly limited.

The most significant deficit relates to the DRMs' limited administrative independence. There is a conflation in the relationship between the judiciary, that is, the UNDT and the UNAT with the OAJ. The OAJ, a supposedly independent office, headed by the Senior Administration Official, is not only charged with the overall responsibility for the coordination of the UN system of administration of justice, but also as providing 'substantive, technical and administrative support to the United Nations Dispute Tribunal and the United Nations Appeals Tribunal through their Registries'.[24] Such an arrangement demonstrably undermines the operational independence of the UN tribunals and is inconsistent with the doctrine of the separation of powers.

In particular, issues arise due to the uneasy relationship between the OAJ and the judicial branches at the UN. The Executive Director heading the OAJ advises and reports to the Secretary-General,[25] who is always the respondent before the UNDT.[26] At the same time, the Executive Director is also mandated to provide support to the UN tribunals ultimately questioning the operational independence of the latter. The UNDT itself has observed that:

> The Executive Director cannot *bona fide* serve two masters whose interests are in conflict. Obviously, the Executive Director cannot give the judges substantive advice, neither directly nor through the Registries. Practical consequences of that built-in conflict are numerous and are present all along the administrative hierarchy of the Office of Administration of Justice.[27]

a three-member panel in complex or important cases (the default position being that a case is to be heard by one judge), it limits the UNDT's administrative freedom by requiring prior authorisation from the President of the UNAT before a three-judge panel can be instituted. See UNDT Statute (n 15), art 10(9); UNDT Rules of Procedure, art 5; and also see UNDT, 'Practice Direction No 1 on Three Judge Panels' (17 December 2010) <www.un.org/en/internaljustice/undt/forms-filing-guidelines.shtml> accessed 3 June 2018. The UNAT has said, the consideration of the President of the UNDT regarding the permissibility of a three-judge panel should suffice: 'Report of the Internal Justice Council – Administration of Justice' UNGA Res 72/210 (24 July 2017) UN Doc A/72/210 (IJC 2017 Report), Annex II (Views of the UNDT), paras 64–5.

24 Through UNGA Res 62/228, 'Administration of Justice at the United Nations' (6 February 2008) (62nd session) UN Doc A/RES/62/228, para 10, the GA established 'the Office of Administration of Justice, comprising the Office of the Executive Director and the Office of Staff Legal Assistance, as well as the Registries for the United Nations Dispute Tribunal and the United Nations Appeals Tribunal'; also see UNGA Res 61/261 (n 20), para 28; also see UN Secretariat, 'Secretary-General's Bulletin – Organization and Terms of Reference of the Office of Administration of Justice' (7 April 2010) UN Doc ST/SGB/2010/3, section 2.1.

25 UN Doc ST/SGB/2010/3 (n 24), sections 3.1, 3.4–.5.

26 UNDT Statute (n 15), art 2(1).

27 IJC 2017 Report (n 23), para 34.

For instance, the role of the Principal Registrar of the UN tribunals is problematic. The Principal Registrar is charged with overseeing the operation of both UN tribunals,[28] which creates conflicts in its own right.[29] Concerningly, the fact that the Principal Registrar is based within the OAJ,[30] and placed under the authority of the OAJ's Executive Director (whose position is already conflicted),[31] seriously undermines the DRMs' operational independence. This is because the Principal Registrar is ultimately answerable to the Secretary-General, who is a party to every case adjudicated by the UNDT or the UNAT.[32] The risk of undue executive interference into the judicial branch is high. Experience has borne this out.

Pointing to the persistent interferences into its administrative independence, the UNDT recently said:

> Some of the challenges that the Tribunal faced in 2019 stem from the very structure of the Office of Administration of Justice and the inevitable tension between the principle of the independence of judges and some interference by the Executive Director and the Principal Registrar in the action of the Tribunal, as well as from the structural ambiguity between the authority of the judges and that of the Executive Director and the Principal Registrar over the registry staff. . . . It therefore remains essential, for the future of the Tribunal and the internal justice system of the United Nations, that, as previous judges mentioned in their reports, the General Assembly, the Internal Justice Council and the judges address the key challenge of judicial independence to ensure that both the mandate of the Tribunal and the universal principle of the separation of powers are properly understood and respected.[33]

In fact, the UN tribunals cannot recruit Registry staff independently of the Administration.[34] And the practice of the Administration to second lawyers to

28 UN Doc ST/SGB/2010/3 (n 24), sections 4.2–.3.

29 The Principal Registrar performs their functions in respect of both the UNDT and the UNAT, creating conflicts of interest and the potential of undue influence: IJC 2017 Report (n 23), Annex II (Views of the UNDT), paras 37–8. Ibid, section 4.3(a). This becomes especially problematic as the Principal Registrar is also seemingly empowered to enforce the Rules of Procedure (n 23) (that power belongs to the relevant tribunal only and cannot belong to the Registrar).

30 All registrars are in fact based within the structures of the OAJ: see Office of Administration of Justice, 'Organizational Structure' <www.un.org/en/internaljustice/oaj/organizational-structure.shtml> accessed 15 April 2021.

31 UN Doc ST/SGB/2010/3 (n 24), section 4.1–.2.

32 IJC 2017 Report (n 23), Annex II (Views of the UNDT), para 38.

33 'Report of the Internal Justice Council – Administration of Justice' UNGA Res 75/154 (10 July 2020) UN Doc A/RES/75/154 (IJC 2020 Report), Annex 2 (Views of the UNDT), paras 7 and 11.

34 IJC 2017 Report (n 23), Annex II (Views of the UNDT), para 40.

the Registry of the tribunals who have previously acted for the respondent[35] further undermines the already weakened regime.[36] In recent times, even the UNAT has pointed to undue interferences into its work, saying:

> Starting in the 2018–2019 period, the Administration has begun to get involved in the way that the Appeals Tribunal manages its proceedings. Most notably, the Office of Administration of Justice imposes restrictions on the number of sessions. While under article 4 of the statute of the Appeals Tribunal, the number of sessions depends on the caseload and the decision lies solely at the discretion of the President, the Office of Administration of Justice now requests that the Appeals Tribunal hold only two sessions per year, even though addressing the number of appeals, as in previous years, clearly requires the holding of three sessions.[37]

Evidently, the operational independence of the UN tribunals suffers from structural deficiencies that make undue interference into the work of the judicial branch possible. Apart from the structural deficits identified earlier, the UN tribunal's physical and virtual locations do not in any way protect their operational independence either. One of the Registries of the UNDT is located within the same building as the OAJ with no physical differentiation created: the 'sharing of premises has given rise to the impression that the judges are subservient to and accountable to the Administration through the Executive Director'.[38] And a perception has been created through, amongst other things, the website of the OAJ that the tribunals are merely a part of the former (which they are not).[39] To make matters worse, the limitations on the DRMs' financial independence also create a perception that the judges are simply an extension of the Administration as opposed to constituting a distinct judicial branch.

When it comes to its funding, a degree of interaction between the UN tribunals and the Administration is of course inevitable.[40] Pursuant to Article

35 Ibid, paras 41–2.

36 Similar criticisms have also been levelled against other international courts: see generally, R Gulati, 'Judicial Independence at International Courts and Tribunals: Lessons Drawn from the Experiences of the International Court of Justice and the Appellate Body of the World Trade Organisation' in Berlin Potsdam Research Group, *The International Rule of Law – Rise or Decline?* (2020) KFG Working Paper Series, No 41.

37 IJC 2020 Report (n 33), Annex 1 (Views of the UNAT), para 10; also see, UNAT Statute (n 18), art 4.

38 IJC 2017 Report (n 23), Annex II (Views of the UNDT), paras 28 and 55.

39 Ibid, para 28.

40 Such interaction would occur through the UN General Assembly, 'Administrative and Budgetary Committee (Fifth Committee)' <www.un.org/en/ga/fifth/rl.shtml> accessed 22 April 2021.

6(1) of the UNDT Statute, the UN is responsible to make arrangements for the overall functioning of the UNDT (including funding its operations).[41] Leaving to one side concerns about the UN justice system's chronic underfunding,[42] instances of the Administration exercising undue control on the resources and finances of the UN tribunals are much too apparent. These issues have especially come to the fore most prominently in the context of the UNDT's operations.

In addition to concerns relating to the denial of the UNDT's 'role in deciding budget, training needs and staffing',[43] a significant intrusion into its institutional independence is caused by treating UNDT judges as UN staff members, and equating them with a Director-level (D-2) UN official.[44] Doing so has resulted in compromising the UNDT's operational independence considerably. In certain cases, the UNDT even declared that it does not provide an objectively independent and impartial forum.[45]

The key structural deficiency concerns the Administration's ability to affect changes to the emoluments of an UNDT judge by reference to the pay scale applying to the Director-level (D-2) at the UN.[46] This means that whenever the Administration affects a change to the salary of a D-2, the salary of an UNDT judge is also affected. This compromises the financial independence of the judiciary at large, impacts the personal independence of individual judges and creates a risk of apprehended bias in relevant cases.[47] The UNDT has found itself between a rock and a hard place on too many occasions.

For example, where a UN staff member approached the UNDT contesting a reduction of their salary,[48] the UNDT embarked on an analysis of whether the judge seized of the case should recuse himself for the process reducing the

41 UNDT Statute (n 15), art 6.
42 M Struyvenberg, 'New Trends in the Administration of Justice of International Organisations, Proceedings of the Annual Meeting' (American Society of International Law) (2012) 106 Confronting Complexity 353–5, 354.
43 IJC 2017 Report (n 23), Annex 2 (Views of the UNDT), paras 29 and 50–1.
44 Report of the Secretary-General, 'Compensation for Judges of the United Nations Dispute Tribunal' A/63/314 – as approved by the Assembly in UNGA Res 63/253 'Administration of Justice at the United Nations' UN Doc A/RES/63/253, para 30.
45 IJC 2017 Report (n 23), Annex II (Views of the UNDT), para 30.
46 Ibid, para 55.
47 As the UNDT has expressed: 'A conflict of interest is inherent in the arrangement in which judges of the Tribunal, when subject to the Staff Rules regime, as augmented, modified and interpreted by the Office of Human Resources Management, are exposed to the risk of disputing those rules and interpretations in their own cases and taking positions which would then compromise their impartiality in all similar disputes': IJC 2017 Report (n 23), Annex II (Views of the UNDT), para 48.
48 *Lloret Alcaniz* UNDT/Order No 113 (16 May 2017) GVA/2017 (UNDT Order No 113), para 1.

complainant's salary equally caused a reduction to the emoluments of the judge, giving rise to an apprehension of bias.[49] Relying on human rights jurisprudence concerning the standards of independence and impartiality,[50] while the UNDT concluded that 'the Dispute Tribunal, as a whole, is not in a position to provide the Applicant the guarantees of independence and impartiality to which she is entitled under art. 19 of the Universal Declaration of Human Rights and art. 14(1) of the International Covenant on Civil and Political Rights',[51] the judge nevertheless decided not to recuse himself as doing so would have resulted in denying the applicant justice due to the UN's jurisdictional immunities.[52] Based on the 'principle of necessity', the UNDT retained carriage of the complainant's case despite the obvious structural deficits in the UNDT's independence and impartiality.[53] If the UNDT had refused to hear the case, the complainant would have been left with no recourse. The UNDT itself has suggested a solution to address the deficit relating to its institutional independence, stating:

> [I]f the judges of the Dispute Tribunal had their conditions of service determined independently, not having their remuneration linked to that of staff members, this matter would not have arisen. It is noted that independence is not for the benefit of the judges of the Dispute Tribunal, but rather for the benefit of those they serve.[54]

Similarly, calling for a revised compensation package for UNDT judges,[55] the UN's own IJC has said that '[w]hen remuneration for judicial service is expressly linked to staff remuneration, litigants may well perceive the judges as simply another branch of the staff, not the independent and impartial arbiters of justice that they are'.[56] Ultimately, the judicial branch has very

49 Ibid, para 6, relying on the European Court of Human Rights in *Harabin v Slovakia* App no 58688/11 (ECtHR, 20 November 2012), para 131.

50 Ibid, paras 6 and 14.

51 Ibid, para 22.

52 Ibid, paras 16 and 19.

53 Ibid, at para 29, Judge Downs stated: 'This situation forces the undersigned Judge to consider applying the doctrine of necessity, which enables a judge, who would otherwise be disqualified, to hear and determine a case where failure to do so may result in an injustice through an inability to adjudicate the matter'; also see Judicial Group on Strengthening Judicial Integrity, 'The Bangalore Draft Code of Judicial Conduct' (2002) <www.unodc.org/pdf/crime/corruption/judicial_group/Bangalore_principles.pdf> accessed 4 June 2018, (Bangalore Principles), Value 2.5. In later cases, UNDT judges even recused themselves due to conflicts of interest: see *Chaoui, Kalotay and Richards v Secretary-General* UNDT/Order No 128 (20 August 2018) GVA/2018 (Order No 128).

54 UNDT Order No 113 (n 48), para 14.

55 IJC 2017 Report (n 23), para 57.

56 Ibid, para 56.

limited opportunity to correct this serious independence deficit. The UN tribunals are denied any role in the legislative process concerning laws related to the functioning of the tribunals[57] and they are unable to pursue direct dialogue with the General Assembly.[58] The independence deficits identified can only be addressed if the UN General Assembly takes meaningful action to remedy them.

For present purposes, the point of note is that as the operational independence of the UN tribunals is overall compromised, the answer to the question whether the UNDT and the UNAT can be said to satisfy the applicable standards for delivering institutionally independent justice can only be answered in the negative. The UNDT judges have themselves tellingly concluded that in all aspects relevant to the tribunals' operational independence, 'international standards of judicial independence are being breached',[59] further observing that:

> [t]he Dispute Tribunal judges have serious concerns about the persistent lack of institutional autonomy and independence of the Dispute Tribunal. … The Administration appears to operate upon an assumption that independence is protected as long as it refrains from exerting pressure on the results in individual cases. Judicial independence in a broader, institutional sense of autonomy and independence is structurally and practically absent, and has the effect of impeding justice being done and being seen to be done.[60]

All in all, as things stand, the UN tribunals do not constitute judicial institutions that are sufficiently free from the undue control of the UN's non-judicial organs. With their institutional independence so compromised, one may already conclude that unless improvements are made to the DRMs in question, just based on the limits to their operational independence, they are unlikely to constitute an 'appropriate' mode of dispute resolution in general. For the sake of a fuller analysis, it is nevertheless important to go on to assess those DRMs against other key fair trial criteria.

(B) DECISIONAL INDEPENDENCE AT THE UN TRIBUNALS A DRM can only be decisionally independent if it has the jurisdiction to conclusively determine its own jurisdiction. The DRM should also decide a case based on its merits alone, as opposed to any extraneous factors. Because no rational court or tribunal would ever admit to deciding a case based on anything but its

57 Ibid, paras 29 and 52–4.
58 Ibid.
59 Ibid, para 29.
60 Ibid, Annex II (Views of the UNDT), para 27.

inherent merits, to assess decisional independence reliance ought to be placed on the situation de jure. If the factual situation suggests that a court's decisional independence is compromised, then obviously decisional independence will not exist regardless of what legal guarantees are present.[61] Moreover, as was clarified in Chapter 2, international courts are DRMs of limited jurisdiction, meaning that decisional independence is circumscribed by the terms of their constituent instruments. Within the scope of its jurisdictional scheme, as long as an international court or tribunal can autonomously and conclusively determine the totality of a claim before it, on its face, a court will be decisionally independent.

The jurisdiction of IATs, such as the UNDT and UNAT, tends to be highly confined. They are only open to persons who qualify as UN staff members,[62] and whose conditions or contracts of employment have been breached through an administrative decision taken by the organisation that personally impacts a complainant.[63] Specifically, the UNDT, the first instance tribunal,[64] is open to individuals having a permanent or fixed-term contract with the organisation, thus leaving out contractors, consultants and interns from judicial protection. The UNAT is the second instance appellate tribunal and hears appeals from the UNDT.[65]

Some commentators seem to suggest that the highly circumscribed jurisdiction of IATs unduly limits their autonomy, creating a gap relating to the broad range of private law claims that aggrieved individuals may wish to raise.[66] Properly understood, such matters concern whether or not an IO complies with its obligation to provide for a mode of dispute resolution to all those individuals whose legal rights it adversely impacts, as opposed to whether or not a particular DRM can be said to be decisionally independent. Within the bounds of their limited competence, the UN tribunals can indeed conclusively rule on their own jurisdiction. Article 2(6) of the UNDT Statute states that '[i]n the event of a dispute as to whether the Dispute Tribunal has competence under the present statute, the Dispute Tribunal shall decide on the matter'.[67] The UNAT also possesses a similar power.[68]

61 However, as was discussed in Chapter 2, establishing impartiality can be onerous.
62 UNDT Statute (n 15), art 3.
63 See ibid, art 2.
64 Ibid, art 1.
65 See UNAT Statute (n 18), art 2.
66 R Silverstein, 'Revisiting the Legal Basis to Deny International Civil Servants Access to a Fundamental Human Right' (2017) 25 Michigan State International Law Review 375.
67 UNDT Statute (n 15), art 2(6).
68 For the UNAT, see, UNAT Statute (n 18), art 2(8).

It is a different thing altogether that so far the UN tribunals have read their own personal jurisdiction narrowly. Whereas the old UN Administrative Tribunal was willing to exercise its jurisdiction over non-staff members to ensure access to justice for such individuals, the UN tribunals have refused to do so.[69] Such an approach may be questioned for international courts open to individuals, and thus performing a protective function, should not take an unduly restrictive approach to their own competence.[70] But this does not imply that the UN tribunals are not decisionally independent. All it means is that the DRMs take a limited view of their own jurisdiction. The UN tribunals can be said to be decisionally independent as they possess the competence to conclusively determine jurisdictional questions.

However, neither the statute of the UNDT nor that of the UNAT expressly provides that those tribunals ought to determine cases independently and impartially.[71] The Burgh House Principles state in their preamble that international courts and tribunals must 'enjoy independence from the parties to cases before them, their own states of nationality or residence, the host countries in which they serve, and the international organisations under the auspices of which the court or tribunal is established'. It is crucial that such a significant structural fair trial guarantee is expressly formulated in a court's statute itself.[72] The absence of such a provision does not imply that UNDT and UNAT judges lack decisional independence in practice, but the absence of an express requirement as to independent decision-making is nevertheless a gap in the constituent arrangements of both these tribunals.

It can only be concluded that the decisional independence of the UN tribunals is lacking. While they can conclusively determine jurisdictional questions, there are gaps in their constituent arrangements. Moreover, as the institutional independence of the UN tribunals is so limited, objective fears

69 As a result, the human rights of IO consultants and contractors, including the right to access a court, are being infringed: see MC Herrera, 'Is the UN Violating International Labour Standards?' (*EjilTalk*, 29 October 2019) <www.ejiltalk.org/is-the-un-violating-international-labour-standards/> accessed 22 April 2021.

70 See Chapter 2.

71 Although, according to their statutes, UNDT and UNAT judges operate in their personal capacity and enjoy full independence: UNDT Statute (n 15), art 4(8); and UNAT Statute (n 18), art 3(8).

72 This, for example, could be achieved by implementing the provisions found in the UNGA, 'Code of Conduct for the Judges of the United Nations Dispute Tribunal and the United Nations Appeals Tribunal' UN Doc A/RES/66/106 (2012) ('Code of Conduct'), section 1: '(a) Judges must uphold the independence and integrity of the internal justice system of the United Nations and must act independently in the performance of their duties, free of any inappropriate influences, inducements, pressures or threats from any party or quarter'.

about the extent to which the UNDT and UNAT may actually enjoy decisional independence are naturally raised.

(C) INDIVIDUAL OR PERSONAL INDEPENDENCE AT THE UN TRIBUNALS The mode of judicial appointment and considerations around the security of tenure constitute the key factors in assessing personal independence. As to the former, judges of the UN tribunals are appointed by the General Assembly on the recommendation of an independent IJC chaired by a distinguished jurist.[73] The IJC invites individual applications from potential candidates, and following a competitive examination makes recommendations to the General Assembly, suggesting two candidates for each available post.[74] The General Assembly then elects one person out of the two options presented.[75] The mechanism at the UN internal justice system removes the influence of states in the appointment of judges to a significant extent.[76] Concerning judicial appointments at the UNDT, Judge Memooda Ebrahim-Carstens pointed out extra-curially: 'it is evident from the applications received that this procedure ensures a larger pool of global competitors who can apply independently and freely, ruling out state politics, bias, and favouritism, and also assures a more representative candidature'.[77] Further, there are minimum qualifications necessary to qualify as a candidate for appointment to either tribunal, requiring at least ten years of judicial experience for an UNDT judge and fifteen for an UNAT judge.[78] In so far as the mode of selection of judges is concerned, the UN system appears to be robust, and may also be worth replicating elsewhere.

Concerning the security of tenure, while the UN tribunals adopt certain positive features, deficiencies nevertheless exist. Before discussing the

73 See UNDT Statute (n 15), art 4(2); see also UNGA Res 62/228 (n 24), paras 35–8, which creates the IJC as a body aimed at enhancing the independence of the UNDT and the UNAT, and comprises of a staff representative, a management representative and two distinguished external jurists, one nominated by the staff and one by management, and chaired by a distinguished jurist chosen by consensus by the four other members, and makes recommendations to the General Assembly regarding candidates for vacancies in the UNDT and the UNAT.

74 See the summary provided in, M Ebrahim-Carstens, 'Gender Representation on the Tribunals of the United Nations Internal Justice System: A Response to Nienke Grossman' (2016) 110 AJIL Unbound 98.

75 See UNGA, 'Appointment of Judges of the United Nations Appeals Tribunal and of the United Nations Dispute Tribunal – Memorandum by the Secretary-General' (4 November 2015) UN Doc A/70/538.

76 Ebrahim-Carstens (n 74).

77 Ibid.

78 UNDT Statute (n 15), art 4(3).

shortcomings, to give credit where it is due, the positive aspects should be first pointed out. The three full-time and six half-time judges of the UNDT, and the seven UNAT judges, are appointed for one non-renewable seven-year term, enhancing structural independence.[79] Further, a judge may only be removed in cases of misconduct or incapacity,[80] although there remain issues as to whether an affected judge will be granted a fair process when contesting their removal should the situation arise.[81] The introduction of a Code of Conduct for the judges of both the UNDT and the UNAT (expressly incorporating human rights standards of independence and impartiality) goes on to strengthen the legal infrastructure as well.[82]

However, significant deficiencies are apparent. Three issues are especially worth stating. First, since the creation of the UNDT, there has been a practice of appointing ad litem judges (temporary judges). These judges, who have short-term contracts, do not possess security of tenure.[83] Struyvenberg has observed that:

> [t]hese judges, appointed by the General Assembly initially for a one-year period ... have received further extensions ranging from one year to six months at a time. These short-term extensions have made it difficult, if not impossible, for these judges to arrange their stays at the duty stations. ... Moreover, the irregular extensions of the ad litem judges may also affect their independence. The system is best served by judges who have security of tenure than by judges appointed for short terms, who are thus subject to frequent reelection or reappointment.[84]

Second, a grave issue at the UNDT arose due to the lack of the UNDT President's security of tenure. The President of the UNDT is elected for

79 Ibid, art 4(4); and UNAT Statute (n 18), art 3.

80 UNDT Statute (n 15), art 4(10).

81 UNGA Res 67/241, 'Mechanism for Addressing Complaints Regarding Alleged Misconduct or Incapacity of the Judges of the UNDT and the UNAT' (24 December 2012) UN Doc A/RES/67/241, section 19(c); for best practice concerning the processes that must be followed when removing a judge, see generally, J van Zyl Smit, 'The Appointment, Tenure and Removal of Judges under Commonwealth Principles: A Compendium and Analysis of Best Practice' (British Institute of International and Comparative Law, 2015), 19–20.

82 The Code of Conduct for the Judges of the UNDT and the UNAT (n 72) was adopted through UNGA Res 66/106 (9 December 2011) UN Doc A/RES/66/106. It incorporates the principles of independence and impartiality as provided for in human rights treaties and other instruments developed by the international community; also see UNDT Order No 113 (n 48), para 11, where a UNDT judge declared a conflict of interest due to the case raising issues that would affect the personal circumstances of the judge demanding disclosure under Code of Conduct (n 72), art 2(e).

83 UNGA Res 74/172, 'Report of the Secretary-General on the Administration of Justice at the United Nations' UN Doc A/74/172 (2019), para 100.

84 See Struyvenberg (n 42), 354.

one-year periods. Remarkably, in 2019, there was a breakdown within the UNDT's judiciary, where two judges of the UNDT simultaneously claimed to be its President, and it was also reported that certain judges filed a formal complaint against one of their colleagues under the mechanism for addressing complaints regarding alleged misconduct or incapacity of the judges of the UNDT and UNAT.[85] A recent report of the Secretary-General on the Administration of Justice at the UN noted that the 'competing assertions made to the presidency of the Tribunal ... highlight the insecurity of tenure of a duly elected President in circumstances where the role requires the exercise of administrative authority within the Tribunal'.[86]

And third, the judges of the UN system do not enjoy appropriate levels of financial independence. As has already been observed, UNDT judges are equated with UN staff members resulting in impermissible intrusions into the financial security of individual judges. The IJC recommended that 'in accordance with the United Nations standards on independence of the judiciary, the status of the judges of the Tribunal, including remuneration, be sufficiently "secured by law"'.[87] If individual independence of the UN's justice machinery is to be secured, reforms are required and the deficits identified ought to be rectified. Or else, the personal independence of the judges will continue to be compromised.

In the final analysis, the UN tribunals lack the necessary institutional, decisional and individual independence expected from a modern international court or tribunal. As a result, the two-tier justice system, just based on the independence shortfall, may not constitute an appropriate mode of dispute resolution.

3.2.1.2 Judicial Impartiality at the UN Tribunals

Impartiality requires that judges do not favour one party over another in a given case. If judges have a conflict of interest, then a recusal mechanism must exist. In so far as the UNDT is concerned, its Statute provides for various guarantees of judicial impartiality.[88] This includes a litigant's ability to seek a recusal on grounds of subjective or objective bias on the part of a judge.[89]

85 See paras 15 and 42 of the IJC 2020 Report and its annexures (n 33).

86 UNGA Res 74/172 (n 83), para 17.

87 IJC 2017 Report (n 23), para 49.

88 UNDT Statute (n 15), art 4(3)(a) states that a judge shall be of high moral character and impartial; art 4(6) avoids situations of perceived conflicts by disallowing a UNDT judge to be employed at the UN for a period of five years following their term of judicial appointment.

89 UNDT Statute (n 15), art 4(8) states: 'A judge of the Dispute Tribunal who has, or appears to have, a conflict of interest shall recuse himself or herself from the case. Where a party requests such recusal, the decision shall be taken by the President of the Dispute Tribunal'; also see UNDT Rules of Procedure (n 23), art 28(2).

Those provisions are further boosted by the Rules of the UNDT, and the applicable judicial Code of Conduct.[90]

More specifically, the UNDT Rules of Procedure define a conflict of interest as situations where a judge has a personal, familiar or professional relationship; previous involvement in a case, such as in the role of counsel or an expert; and any other situation that would objectively doubt the impartiality of the judge.[91] The Code of Conduct further clarifies the meaning of a conflict of interest,[92] requiring that a judge's conduct inside and outside of the court must not indicate bias on the part of a judge. Such bias may become apparent where amongst other things, a judge receives gifts or benefits from one party to litigation.[93]

Indeed, applications for judicial recusal are increasingly a regular feature of the UN system, with judges even making disclosures as to conflicts of interests of their own accord.[94] As individuals can lodge complaints against a judge for alleged breaches of the Code of Conduct, another potential mechanism that could play a useful role in keeping the judiciary impartial exists.[95] De jure guarantees as to judicial impartiality at the UN tribunals are relatively strong. However, the extent of interference into all aspects of the UN tribunals' independence by the non-judicial organs of the organisation is stark. And where one party to a case before the UNDT or UNAT is always the UN itself, it may be questioned whether those tribunals can be said to be objectively impartial.[96] Thus, despite the presence of de jure guarantees as to judicial impartiality, structurally speaking, the UN tribunals' objective impartiality is debatable. This is why an intense focus ought to be placed on whether or not the UN tribunals deliver justice 'fairly'. If the administration of justice lacks fairness and does not maintain an equal distance from the parties to litigation, the likelihood that the forum is in fact partial towards one party to litigation is high.

90 Code of Conduct (n 72), section 6.

91 UNDT Rules of Procedure (n 23), art 27(2).

92 Code of Conduct (n 72), section 2.

93 Ibid, see especially section 2(h).

94 Order No 128 (n 53).

95 Complaints mechanism, as adopted by the General Assembly, under resolution UNGA Res 70/112, 'Mechanism for Addressing Complaints Regarding Alleged Misconduct or Incapacity of the Judges of the United Nations Dispute Tribunal and the United Nations Appeals Tribunal' UN Doc A/70/112 (2015).

96 R Downing, 'The Judge's View: The UN Justice System is Not Independent and Needs to Be Fixed' (*UN Today*, 8 April 2021) <https://untoday.org/the-judges-view-the-un-justice-system-is-not-independent-and-needs-to-be-fixed/> accessed on 23 April 2021.

3.2.1.3 Fairness at the UN Tribunals

As was said in Chapter 2, fairness is a broad concept that is closely linked to the principle of 'equality' in the administration of justice. It incorporates within its domain several subcomponent fair trial guarantees. The UN's internal justice system has made progress in terms of ensuring fairness in some respects. For instance, the UNDT Statute and its Rules of Procedure require the provision of reasons,[97] all judgments must be published,[98] oral hearings should be provided[99] and the complainant can access a second instance UNAT to challenge UNDT decisions, implementing the right to appeal. However, other fairness deficits exist. In this section, I canvass those key deficiencies. These are infringements of (a) the right to equal access to the courts; (b) equality of arms; (c) right to justice without undue delay; and (d) right to an effective remedy.

(A) EQUAL ACCESS TO THE UN TRIBUNALS The personal jurisdiction of the UN tribunals is limited to those individuals who are classified as UN staff members.[100] UN contractors and consultants are not classified as staff members, and so do not have access to the UNDT and UNAT. With the UN tribunals unwilling to read the scope of their personal jurisdiction broadly, and the pace of reform being glacial, a significant equality deficit prevails within the UN's internal justice system. The UN tribunals themselves lament this state of affairs.[101]

97 See UNDT Statute (n 15), art 11(1); and UNDT Rules of Procedure (n 23), art 25(1), which provides that '[j]udgements shall be issued in writing and shall state the reasons, facts and law on which they are based'.

98 See UNDT Rules of Procedure (n 23), art 26, regarding the publication of judgments, which requires that all judgments of the UNDT be published on the website of the UNDT and personal data must be protected.

99 See UNDT Statute (n 15), arts 7(e) and (f), which empower the UNDT to make rules of procedure regarding oral hearings and publication of judgments; art 9(3) requires that oral hearings are held in public unless exceptional circumstances exist; and see ibid, arts 16(1) and (2) giving the judge a discretion to hold an oral hearing; and providing that in disciplinary cases, '[a] hearing shall normally be held following an appeal against an administrative decision imposing a disciplinary measure'.

100 The lack of access for consultants, contractors and interns to the UN's internal justice system is by legislative design: see Report of the Secretary-General, 'Administration of Justice at the United Nations' (16 September 2010) (65th session, Items 131 and 142) UN Doc.A/65/373, para 179.

101 The UN tribunals have relied on a formalist understanding of the definition of a 'staff member' having access to the UN's internal justice system, narrowly interpreting UNDT Statute (n 15), art 3(1). The effect is that even if consultants and contractors perform materially the same work as individuals retained by the UN in the formal category of a permanent or

Accordingly, perhaps the most prominent equality deficit at the UN's internal justice system concerns the lack of judicial protection for so-called non-staff personnel that include consultants and contractors. Such individuals now constitute more than 45 per cent of the UN's workforce, and their substantive relationship with the organisation is no different to the one existing between the UN and its staff members as both those category of personnel perform materially the same type of work.[102]

Denying access to judicial protection on the basis of an individual's employment status as a consultant or contractor is a manifest breach of the equality principle where such persons are fundamentally in the same position as UN staff members.[103] Such difference in treatment is arbitrary and unjustifiable for there is no rational reason as to why such a distinction ought to be made. Some IATs have indeed held that individuals working for IOs as consultants on rolling contracts may be considered as de facto employees who may access the protection of an IAT.[104] The old UN Administrative Tribunal did take jurisdiction over cases advanced by such claimants on the basis that without its intervention, the complainants would suffer a denial of justice.[105] The UNDT and UNAT have not taken the same approach.[106] The position of so-called non-staff personnel is already precarious to start with, and the lack of judicial

fixed staff member under the relevant contract of employment, the former do not have access to the UN's internal justice system. It has been said that the lack of a remedy for such individuals is most 'unfortunate': see especially, *El Moctar v Secretary General of the United Nations* (24 July 2012) Judgment No UNDT/2012/113, paras 13–36.

102 Significant reforms to secure access to justice for contractors and consultants of IOs are thus needed: see R Gulati, 'Advancing International Administrative Law: A Four-Point Agenda' (FICSA Magazine, 2020).

103 See Chapter 2; International Covenant on Civil and Political Rights (adopted 16 December 1966, entered into force 23 March 1976) 999 UNTS 171 (ICCPR), art 26, providing for a general right to equality before the law which prohibits an unjustifiable difference in treatment between similarly situated persons based on the 'status' of a person. Unjustifiable distinctions made between individuals based on their status as holding temporary employment compared to those holding more permanent employment, especially in the context of the right to access to courts, is impermissible. The Inter-American Court stated that the right to judicial protection must be granted to all categories of workers regardless of their status, concluding that the 'status of a person cannot constitute a justification to deprive him of the enjoyment and exercise of human rights, including those of a labor-related nature': see *Juridical Condition and Rights of Undocumented Migrants* (Advisory Opinion) OC-18/03 (17 September 2003, Inter-American Court of Human Rights), para 109 and conclusion 8.

104 See, *Amora v Asian Development Bank* (6 January 1997) ADBAT Decision No 24, which sets out the series of factors to be considered to determine whether an individual could be considered to be a de facto employee despite being retained as a consultant or contractor.

105 See *Teixeira v the Secretary General of the United Nations* (14 October 1977, UN Administrative Tribunal) Judgement No 230.

106 See (n 101).

protection makes a bad situation even worse. Because similarly situated persons are not being granted access to the UN tribunals on an equal basis, a vast category of individuals working for the UN are not being accorded their right to equal access to the courts. Assuming that the UN tribunals continue to uphold a narrow view of personal jurisdiction, only legislative reform can correct this injustice.[107]

It is worth pointing out that the UN in fact recognises that it has the obligation to provide appropriate modes of dispute settlement to so-called non-staff personnel. Citing resource constraints, it so far has refused to provide access to the UN tribunals to that category of individuals.[108] First, restricting the right to access a fair trial for a particular group of persons based on resource constraints is impermissible and does not justify treating similarly situated individuals differently.[109]

Second, if non-staff personnel are not granted access to a judicial body, then other appropriate alternatives must be provided. Purporting to comply with its access to justice obligations, in respect of its consultants and contractors, the UN provides the possibility of arbitration. Such an arbitral procedure can only be considered an appropriate mode of dispute settlement if it does not place relevant individuals at a disadvantage, which it does (see Section 3.3). Unless consultants, contractors and interns are given access to the UN tribunals (through legislative amendments, or the UNDT and UNAT start to read their personal jurisdiction more broadly), or an effective arbitral scheme is implemented, the right of such individuals to practically realise a fair trial on an equal basis will continue to be contravened.[110]

(B) EQUALITY OF ARMS That a marked factual inequality between the UN and its personnel exists is obvious. The institution has available to it the vast resources of the organisation, and is invariably represented by the organisation's lawyers.[111] Relative to the individual applicant, the UN has considerably deeper pockets. The provision of legal aid or affordable legal representation to

107 See, UNGA Res 74/172 (n 83), para 95(d).

108 Report of the Secretary-General, 'Review of the Efficiency of the Administrative and Financial Functioning of the United Nations' (24 April 1995) UN Doc A/C.5/49/65, para 3.

109 HRC, 'General Comment No 32: Right to Equality before Courts and Tribunals and to a Fair Trial' (23 August 2007) UN Doc CCPR/C/GC/32 (General Comment No 32), para 27.

110 See R Gulati and T John, 'Arbitrating Employment Disputes Involving International Organisations' 3 AIIB Yearbook of International Law (Brill Nijhoff 2020).

111 Such assistance is provided through the General Legal Division of the UN – Office of Legal Affairs: see J Pozenel, 'General Legal Division' (*OLA*) (2010) <https://legal.un.org/ola/div_gld.aspx?section=gld> accessed on 24 April 2021.

UN staff wishing to raise claims against their employer IO is, thus, of immense importance if equality of arms and fairness are to be realised.

Assuming that a claimant does not retain private counsel at his or her own expense, an aggrieved employee having a prima facie meritorious case should be accorded legal assistance when seeking justice against an employer IO in relation to their employment-related disputes. This must be done to guarantee that such individuals can put forward their case in full equality with the respondent, and also to ensure that other litigants can receive justice without undue delay. Unrepresented litigants 'have a negative impact on the workload of the Tribunal … often do not understand the legal process and tend to file numerous irrelevant documents and submissions, inundate the Registries with unnecessary or inappropriate queries and requests and generally slow down the system, causing delays in proceedings'.[112] This is why the Redesign Panel charged to reform the UN internal justice system had suggested the creation of a legal aid scheme for UN staff members. As a result, the UN's internal justice system has taken steps to strengthen access to legal representation for UN staff members who have access to the UNDT and UNAT. This has largely been accomplished through the creation of the OSLA, based at the OAJ.[113]

Pointing to the role of OSLA in ensuring the equality of arms, the UNDT has observed:

> The right to representation, guaranteed by the Universal Declaration of Human Rights and enshrined in the principle of equality of arms, is an essential element of the new system of administration of justice, and the role of the Office of Staff Legal Assistance should continue to be that of assisting staff members not only in processing claims, but in representing applicants before the Tribunals.[114]

OSLA can only help realise the equality of arms if it is appropriately staffed and resourced. OSLA suffers from serious underfunding, lacks sufficient staff and is in need of urgent budgetary and personnel enhancement.[115] The lack of resources prevents OSLA from providing representation to a large number of aggrieved individuals. For example, in 2019, roughly 40 per cent of claimants before the UN tribunals were self-represented, undermining the equality of arms and causing delays in the administration of justice.[116] This significant

112 IJC 2017 Report (n 23), Annex II (Views of the UNDT), para 66.
113 See 'The Office of Staff Legal Assistance (OSLA)' <www.un.org/en/internaljustice/osla/> accessed 24 April 2021.
114 IJC 2017 Report (n 23), Annex II (Views of the UNDT), para 68.
115 Ibid, para 79.
116 IJC 2020 Report (n 33), para 53.

problem is even more acute for staff in the field who may be further disadvantaged due to reasons of geography and language. The IJC found in 2020:

> [T]he Council has received consistent comments from various interlocutors that staff in the field self-represent largely because there is little alternative. Engaging a private counsel is expensive and such a counsel may simply not be readily available. The Office of Staff Legal Assistance does its best but lacks the necessary resources and presence in the field to fully handle the demand for legal assistance. This point has been made to the Council by the Office itself, and its validity has been corroborated in separate comments received from field staff unions that the Office is overwhelmed and that field staff therefore end up representing themselves.[117]

Despite the presence of the OSLA, for a significant number of claimants before the UN internal justice system, the principle of equality of arms is not being realised. This state of affairs not only adversely impacts the right to equality for persons unable to access legal representation in particular cases but also contributes to undue delays in the administration of justice generally. Increasingly, delays are becoming a feature of the delivery of justice at the UN.

(C) UNDUE DELAY IN THE ADMINISTRATION OF JUSTICE Employment cases, which tend to be relatively less complex compared to other types of international claims, ought to be heard and decided within months and not years,[118] unless the behaviour of the claimant does not allow for this to happen.[119] Indeed, domestic employment tribunals are required to adjudicate disputes within months, with harassment claims even requiring urgent attention (sometimes within twenty-four hours of a complaint being raised).[120] In a comparative study of national employment tribunals, a study by the ILO observed:

> In 2013–14, Australia's [Fair Work Commission] rendered decisions within eight weeks of a hearing in almost 84 per cent of cases, and within 12 weeks in

[117] Ibid, para 54.

[118] See *Re Mrs K JL* (2011) ILOAT Judgment No 3092, para 15: where the WHO did not process a claim for a service-incurred injury within forty-two months, the ILOAT awarded moral damages as the delay was said to be manifestly unfounded. Any delay (of even a few months) that cannot be objectively justified will be undue; in *Re Mr JA C* (2013) ILOAT Judgment No 3168, para 18, where there was an unjustifiable delay of approximately nine months, it was found to be undue.

[119] See General Comment No 32 (n 109), para 27, where the HRC states that '[a]n important aspect of the fairness of a hearing is its expeditiousness ... [delays] that cannot be justified by the complexity of the case or the behaviour of the parties detract from the principle of a fair hearing enshrined in [art 14(1) of the ICCPR]'; also see the discussion in Chapter 2.

[120] See A Forsyth, 'Australia' in International Labour Organisation: Resolving Individual Labour Disputes (Geneva, 2016) (ILO: Resolving Individual Labour Disputes), 46.

> over 93 per cent of cases. In Germany, the importance of speedy procedures at all levels of labour court matters is explicitly referred to in the Labour Court Act. In addition, the Act provides that disputes concerning the existence, non-existence or termination of the employment relationship must be dealt with as a matter of priority. In 2012, more than 85 per cent of all cases lodged were settled within six months. Japan's Labour Tribunal Act requires the tribunal panel to complete its procedures within three hearing sessions. Average disposal time was nearly 75 days in 2013, while under the first-instance civil procedure it was just over 13 months. In the United Kingdom, the average disposal time for a single claim at the [Employment Tribunal] is 27 weeks. ... In Sweden, cases adjudicated through the labour courts took around 12 months.[121]

Even a delay of mere months in the determination of an employment claim, thus, ought to attract very close scrutiny vis-à-vis compliance with the right to a fair trial. Resource constraints are no excuse for not rendering justice without undue delay. It is the responsibility of the authorities charged with setting up the justice system to ensure that enough resources (in terms of number of judges, registry staff and budgetary allocations) are made so that the individual right to a fair trial without undue delay can be practically realised.[122] Despite reform attempts at the UN though, the right to receive justice without undue delay is being undermined. This is especially concerning as the whole point of the reform efforts was to address the excessive delays in the administration of justice at the UN. In fact, one of the most severe criticisms of the pre-2009 UN internal justice system concerned the length of time it took to resolve cases.[123] According to some estimates, cases took more than five years from start to finish.[124] Of course, such a lengthy period of time to resolve employment claims was manifestly excessive and egregious, resulting in the breach of the right to a fair trial. Unfortunately, exceptional delays in the delivery of justice continue to be a significant issue in the post-2009 UN internal justice system too.

In its most recent report, the IJC noted that the UN internal justice system was suffering from persistent backlogs, and that just clearing it is likely to require more than eighteen months.[125] As the UNDT receives around 300

[121] Ibid, 20.

[122] See Chapter 2.

[123] A delay of three years in processing of claims in the old UN internal justice system was said to constitute an 'egregious delay': 'Report of the Redesign Panel on the United Nations System of Administration of Justice' (28 July 2006) (61st session) UN Doc A/61/205 (Redesign Panel Report), para 67.

[124] Ibid, paras 67–70.

[125] IJC 2020 Report (n 33), paras 17–19.

cases per year, it is likely that more and more delays will be a feature of the UN's internal justice system.[126] The IJC went on to conclude:

> [T]he United Nations Dispute Tribunal, as an institution, has not only underperformed . . . but also, that underperformance has not been effectively acknowledged and sufficiently addressed by the judges. That has been manifest both in the persistent backlog of old cases and in the absence of internal rules or mechanism to monitor and improve the judicial and operational performance of the Tribunal. The Council also notes that the Tribunal assigns only 10 to 15 cases to a judge at any given time, without establishing deadlines for disposing of those cases and leaving all other cases unaddressed until the 10 to 15 cases have been resolved. More than half of the caseload therefore usually remains unassigned (62 per cent of cases were pending assignment as at 1 July 2020), effectively adding to the backlog of cases and perpetuating it for the future.[127]

It is all well and good for the UN General Assembly to amend the UNDT and UNAT Statutes authorising the President of each Tribunal to monitor the timely delivery of judgments[128] and express its concerns about the delays in the administration of justice.[129] However, if in practice cases are taking excessive amounts of time to resolve, then for the individual litigant stuck in the justice machinery, the right to access justice without undue delay is being demonstrably compromised. The UNDT and UNAT's own Code of Conduct says that claims ought to be disposed efficiently and promptly, stating in section 7:

> (a) Judges must perform all assigned judicial duties, including tasks relevant to the judicial office or the operation of the Tribunals, diligently and dispose of judicial work promptly in an efficient and professional manner.
>
> (b) Judges must give judgement or rulings in a case promptly. Judgements should be given no later than three months from the end of the hearing or the close of pleadings or, in the case of the United Nations Appeals Tribunal, from the end of the session in which the matter is decided, unless there are exceptional circumstances.[130]

If the UN tribunals live up to their own set of standards, the right to a fair trial without undue delay will be realised. If lengthy delays in adjudicating claims

126 Ibid, para 18; and for reforms proposed by the IJC, see ibid, para 26 (Recommendation 1).

127 Ibid, para 15.

128 UNAT Statute (n 18).

129 UNGA Res 73/276, 'Administration of justice at the United Nations' UN Doc A/RES/73/276 (22 December 2018).

130 Code of Conduct (n 72), section 7.

continue to occur, then in cases where such delays cannot be justified due to the complexity of a case or the behaviour of the claimant, the UN's internal justice system will not constitute an appropriate mode of dispute resolution. Moreover, undue delays in the realisation of a fair trial also undermine the right to an effective remedy,[131] which is an independent right closely linked to the right to a fair trial.

(D) THE RIGHT TO A FAIR TRIAL AND EFFECTIVE REMEDY AT THE UN TRIBUNALS The interlinkages between the right to a fair trial and effective remedy have already been clarified in Chapter 2. It should be recalled that for the right to a fair trial and effective remedy to be implemented in conjunction, an individual must be given access to a judicial or functionally equivalent mechanism to resolve their legal claims. Moreover, the relevant forum approached should have the appropriate jurisdiction to adjudicate the substance of the claims advanced. The forum must be empowered to provide appropriate relief. And crucially, any decisions made by that forum must be final, binding and enforceable. As the UN tribunals clearly constitute judicial mechanisms, although their independence and impartiality is questionable, to determine whether they otherwise provide an appropriate mode of dispute resolution requires considering whether they are vested with sufficient powers to grant appropriate relief that is final and binding.

First, the subject matter jurisdiction of the UN tribunals is limited to employment claims. Within the scope of their subject matter jurisdiction, the UN tribunals' limited powers in terms of what relief may be granted adversely impact the realisation of an effective remedy. Article 10(5) of the UNDT Statute limits its powers in terms of the relief that may be granted, stating:

> 5. As part of its judgement, the Dispute Tribunal may only order one or both of the following:
>
> (a) Rescission of the contested administrative decision or specific performance, provided that, where the contested administrative decision concerns appointment, promotion or termination, the Dispute Tribunal shall also set an amount of compensation that *the respondent* may elect to pay as an alternative to the rescission of the contested administrative decision or specific performance ordered, subject to subparagraph (b) of the present paragraph;
>
> (b) Compensation for harm, supported by evidence, which shall normally not exceed the equivalent of two years' net base salary of the

[131] Undue delay and effective remedy.

> applicant. The Dispute Tribunal may, however, in exceptional cases order the payment of a higher compensation for harm, supported by evidence, and shall provide the reasons for that decision (emphasis added).[132]

The reason for placing limits on the amount of compensation that the UN tribunals are empowered to grant has a historical explanation, stemming from the organisation's displeasure with the extent of damages provided by the old UN Administrative Tribunal.[133] This history dictates that such generic caps on compensation ought to be treated with caution.[134] Given the inbuilt discretion in Article 2(6), the situation would have been consistent with the right to a fair trial and effective remedy but for the attitude shown by the Administration. A three-judge bench in the case of *Nakhlawi v Secretary-General of the United Nations*[135] noted that:

> [T]he reality is that in cases where the Tribunal found that a staff member had been wrongly separated, through no fault of his/her own but rather as a result of managerial error, the decision was systematically taken to pay compensation, instead of considering the reintegration of the staff member. . . . There may, thus, be cases in which the career of staff members, who dedicated their entire professional life to the Organization and its mission, is completely ruined by an act carried out by the Respondent and found to be unlawful.[136]

Moreover, for a remedy to be effective, it must be commensurate with the harm suffered by a claimant. In respect of the UN's scheme that creates a two-year cap to the compensation that may be ordered, the IJC has noted:

> [T]he 'no rescission, no reinstatement' approach does not serve justice in every instance. . . . The chronic backlog of cases and the delays in delivering judgments, often two or more years after the submission of an application, inflict further harm on applicants found to have been unlawfully terminated. Depending on the circumstances involved in specific cases, including the difficulty of finding comparable alternative employment and whether delays

[132] UNDT Statute (art 15), art 10(5).

[133] R Gulati, 'An International Administrative Procedural Law of Fair Trial: Reality or Rhetoric?' (2018) 21 Max Planck Yearbook of United Nations Law 210–70, 242.

[134] The UNAT recalled in *Hersh v Secretary-General of the United Nations* (2014-UNAT-433, 27 June 2014) that it had held in *Mmata v Secretary-General of the United Nations* (2010-UNAT-092, 29 October 2010), namely that 'art 10.5(b) of the UNDT Statute (n 15) does not require a formulaic articulation of aggravating factors; rather it requires evidence of aggravating factors which warrant higher compensation'.

[135] *Nakhlawi v Secretary-General of the United Nations* (UNDT/2016/204, 11 November 2016).

[136] Ibid, paras 104–5.

> in adjudication were attributable to systemic inefficiencies, the Dispute Tribunal should consider whether justice requires an award of compensation in excess of the two years of net base salary which is provided for in normal situations.[137]

To address these deficits, the most effective option would be to grant the UN tribunals the power to make orders that leave no choice concerning the applicable remedy, and reconsider whether the two-year cap to the compensation that may be ordered should be done away with. Another solution recommended is that 'the statute of the Dispute Tribunal be amended to provide that, prior to opting for payment of compensation in lieu of rescission or reinstatement, the respondent should provide satisfactory evidence to the Tribunal that rescission or specific performance is not feasible owing to compelling operational, administrative or budgetary reasons'.[138] As the situation now stands, given the limitations on relief that the UN tribunals may grant, and the practice of the organisation, the risk that in individual cases the right to an effective remedy may be breached is high.

Second, on the question of the bindingness and enforceability of the orders and decisions of the UN tribunals, as a matter of law, they are final, binding and must be enforced.[139] In practice, however, issues with enforcement have been a prevailing feature of the UN internal justice system since its inception, rooted in a culture where the senior most members of the Administration do not seem to consider the UNDT and UNAT's decisions as binding. Where the UN failed to disclose documents pursuant to the UNDT's orders in numerous cases,[140] the Secretary-General was reported as saying: 'Sometimes there may be some cases of decisions which are not totally in line with what the Secretariat has been doing. ... But we will try to respect all the decisions.'[141] The use of such ambiguous language by the Chief Administrative Officer of the UN is unfortunate as it seriously undermines the right to an effective remedy and fair trial. Remarkably, at the end of his term as an UNDT judge,

[137] IJC 2020 Report (n 33), paras 63–4.

[138] Ibid, para 65.

[139] See UNDT Statute (n 15), art 9(1), on the power of the UNDT to order production of documents; art 11(3) provides that the 'judgments and orders of the Dispute Tribunal shall be binding upon the parties, but are subject to appeal in accordance with the UNAT Statute (n 18). In the absence of such appeal, they shall be executable following the expiry of the time provided for appeal in the statute of the Appeals Tribunal. Case management orders or directives shall be executable immediately'.

[140] See the discussion in Gulati (n 21), especially jurisprudence cited at footnotes 178–82 of that work.

[141] The New York Times, 'Review Panel Judges See a Culture of U.N. Secrecy' (16 June 2010) <www.nytimes.com/2010/06/17/world/17nations.html?pagewanted=all&_r=0> accessed 19 May 2018.

Judge Adams reportedly said: 'You have to look at the culture here. Someone in the position of undersecretary general is never confronted with the requirement that particular questions be answered.'[142] The fact that judges of the UN tribunals are equated with the D-2 rank does not help the situation either as this can create a perception that staff members ranked D-2 or higher can simply ignore the decisions of the UN tribunals.[143]

Until this day, issues with enforceability subsist. On several occasions, the UN has failed to comply with the UNDT's orders relating to protective measures aimed at preventing retaliation against witnesses.[144] Orders as to the production of documents can be left unenforced.[145] And often, the UN fails to follow-up on referrals for accountability by the UNDT where the tribunal has found that officials may have engaged in serious wrongdoing, including corruption and sexual assault.[146] Such an attitude by the Administration defies the UNDT's Statute, and is squarely contrary to the right to a fair trial and effective remedy. While a litigant can apply to the UNDT for the execution of its orders and decisions,[147] if the Administration refuses to comply, in the absence of a meaningful enforcement power vested in the UN tribunals, there is little an applicant, or for that matter the relevant tribunal can do to seek enforcement of its orders and decisions. In the final analysis, significant structural and factual deficiencies mean that a claimant's right to an effective remedy and fair trial may not be realised at the UN tribunals.

3.2.1.4 A Comment on the UN Tribunals

The UN internal justice system is deficient. A vast number of so-called non-staff personnel working for the UN have no access to the UNDT and UNAT. These individuals are unable to access justice on an equal footing with those officials who perform materially similar work. For such individuals, the UN tribunals do not provide for an appropriate mode of dispute resolution for the simple reason that access to the tribunals is completely denied. For individuals with access to the UN tribunals, the situation is also concerning. In theory,

142 Ibid.

143 One article noted that the 'judges were assigned an administrative rank that puts them below an assistant secretary general, so those who rank higher often feel that answering the tribunal is beneath them': see ibid.

144 IJC 2017 Report (n 23), para 27 pointed out that contractors are especially vulnerable in such situations.

145 Ibid, Annex II (Views of the UNDT), para 59.

146 Ibid, paras 54 and 58; the UNDT's power to refer cases to the UN to enhance accountability is provided for in UNDT Statute (n 15), art 10(8).

147 UNDT Statute (n 15), art 12(4).

access to a two-tier judicial system exists. However, the forums lack institutional, decisional and individual independence. Objective fears about the UN tribunals' impartiality are apparent. Moreover, fairness and equality are increasingly being undermined due to OSLA's chronic underfunding and the undue delays in the administration of justice. Serious concerns about the effectiveness of the remedies that the UN tribunals can grant also prevail. Perhaps one of the most significant issues still lies in the culture prevailing at the organisation, which can let judicial orders go unenforced from time to time. Even more concerning is the significant discord that has recently been evident amongst the UNDT's judges, bringing the internal justice machinery at the UN into disrepute. Resolving the fair trial deficiencies pointed out requires significant structural and cultural reforms. With budgetary pressures on the UN immense,[148] the prospects of large-scale reforms at this time are not bright. Of course, this may change in the future. But as things stand, even though the UN's internal justice system has witnessed much reform, the UN tribunals do not generally constitute an appropriate mode of dispute settlement.

3.2.2 *The ILOAT*

The ILOAT, originally known as the League of Nations Administrative Tribunal, is the oldest IAT and has been in operation for more than ninety years.[149] The ILOAT exercises jurisdiction over close to sixty IOs,[150] is open to approximately 60,000 international civil servants[151] and has delivered more than 4,000 judgments so far.[152] Its potential significance to the realisation of the right to a fair trial for a vast number of individuals impacted by IO conduct is obvious. Structurally though, the ILOAT has not materially changed since

148 See generally IJC 2020 Report (n 33).

149 The ILOAT succeeded the League of Nations Administrative Tribunal: see D Petrovic, 'Longest-Existing International Administrative Tribunal: History, Main Characteristics and Current Challenges' in D Petrovic (ed), *90 Years of Contribution of the Administrative Tribunal of the International Labour Organization to the Creation of International Civil Service Law* (International Labour Organization 2017) (90 Years of ILOAT), 23.

150 Organisations other than the ILO can join the ILOAT regime if they accept its jurisdiction pursuant to the provisions of the Annex to the Statute of the Administrative Tribunal of the International Labour Organization; see ILO 'ILO Administrative Tribunal' <www.ilo.org/tribunal/lang–en/index.htm> accessed 3 June 2018 (the tribunal, amongst others, is open to several UN Specialized Agencies), and currently exercises jurisdiction over at least fifty-eight international organisations: see ibid, 25.

151 90 Years of ILOAT (n 149), 28.

152 See the ILOAT's case law database known as Triblex: ILO, 'Triblex: Case-Law Database' (2021) <www.ilo.org/dyn/triblex/triblexmain.bySession> accessed 3 June 2018.

its inception.[153] The ILOAT has failed to adopt modern fair trial standards in its practice and procedure.

The ILOAT's persisting deficiencies have already been subjected to detailed studies, including in a report by the Amsterdam Centre for International Law (Amsterdam Report), as well as this author.[154] Still, it is important to point out the ILOAT's key deficits relating to independence (Section 3.2.2.1), impartiality (Section 3.2.2.2) and fairness (Section 3.2.2.3).

3.2.2.1 Assessing Judicial Independence at the ILOAT

As is shown next, the ILOAT cannot be said to be (a) institutionally; (b) decisionally; or (c) individually independent. The tribunal cannot constitute an appropriate mode of dispute resolution based on the independence deficits alone.

(A) ASSESSING INSTITUTIONAL INDEPENDENCE AT THE ILOAT Concerning the ILOAT's institutional and operational independence, any meaningful de jure guarantees in its constituent arrangements are generally absent.[155] Article 2 of the ILOAT Statute creates a Registry and states that the Registrar is appointed by the Director-General of the International Labour Office.[156] The Registrar

[153] The ILOAT's competences ratione materiae and ratione personae have not been modified; see 90 Years of ILOAT (n 149), 21–2.

[154] See generally, E Cannon and I Warlam, 'The Judicial Independence of the International Labour Organization Administrative Tribunal: Potential for Reform' (Report, Amsterdam International Law Clinic, 2007) (Amsterdam Report); for the independence deficits identified, see G Robertson QC, 'Opinion for the Information Meeting on the ILO Administrative Tribunal Reform and Related Matters' (2002) <www.ilo.org/public/english/staffun/info/iloat/robertson.htm> accessed 3 June 2018; L Doswald-Beck, 'ILO: The Right to a Fair Hearing Interpretation of International Law' (13 November 2002) <www.ilo.org/public/english/staffun/info/iloat/doswald.htm> accessed 3 June 2018; I Seiderman, 'Does the ILO Administrative Tribunal Meet the Standards of an Independent and Impartial Judiciary?' (2002) <www.ilo.org/public/english/staffun/info/iloat/seiderman.htm> accessed 3 June 2018; OA Jefferson and I Epichev, 'International Organisations as Employers: Searching for Practices of Fair Treatment and Due Process Rights of Staff' in K Rubenstein and KG Young (eds), *The Public Law of Gender: From the Local to the Global* (Cambridge University Press 2016), 489–513, 496–7.

[155] ILOAT Statute, (International Labour Conference, 105th session) <www.ilo.org/global/about-the-ilo/how-the-ilo-works/departments-and-offices/jur/legal-instruments/WCMS_498369/lang–en/index.htm> accessed 18 April 2021 (ILOAT Statute), art X, is in general terms giving the ILOAT a degree of freedom in terms of enacting rules of procedures and on operational aspects.

[156] 'Rules of the Administrative Tribunal of the International Labour Organization' (2021) <www.ilo.org/tribunal/about-us/WCMS_249195/lang–en/index.htm> accessed 18 April 2021 (ILOAT Rules of Procedure), art 2.

and key officers of the ILOAT are ILO staff members who report to the ILO's Director-General. Article IX of the ILOAT Statute simply provides that the 'administrative arrangements necessary for the operation of the Tribunal shall be made by the International Labour Office in consultation with the Tribunal'.[157] Because de jure guarantees as to institutional independence are for most part absent, one must look at the factual situation prevailing at the ILOAT. Unfortunately, the factual situation cannot be readily ascertained either. The 'governance functions over ILOAT are ... performed by ILO organs. Its seven judges are appointed by the International Labour Conference, and its expenses are borne by the International Labour Office'.[158] But there is little transparency as to how the ILOAT's operational independence is secured. The Amsterdam Report concluded:

> The ILOAT is not transparent with regard to how it is funded and how those funds are paid out to judges and used for ensuring the proper functioning of the Tribunal. Cases are financed by the defendant in a given case. This means that all cases are financed by the international organization at bar. These concerns are increased when one considers the [very low] success rates of complainants before the Tribunal.[159]

It can hardly be said that the ILOAT constitutes an operationally independent judicial body.[160] Not only is there a real deficiency concerning the ILOAT's institutional independence, but significant deficits also continue to prevail concerning decisional and individual independence.

(B) ASSESSING DECISIONAL INDEPENDENCE AT THE ILOAT Concerning the first aspect of decisional independence, that is, the ability to conclusively determine its own jurisdiction, the ILOAT can be said to be sufficiently independent. Article II(7) of the ILOAT's Statute provides that '[a]ny dispute as to the competence of the Tribunal shall be decided by it'. The ILOAT thus can conclusively determine questions of jurisdiction. Of course, the ILOAT's jurisdiction is circumscribed by its Statute. Article II of the ILOAT's Statute prescribes its personal and subject matter jurisdiction. As to the ILOAT's

157 ILOAT Statute (n 155), art X, empowers it to enact rules governing the conduct of proceedings and any matters not covered by the Statute. However, the ILOAT's operational independence is not guaranteed.

158 N Blokker, 'The Governance of International Courts and Tribunals: Organizing and Guaranteeing Independence and Accountability' in A Follesdal and G Ulfstein (eds), *The Judicialization of International Law: A Mixed Blessing?* (Oxford University Press 2018), 35.

159 Amsterdam Report (n 154), 60–1, with the authors noting that the success rate of complainants in the previous sixteen years from the date of writing was less than 25 per cent.

160 Ibid, 1; also see Jefferson and Epichev (n 154), 489–513.

personal jurisdiction, under Article II(6)(a), the ILOAT is competent to determine complaints from an ILO official or an official of any other organisation who has joined the ILOAT regime. In terms of subject matter jurisdiction, the tribunal is empowered to hear and determine cases that impugn the employment rights of an official as provided by the applicable international administrative regime, including disputes about the compensation to be paid for workplace injury.[161] The ILOAT can also adjudicate claims about the execution of contracts to which the organisation is a party where the ILOAT's jurisdiction is recognised, presumably through a choice of court clause.[162] While the ILOAT's subject matter jurisdiction in theory is somewhat broader from what one may expect from an employment tribunal, in practice, the focus of its work has been on labour cases.

Concerning the second aspect of decisional independence, that is, that a DRM should decide a case based on the facts and law alone, the ILOAT's mode of delivering justice is deficient. The ILOAT does not tend to conduct its own factual inquiry even though under its Statute it has the capacity to do so.[163] Due to the way in which the ILOAT chooses to discharge its judicial function, a claimant before that tribunal is unable to access a truly first instance judicial mechanism.

It is important to understand how a claim makes its way to an IAT in general, and the ILOAT in particular. Generally, internal justice systems at IOs require that a complaint against an administrative decision is first filed with an arm of the Management (such as with the human resources department). If the complainant is not satisfied, they may appeal to an internal appeals body, which is a peer review body, such as a grievance committee or appeals committee/board.[164] In the case of the ILOAT specifically, unless an internal body has been first approached, the claim is not receivable at the level of the tribunal.[165] Crucially for our purposes, such committees usually do not consist of professional judges and are constituted by members of the Administration.[166]

161 ILOAT Statute (n 155), art II(2). This provision does not seem to have attracted jurisprudence. On the language of the provision, it would seem that it applies not to determine fault but only disputes about the compensation to be paid.

162 Ibid, art II(4).

163 See ILOAT Rules of Procedure (n 156), arts 11–12.

164 See L Fauth, 'Due Process and Equality of Arms in the Internal Appeal: New Developments from Judgments 3586 and 368', in D Petrovic (ed), *90 Years of Contribution of the Administrative Tribunal of the International Labour Organization to the Creation of International Civil Service Law* (International Labour Organization 2017).

165 ILOAT Statute (n 155), art VII.

166 Some organisations have taken steps to appoint non-staff members and independent persons with relevant legal expertise to carry out administrative reviews internally, such as the OECD.

Amongst other deficits, their recommendations are not binding. In such a system, perversely, the ultimate decision-maker is the very person whose decision is often challenged, that is, the executive head of an organisation. These mechanisms cannot and do not constitute fair trial compliant modes of dispute resolution as they demonstrably lack independence and cannot render binding decisions.[167]

Accessing the ILOAT is then the only opportunity for a claimant to approach a judicial mechanism to resolve their claim. The ILOAT should be playing the role of a first instance court, unless internal appeal mechanisms at IOs are made due-process-compliant. But the ILOAT's role is confused. It is somewhere between a truly first instance court that ought to make its own independent findings of fact (which the ILOAT does not tend to do) and an 'appellant court'. In practice, the ILOAT gives 'significant deference to the findings of fact and conclusions on the merits of the internal appeal bodies', meaning that no real scrutiny of the facts is undertaken.[168] The ILOAT itself has said that it is 'ill-equipped to act as a trial court' or a first instance court.[169] It states:

> An internal appeal procedure that works properly is an important safeguard of staff rights and social harmony in an international organisation and, as a prerequisite of judicial review, an indispensable means of preventing the dispute from going outside the organisation. In the event of a complaint it greatly helps the Tribunal in identifying the material issues of fact and law.[170]

The ILOAT primarily sees itself as an appellate court. This perhaps is due to reasons of practicality as opposed to any limitations as to its competence.[171] The ILOAT has one Registry in Geneva where the judges meet for the sessions of the tribunal, with respondent organisations and complainants spread

For a discussion, see AM Thevenot, 'Effective Individual Dispute Resolution Mechanisms Prior to Judicial Appeals in International Organizations' in A Talvik (ed), *Best Practices in Resolving Employment Disputes in International Organizations* (Conference Proceedings, ILO Geneva 2015) (Best Practices in Resolving Employment Disputes), 31; for a study of the work of the independent Management Evaluation Unit within the UN's internal justice system, see generally, Gulati (n 21).

167 Best Practices in Resolving Employment Disputes (n 166), 33.

168 Fauth (n 164), 184.

169 See *Re Mr AR BB* (2013) ILOAT Judgment No 3222, para 10, where the ILOAT said '[a]nother purpose of art VII (1) of the Statute is to ensure that the Tribunal does not become, de facto, a trial court of staff grievances and to ensure it continues as a final appellate tribunal. The Tribunal is ill-equipped to act as a trial court and its workload could, potentially, become intolerable or unmanageable if its role was not confined in this way'.

170 In *Re Amira* (1994) ILOAT Judgment No 1317, para 31.

171 In principle, there is nothing stopping the ILOAT from playing a first instance role.

around the world. Engaging in fact-finding in such circumstances can be a challenge, although the advent of technology can deal with this challenge well. In fact, due to the COVID-19 pandemic that obstructed normal business, the ILOAT did take some initial steps to use electronic methods of communication. It is not clear whether such a development is to be continued.[172] Whatever the reason, the point is that the ILOAT currently does not provide justice to claimants consistent with their right to access a decisionally independent court. If internal justice mechanisms at IOs see significant reform where first instance judicial mechanisms are created, then the ILOAT could very well limit itself to play the role of an appellate court. Unless such reforms occur, it is questionable whether the ILOAT provides for an appropriate DRM, especially where the facts of a case are disputed.

(C) ASSESSING INDIVIDUAL/PERSONAL INDEPENDENCE AT THE ILOAT At the ILOAT, neither the mode of judicial selection is transparent, nor security of tenure historically present. The deficits at the ILOAT concerning the judicial appointment process are significant and have been well traversed. In 2007, it was noted in the Amsterdam Report that the selection process involves 'the ILO Director-General first consult[ing] with the ILO Governing Body and then select[ing] candidates on the following criteria: (1) experience in a court of high national jurisdiction or equivalent status at the international level; (2) nationality; and (3) balance in linguistic ability'.[173] More recently, the process was explained as follows:

> While the original text of the Statute adopted in 1927 provided that three judges and three deputy judges would be appointed by the Council of the League of Nations, which would be equivalent to the ILO Governing Body, the ILO decided that judges should be appointed by the International Labour Conference. By entrusting the task of appointing judges to the Conference, which is not only the highest body of the Organization but, more importantly, is a tripartite body entrusted with the mandate of dealing with international labour issues, the ILO pre-empted any serious challenge to the judges' legitimacy. Who else would be better placed than the 'World Parliament of Labour' to choose judges for this type of jurisdiction?[174]

But according to modern standards, judicial appointments must entail a significant role for an independent body operating transparently. The

172 See, ILO, 'Filing of Written Submissions during the COVID-19 Crisis' (2020) <www.ilo.org/tribunal/news/WCMS_742882/lang–en/index.htm> accessed 24 April 2021.

173 Amsterdam Report (n 154), 38.

174 See 90 Years of ILOAT (n 149), 29.

absence of an independent commission or mechanism, as well as transparency in the appointment process, undermines the perception of the individual independence of ILOAT judges. That being said, so far, more than fifty judges and deputy judges of at least twenty-nine different nationalities have sat on the ILOAT since 1946.[175] The practice whereby only existing judges of superior courts are appointed to the ILOAT tempers to a degree the opaque nature of the judicial appointment process. Still, the perception of an independence deficit remains.

What is more, it must be acknowledged that for most of its history, issues around the security of tenure at the ILOAT have been grave. Until recently, ILOAT judges were appointed for short three-year renewable terms. As was clarified in Chapter 2, short renewable terms undermine judicial independence. Specifically concerning the ILOAT, Robertson had commented:

> [T]he Tribunal members are 'contract judges', whose well-remunerated employment is contingent upon the regular approval of the very body which is a defending party to their proceedings. This position is plainly incompatible with the rule that requires the judiciary to be independent.[176]

In a welcome development, on 18 June 2021, Article III of the ILOAT Statute was amended with ILOAT judges now 'appointed for a term of five years, renewable once by the International Labour Conference'. Security of tenure in terms of its length has thus been largely accomplished. However, deficits remain. There seem to be no provisions guaranteeing financial security of the judges in place. And rules around the removal of judges are also absent. In sum, until further significant reforms are pursued, the ILOAT regime continues to be deficient. .[177]

3.2.2.2 Assessing Judicial Impartiality at the ILOAT

The ILOAT's Statute and Rules of Procedure also fail to ensure impartiality in an objective sense. There exists no possibility of seeking a judge's

[175] Ibid, 27. It is also noted that several former presidents of the Tribunal – Judges Gentot, Ba, Gaudron and Rouiller, for instance – stayed with the Tribunal for between ten and fifteen years each.

[176] Robertson (n 154), para 6.

[177] Amsterdam Report (n 154), 61; also note, steps to enhance judicial independence have been contemplated and to an extent, enacted: see the amendments proposed by the ILO's Governing Body to the ILOAT Statute seeking to strengthen judicial independence at the ILOAT in ILO, 'Matters Relating to the Administrative Tribunal of the ILO. Proposed Amendments to the Statute of the Tribunal' (19 February 2021) GB.341/PFA/15/1 (ILO Document).

recusal where impartiality might be an issue. Remarkably, the parties to the proceedings at the ILOAT do not even know the identity of the judge determining the case. Until judgment is rendered, for all intents and purposes, the trial is before a faceless court.[178] To add to that, the absence of the right to appeal within the ILOAT system makes it impossible to seek review from a second instance judicial mechanism where a party wishes to challenge the independence and impartiality of a judge(s). It is manifest that the ILOAT presently does not deliver impartial justice in an objective sense. What is more, the significant fairness deficits prevailing at the ILOAT render an already deficient regime even more 'inappropriate'.

3.2.2.3 Assessing Fairness at the ILOAT

The ILOAT does provide for some fairness guarantees in its Statute and Rules of Procedure. They must provide a reasoned judgment.[179] These judgments are also made publicly available through the most sophisticated public facing international administrative law case law database.[180] The right to appoint counsel of one's own choosing is also stated in the ILOAT's Statute.[181] However, significant structural deficits exist. These include (a) the breach of the right to equality; (b) the routine denial of oral hearings; (c)the undue delays in the administration of justice; and (d) the denial of the right to appeal.

(A) ASSESSING EQUALITY AT THE ILOAT As is the case at the UN internal justice system, perhaps the gravest equality deficit at the ILOAT concerns the lack of access to judicial protection for non-staff personnel. In particular, international civil servants categorised as non-staff members cannot access the ILOAT unless that tribunal is expressly selected as a forum of choice. In its case law, where no alternative mechanisms for so-called non-staff members exist, the ILOAT has shown a willingness to take jurisdiction to ensure that

178 Amsterdam Report, 49 and 55.

179 ILOAT Statute (n 155), art VI(2).

180 ILOAT judgments are available at ILO, 'Advanced Search in Triblex: Case-Law Database' (2021) <www.ilo.org/dyn/triblex/triblexmain.advancedSearch?p_lang=en> accessed 26 April 2021.

181 Although, it remains unclear whether the IOs subscribing to the ILOAT's jurisdiction provide a UN-style OSLA to their staff members. This would raise issues of equality of arms given that the factual inequality between the claimant and an employer is stark: see *Judgment No 2867 of the Administrative Tribunal of the International Labour Organization Upon a Complaint Filed against the International Fund for Agricultural Development* (Advisory Opinion) [2012] ICJ 10 (*IFAD Advisory Opinion*), (Judge Greenwood), para 6.

access to justice is maintained.[182] However, where an alternative mechanism, such as an arbitration clause, exists, the ILOAT refuses to take jurisdiction.[183] This the ILOAT seems to do without satisfying itself that the arbitral mechanism is in fact effectively implemented. Such an approach can result in the bizarre outcome that an IO could oust the jurisdiction of the ILOAT by simply incorporating an arbitration clause in its contractual arrangements with consultants and contractors,[184] with no intention of ever subjecting any dispute that may arise to an arbitral process. A fair trial in such circumstances cannot be practically realised. A significant equality deficit, thus, prevails at the ILOAT when it comes to the right to equal access to the courts and tribunals for a large category of individuals working for IOs. For such persons, the effectiveness of an arbitral process obviously becomes critical (see Section 3.3).

Of course, the right to equality in the administration of justice can also be engaged at other stages in the justice process. For example, equality must be ensured before any internal review mechanisms that a claimant must approach prior to seeking a remedy at the ILOAT. Considering such issues requires an analysis of the internal justice system of every IO that currently subscribes to the ILOAT's jurisdiction. Such an analysis is outside the scope of this work. It suffices to say that if the appropriateness of the ILOAT as a DRM is to be assessed, the fair trial compliance of the entire justice machinery, with the ILOAT sitting at the top of the pyramid, may become necessary when determining whether the right to a fair trial has been practically realised in a particular case.

(B) THE ABSENCE OF ORAL HEARINGS AT THE ILOAT It appears that since 1989, not a single request for an oral hearing has been granted by the ILOAT.[185] The provision in the ILOAT's Statute and Rules of Procedure empowering it to hold oral hearings is devoid of any real meaning, with the ILOAT routinely and cursorily dismissing requests for oral hearings.[186] As the ILOAT is the only judicial mechanism a claimant can approach to resolve

182 See the broad interpretation given to the term 'staff member' by the ILOAT (an approach not adopted at the UN tribunals) in the well-known case of *Re Chadsey v World Postal Union* (15 October 1968) ILOAT Judgment No 122.

183 See for example *Mr J.-D. v ILO* (3 February 2010) ILOAT Judgement No 2888, para 6.

184 However, the ILOAT does treat an individual as constituting a de facto staff member where short-term contractual arrangements are misused, meaning access to the tribunal for such persons is possible: see *Ms P v WIPO* (8 February 2012) ILOAT Judgment No. 3090, para 7.

185 Amsterdam Report (n 154), 1.

186 Flaherty identifies common phrases employed by the ILOAT to deny oral hearings: 'Having examined the written pleadings, the Tribunal has decided not to order hearing for which neither party has applied.' 'Having examined the written submissions and disallowed the

their dispute against IOs subscribing to that tribunal's jurisdiction, the right to a fair trial requires that an oral hearing be granted, which is not the ILOAT's practice. Moreover, the denial of an oral hearing arguably constitutes a fundamental breach of procedure where there is a contest on the facts. This would often be the case in international administrative disputes. Accordingly, the ILOAT's routine denial of oral hearings seriously undermines the right to a fair trial. It is alarming that officials can suffer the most serious consequences, including loss of their employment and the destruction of their reputations, effectively based on findings that have not been put through a robust forensic examination by an independent and impartial court. Thus, it has been concluded that the ILOAT's practice of denying an oral hearing is a contravention of the right to a fair trial and contrary to the statutory intention enshrined in the ILOAT's Statute.[187]

The denial of an oral hearing can also lead to the potential breach of other fair trial rights. These include the right to put forward one's case in full equality and the right to defence. The ILOAT's Statute and Rules of Procedure have no meaningful mechanism through which a claimant may seek discovery of relevant documents from an employer IO, substantially hampering a complainant's ability to meet their burden of proof or impairing their 'right of defence when accused of misconduct'.[188] In the absence of an oral hearing, where no witness testimony is heard, and where the IO is in a factually superior position vis-à-vis the claimant, it can hardly be said that the right to put forward one's case in full equality and the right to defence are being practically realised. Access to justice at the ILOAT can be significantly enhanced if the ILOAT starts to grant oral hearings as a matter of right. Any argument that oral hearings are impracticable due to reasons of geography can be readily overcome by the use of technology, which the ILOAT seems reticent to adopt.[189] The ILOAT still relies on antiquated procedures. With

complainants' application for hearings.' 'Having examined the written submissions and disallowed the complainant's application for the hearing of witnesses': see EP Flaherty, 'Legal Protection in International Organisations for Staff – A Practitioner's View' (undated), 4.

187 Robertson (n 154), para 10.

188 See Staff Union of the European Patent Organization, 'Managing the ILO Administrative Tribunal's Workload – Current Challenges and Possible Improvements' (2015) (SUEPO Report), 9.

189 Perhaps the ILOAT's willingness to accept electronic submissions during the COVID-19 crisis the world faced in 2020–2021 may lead to permanent improvements: see 'Filing of Written Submissions during the COVID-19 Crisis' (*ILO*) <www.ilo.org/tribunal/news/WCMS_742882/lang–en/index.htm> accessed 18 April 2021.

no e-filing in place at the ILOAT and the absence of the use of technology to conduct proceedings, the delivery of justice is cumbersome and slow.[190]

(C) UNDUE DELAYS AT THE ILOAT As has already been said, for a fair trial to be realised, employment claims ought to be resolved in months and not years. According to the ILOAT's own case law, a claimant is entitled to an efficient means of redress and to expect a decision on an appeal to be taken within a reasonable time.[191] The ILOAT has found delays of even a few months that cannot be objectively justified due to the complexity of the case or the behaviour of the complainant to be unreasonable.[192] Given the ILOAT's own jurisprudence, it is all the more perplexing that the right to receive justice without undue delay is being seriously compromised.

On one analysis carried out by the Staff Union of the EPO, it could take up to six years before the ILOAT is able to address its backlog.[193] The ILO points to the ever-increasing caseload of the tribunal. It points out that the ILOAT is working at maximum capacity (rendering around 150 judgments per year), and that it does not have capacity to enhance its output without compromising on its quality.[194] Meaning that some cases may take anywhere between four to six

190 Ibid.

191 See *Re Mr JA C* (n 118), para 13 (and cases cited there); in *Re PM (No 2)* (2016) ILOAT Judgment No 3688: where there was a three-year delay attributable to the organisation for delay in the administration of justice, the ILOAT awarded moral damages because the delay breached the complainant's due process rights (see paras 5–12). In that case, even an unexplainable delay in one aspect of the internal appeals process amounting to eight months that could not be explained by the organisation was considered unjustified (para 6); also see *Re Mrs K JL* (n 118), para 15: where the WHO did not process a claim for a service-incurred injury within forty-two months, the ILOAT awarded moral damages for the delay was said to be manifestly unfounded; it is also apparent that any delay (of even a few months) that cannot be explained or justified due to the complexity of the case, and so on, will be 'undue'. The tribunal has also said that an organisation has a positive obligation to ensure that internal appeal procedures move forward with 'reasonable speed': see ILOAT Judgment No 2197, para 8; and ILOAT Judgment No 2904, para 15.

192 See *Re Mrs K JL* (n 118), para 15: where the WHO did not process a claim for a service-incurred injury within forty-two months, the ILOAT awarded moral damages for the delay which was said to be manifestly unfounded. In that same case, it is also apparent that any delay (of even a few months) that could not be objectively justified was undue; in *Re Mr JA C* (n 118), para 18: where there was an unjustifiable delay of approximately nine months, it was found to be undue.

193 SUEPO Report (n 188), 1–2. The SUEPO pointed out that as of July 2015, the ILOAT had 450 pending cases; and it could take up to six years for the backlog to be cleared, assuming no new backlogs are created; also see ILO, 'Matters Relating to the Administrative Tribunal of the ILO Workload and Effectiveness of the Tribunal' (325th session, ILO Geneva, 2015) (ILOAT Workload and Effectiveness Report), paras 7 and 14.

194 ILOAT Workload and Effectiveness Report (n 193), para 14.

years to be processed from their inception at an internal appeals process until the ILOAT decision is rendered. This assumes that the ILOAT maintains its higher output achieved since 2014, and no further backlogs are created.

In general, the time it takes a case to be completed at the ILOAT demonstrably breaches the right to access a court without undue delay. Similar delays within the UN's internal justice system that preceded the 2009 reforms were found to be 'egregious'.[195] In fact, some IOs have left the ILOAT system because of the undue delays in the administration of justice. When leaving the ILOAT's jurisdiction in favour of the UNAT in 2019, the IFAD said:

> [The] time span for staff and IFAD to await tribunal decisions from the ILOAT is two to three times longer than that of UNAT. . . . Given the context of 'justice delayed is justice denied', members noted that quicker decisions will better protect staff.[196]

Several reasons have been put forward seeking to explain why the delivery of justice at the ILOAT is beset with delays. First, the ILOAT's caseload has exponentially increased.[197] Such an increase has not been matched with enhanced resources so far. This cannot be an excuse to deny a fair trial. It is the IO that must ensure that a DRM is sufficiently resourced so that it can render justice without undue delay. Second, on a related note, it has been claimed that the vast personal jurisdiction of the ILOAT can cause delays. However, there are only a small number of organisations that form the majority of the ILOAT's caseload, with the EPO constituting a significant percentage.[198] Indeed, the EPO has been blamed as a main reason for

195 A delay of three years in processing of claims in the old UN internal justice system was said to constitute an 'egregious delay': Redesign Panel Report (n 123), para 67.

196 See the reasons for IFAD's withdrawal: IFAD, 'IFAD's Withdrawal from the Jurisdiction of the Administrative Tribunal of the International Labour Organization (ILOAT) and Its Submission to the Jurisdiction of the United Nations Appeals Tribunal (UNAT) Based on the Assessment and Recommendations Outlined in EB 2019/126/R.35' (6 May 2019) (126th session) EB 2019/126/C.P.R.1/Rev.2. Given that delays in the administration of justice are also increasingly becoming a problem at the UN's internal justice system, it remains to be seen whether IFAD's decision will ultimately be prudent.

197 As the current Registrar of the ILOAT points out, in the whole period of its operation as the League of Nations Administrative Tribunal, it rendered thirty-seven judgments. Since 2010, the Tribunal has been regularly receiving more than 200 complaints per year: see 90 Years of ILOAT (n 149), 29.

198 ILOAT Workload and Effectiveness Report (n 193), para 24; at para 10, it is noted: 'the EPO has been concerned by 761 judgments out of a total of 3,560 judgments delivered by the Tribunal since its creation. By way of comparison, the Tribunal's second oldest member organization – the World Health Organization – with similar staff numbers has been concerned by 447 judgments in 66 years of membership, that is an average of seven judgments per year'.

excessive delays by the ILO.[199] It has been said that 'it is difficult to see how the Tribunal could continue under its current configuration and arrangements to cope with both its accumulated backlog and increasing workload'.[200]

Finally, the ILOAT's approach to certain issues also contributes to delays in the administration of justice. In particular, the ILOAT does not allow claims from staff associations on behalf of staff members (narrowly interpreting Article 2(6) of its Statute).[201] Thus, test cases that could clarify the law and potentially reduce the number of cases brought before the tribunal become difficult to pursue. Further, challenges to general decisions of the organisation impacting on staff rights have attracted inconsistent jurisprudence, with the ILOAT not allowing for such challenges in recent times.[202] A vast number of claims (which could be determined in one proceeding or test cases supported by a staff association) then end up being subjected to multiple challenges.[203] Surely, if the ILOAT's approach to such questions shifts, the number of cases it has to decide will reduce in number, speeding up the delivery of justice.

The ILOAT has taken marginal steps to improve its efficiency. A fast-track system was recently introduced providing for a more expeditious procedure in cases where the dispute concerns only questions of law, identified by agreement between the parties, and the main facts are uncontested.[204] It is not clear whether this procedure has succeeded in reducing delays at the tribunal. The ILOAT has also increasingly relied on its power to summarily dismiss a complaint,[205] although this has led to the criticism that such a practice further undermines the right of a claimant to a determination on the merits of their claim.[206] It is

199 Ibid, para 10.

200 Ibid, para 24.

201 Robertson (n 154), para 15; also note that in most jurisdictions/national systems as 'individual workers are often reluctant to voice their claims, fearing retaliation or the inability to proceed alone against their employers. In order to reduce this barrier to access, most adjudication systems provide that a claim can be pursued on a claimant's behalf by another individual' and so on: ILO: Resolving Individual Labour Disputes (n 120), 26–7. In another blow to the exercise of collective rights and access by staff associations to a court, in *EPO v. VEOB et al.* (20 January 2017) Dutch SC, First Chamber, paras 3.3, 5.2 and 5.7, the Dutch Supreme Court reversed the decision of the Hague Court of Appeal in *VEOB et al. v. EPO* (17 February 2015) Case no 200.141.812/01 AC of the Hague, which breached the immunities of the EPO for it did not provide the staff their collective rights in accordance with the European Convention on Human Rights.

202 SUEPO Report (n 188), 3.

203 Ibid.

204 ILOAT Rules of Procedure (n 156), art 7 (*bis*).

205 SUEPO Report (n 188), 1 (at footnote 3). That report points out that '[t]he summary procedure provided for in art 7 of the ILOAT Statute was used eighteen times between 1945 and 2014; since July 2014 (as of 2015): it has been used in at least fifty-eight cases'.

206 Ibid.

difficult to see how the problem of delays at the ILOAT can be solved unless significant systemic reforms are made. Currently, the seven ILOAT judges meet for approximately two months a year, several of whom are still in the service of their respective domestic judiciaries.[207] Unless more judicial resources are made available to the ILOAT, excessive delays will continue to occur despite the judges' best efforts.[208]

(D) THE DENIAL OF THE RIGHT TO APPEAL The right to an appeal is now firmly an aspect of what this author has previously referred to as an international administrative procedural law of fair trial.[209] There is little doubt that the right to an appeal is now considered to constitute a key procedural right without which fairness cannot be realised. Most IOs subscribing to the ILOAT's jurisdiction still have not established first instance judicial mechanisms. This means that the ILOAT is the only judicial mechanism that a claimant may access when pursuing their claim against a relevant employer IO. The right to an appeal for such claimants is thus being undermined due to the absence of a two-tier justice system, with no appeal rights existing. To resolve this deficit, three options exist. First, the ILOAT could itself establish an appellate division. This would require significant structural reforms. A second possibility is that IOs could create truly distinct first instance judicial mechanisms, with the ILOAT formally playing the role of an appellate court only. Third, if none of those things are done, the only option before an IO would be to join other international administrative dispute resolution regimes that provide for a two-tier justice system, such as the UN's internal justice regime. As was stated earlier in the chapter, this is already starting to happen.

3.2.2.4 The ILOT's Assessment

The ILOAT is not rendering justice consistently with fair trial standards. It lacks independence in an objective sense. Additionally, assuming access to the ILOAT is provided in the first place, the complete lack of oral hearings and the excessive delays in the delivery of justice, with cases taking years to resolve, on their own are egregious fair trial contraventions. Unless significant changes to the ILOAT's

207 ILOAT Workload and Effectiveness Report (n 193), paras 9 and 14.

208 See 90 Years of ILOAT (n 149), 29, where it is noted to deal with the workload, the tribunal recently organised an extra session and extended the duration of its regular sessions from three to four weeks. This enabled the ILOAT to increase its workload from fifty to eighty judgments per session.

209 IJC 2020 Report (n 33), paras 6–8 (Views of the UNAT), Recommendation 10.

constituent arrangements and practice are made, it is unlikely that individuals having access to the ILOAT can receive justice at an appropriate DRM that delivers justice in compliance with the right to a fair trial.

3.3 INTERNATIONAL ARBITRATION INVOLVING IOS

Thus far, this chapter has analysed the appropriateness of the two leading judicial mechanisms established at IOs seeking to provide access to justice to private claimants. It is important to also consider alternatives to full-fledged courts that are sometimes resorted to. One of them is international arbitration. Because IOs are international legal persons, disputes between IOs and a private actor acquire an international character. Generally, arbitrations against IOs should be considered to constitute an international arbitration as opposed to a purely domestic one. Although arbitration can in principle form an appropriate DRM (Section 3.3.1), it will only do so if it is capable of providing a fair trial (Section 3.3.2). I conclude that arbitration does not constitute an appropriate DRM in the context of resolving claims against IOs as of now (Section 3.3.3).

3.3.1 *International Arbitration in General*

The resolution of disputes through arbitration dates back to ancient Greek and Roman times and has been practiced in one form or another in all cultures around the world.[210] Arbitration provides for a flexible and neutral process for resolving disputes where an independent third party – an arbitrator – makes a binding decision.[211] The parties to a dispute must agree to submit their dispute to arbitration for the arbitral tribunal to have jurisdiction.[212] In modern times, especially when it comes to resolving international disputes, the arbitral process has been highly institutionalised and judicialised. It is now mostly administered by well-established arbitral institutions,[213] with arbitrators performing their role in a manner similar to

210 L Kidane, *The Culture of International Arbitration* (Oxford University Press 2017), 24–6.

211 See 'What is Arbitration?' *(CIArb)* <www.ciarb.org/dispute-appointment-service/arbitration/what-is-arbitration> accessed 23 July 2018.

212 Such agreement can be reflected in contract, or through treaty commitments; but see *Westland Helicopters Ltd and Arab Organization for Industrialization, United Arab Emirates, Kingdom of Saudi Arabia, State of Qatar, Arab Republic of Egypt and Arab British Helicopter Company* (5th March 1984) (Case no 3879/AS, 80 ILR 600, 80 ILR 595), where an arbitral tribunal was willing to lift the corporate veil of an IO.

213 See A Stone Sweet and F Grisel, *The Evolution of International Arbitration: Judicialization, Governance, Legitimacy* (Oxford University Press 2017), 49.

judges, with heavy reliance on past cases.[214] In addition to the well-known arbitral institutions such as the PCA and the ICC, nowadays, numerous institutions around the world aim to provide cost-effective arbitration services.

International arbitration can be an especially attractive DRM for parties who wish to stay out of national courts for one reason or another. IOs are such parties (see Chapter 4).[215] ICA has constituted a forum of choice to resolve transnational commercial disputes for a very long time. In more recent times, and especially since the 1990s, ISA has been used to resolve most international investment disputes predominantly through the mechanism of the ICSID Convention.[216] Thus, arbitration has been used to resolve all types of claims, from typically private law disputes to disputes having a public dimension, as well as employment disputes.[217] Indeed, countless international disputes are now decided through arbitral mechanisms, helping parties to stay out of national courts. At first glance, arbitration should be an instinctively appealing DRM through which IOs may discharge their access to justice obligation. But the issue requires a much more nuanced analysis. Commentators tend to be either strong supporters of arbitral processes (the pro-arbitration lobby)[218] or strongly oppose it, referring to it as a 'mafia' comprising of a limited number of repeat players that arbitrate most major disputes.[219] Ultimately, whether arbitration can constitute an appropriate DRM depends on whether such processes can provide a fair trial, which they can (Section 3.3.2) but presently do not (Section 3.3.3).

214 See A Stone Sweet and F Grisel, 'The Evolution of International Arbitration: Delegation, Judicialization, Governance' in W Mattli and T Dietz (eds), *International Arbitration and Global Governance: Contending Theories and Evidence* (Oxford University Press 2014), 32 and 43.

215 Kidane (n 210), 99–100; DD Caron, SW Schill, A Cohen Smutny and EE Triantafilou, *Practising Virtue: Inside International Arbitration* (Oxford University Press 2016), 1.

216 ICSID Convention (n 8).

217 See S Menon, 'The Transnational Protection of Private Rights Issues, Challenges, and Possible Solutions' (2015) 5 Asian Journal of International Law 2, 219–45, 230. Employment disputes are also increasingly being subjected to arbitration where a claim has connections with more than one legal order: see generally, Permanent Court of Arbitration, 'Internationalization of Labor Dispute Settlement' (Kluwer Law International, 2003).

218 Advocates of international arbitration point to the enforceability of awards across jurisdictions, avoidance of national jurisdiction, flexibility and ability to select arbitrators as its key advantages: Kidane (n 210), 26.

219 See R Michaels, 'Roles and Role Perceptions of International Arbitrators' in W Mattli and T Dietz (eds), *International Arbitration and Global Governance: Contending Theories and Evidence* (Oxford University Press 2014), 53–4.

3.3.2 *Can Arbitration Constitute an Appropriate DRM to Resolve Claims against IOs?*

That arbitration can play a role in providing private parties access to justice against IOs is not controversial. As early as 1954, in its *Effect of Awards* Advisory Opinion, the ICJ said that individuals affected by IO conduct may be delivered justice through a judicial mechanism or through arbitral means, drawing a functional equivalence between courts and arbitration.[220] In more recent times, the European Court has also endorsed arbitration as a viable mode of dispute resolution in claims against IOs.[221] But an arbitral process will only be an appropriate DRM if it satisfies key fair trial criteria. Namely, it must be independent, impartial and fair. Regardless of which set of arbitral rules govern the conduct of a particular arbitration, those requirements would usually be stated explicitly.

For example, concerning independence and impartiality, the UN Commission on International Trade Law (UNCITRAL) Arbitration Rules 2013 provide in Article 11: '[w]hen a person is approached in connection with his or her possible appointment as an arbitrator, he or she shall disclose any circumstances likely to give rise to justifiable doubts as to his or her impartiality or independence'. Moreover, a party can seek the recusal of an arbitrator before a neutral third party if the circumstances give rise to justifiable doubts as to the arbitrator's independence and impartiality.[222] While the applicable arbitration rules would tend to expressly enshrine the requirement of independence and impartiality, what happens in practice is subject to some debate.

International arbitration has been much criticised for alleged lack of arbitrator independence. Where individuals act as counsel as well as arbitrators, 'issue conflicts' can arise.[223] The lack of diversity in the pool of international arbitration specialists available and repeat appointments of arbitrators are also well-known problems. There is an ever-burgeoning literature on arbitrator independence and there is no need to restate that debate here, the point of note being that there would be little point choosing arbitration as a DRM if it is incapable of providing an independent and impartial mechanism to resolve disputes. If arbitrator independence and impartiality cannot be secured,

220 *Effect of Awards of Compensation Made by the United Nations Administrative Tribunal* (Advisory Opinion) [1954] ICJ Rep 47, 57.

221 *Klausecker v Germany* App no 415/07 (ECtHR, 6 January 2015), para 76.

222 See, for example, ICC Rules of Arbitration (entered into force 1 January 2021) <https://iccwbo.org/dispute-resolution-services/arbitration/rules-of-arbitration/#article_2> accessed 24 April 2021, art 14.

223 Menon (n 217), 219–45, 231–2.

a backlash can be the result. A good example of such a backlash is against ISA, where arbitrator independence has been an issue of significant controversy.[224]

In the end, for any arbitral scheme to be considered appropriate, the relevant arbitral procedures must guarantee arbitrator independence and impartiality in law and practice.[225] The same is true for fairness. Most arbitration rules would also require that equality and fairness be maintained during the arbitral process. For instance, Article 17(1) of the PCA Arbitration Rules states:

> [T]he arbitral tribunal may conduct the arbitration in such manner as it considers appropriate, provided that the parties are treated with equality and that at an appropriate stage of the proceedings each party is given a reasonable opportunity of presenting its case. The arbitral tribunal, in exercising its discretion, shall conduct the proceedings so as to avoid unnecessary delay and expense and to provide a fair and efficient process for resolving the parties' dispute.[226]

Indeed, if an arbitration undermines fair trial rights, such as where the arbitral tribunal lacks independence or impartiality, an award fails to provide adequate reasons or the parties are not treated equally and fairly, the enforcement of any resultant award can be jeopardised due to procedural deficiencies.[227] If an arbitral process is unfair, then a potential recourse may be available at the enforcement stage, although such a course of action may prove lengthy and very costly. The costs associated with arbitration are in fact its greatest disadvantage. These costs include legal costs incurred by the parties towards their counsel, as well as costs of the arbitration (including institutional and arbitrator fees). If the expense of commencing or going through with an arbitration process presents unjustified barriers to access justice, then it can hardly be said that a fair trial can be realised.[228]

224 This has led to calls for creating a permanent court in the sphere of ISA. For a brief analysis, see R Gulati and N Lavranos, 'Guaranteeing the Independence of the Judges of the Multilateral Investment Court: A Must for Building the Court's Credibility' (2019) Columbia FDI Perspectives.

225 See, for example, the IBA Guidelines on Conflicts of Interests in International Arbitration (23 October 2014) (Principle 1 enshrines that arbitrators must be independent and impartial); Menon (n 217), 239, notes that establishing accreditation procedures and creating arbitrator databases can enhance transparency in arbitrator choice.

226 See PCA Arbitration Rules 2012 (*Permanent Court of Arbitration*) <https://pca-cpa.org/en/services/arbitration-services/pca-arbitration-rules-2012/> accessed 24 April 2021.

227 See especially Art V of the Convention on the Recognition and Enforcement of Foreign Arbitral Awards (New York, 1958) or the New York Convention; ICSID Convention (n 8), art 52.

228 See the discussion in Chapter 2 pertaining to costs and access to justice.

Claimants against IOs are often not sophisticated litigants and factual inequalities are usually stark. For a claimant pursuing justice against an IO, having to incur, or being at risk of having to incur, potential costs amounting to hundreds of thousands of dollars will almost always undermine the right to a fair trial. Some arbitral tribunals determining claims by private actors against IOs have tried to address this issue by holding that each party to the arbitration should bear its own legal costs.[229] Where a claim concerns a typically commercial dispute between a sophisticated party and an IO, such an allocation of costs is probably fair. However, in other situations where the claimant is a demonstrably weaker party, for an arbitral process to be considered appropriate, the arbitral tribunal should provide costs protection to the claimant. Preliminary rulings by arbitral tribunals on how costs are to be allocated in an arbitration can impact its very progress. Such preliminary determinations ought to take into account the overall context of the claim. Sometimes the claim may be treated as a typical international commercial arbitration and the claimant may not require any special protection as such. This could be the case where there is no stark factual inequality between the parties. Even in this type of case though, indicating how costs are to be allocated at an early stage can be beneficial for the efficient resolution of the dispute in general. As a 2015 ICC report noted:

> The allocation of costs can be a useful tool to encourage efficient behaviour and discourage unreasonable behaviour ... the arbitral tribunal has discretion to award costs in such a manner as it considers appropriate. It is expressly stated that, in making its decisions on costs, the tribunal may take into consideration the extent to which each party has conducted the arbitration in an expeditious and cost-effective manner. The tribunal should consider informing the parties at the outset of the arbitration (e.g. at the case management conference) that it intends to take into account the manner in which each party has conducted the proceedings and to sanction any unreasonable behaviour by a party when deciding on costs.[230]

The stage of the proceedings where costs are addressed is one thing, but who is to bear them is another. Determining how costs are to be allocated requires a close analysis of the circumstances of the parties and the context in which a dispute arises. A tribunal should not fail to appreciate that an arbitration against an IO is after all an alternative to traditional court proceedings, which the claimant cannot access due to an IO's jurisdictional immunities. It is thus

229 *Polis Fondi Immobiliari Di Banche Popolare S.G.R.p.A (Italy) v IFAD*, PCA Case No. 2010-8, para 228.

230 ICC, 'Decisions on Costs in International Arbitration' (2015), section IV.

even more important to ensure that every claimant is being treated equally and fairly. In particular, where a claimant is the weaker party, it will be incumbent on any tribunal to ensure that the costs of seeking justice are not unreasonable, disproportionate or otherwise prohibitive. Prohibitive costs implications can lead to a claimant not commencing or even abandoning their case. There is some evidence of such occurrences. Where a consultant commenced arbitration against an IO in an employment dispute, high arbitrator fees meant that the claimant completely abandoned their claim before the arbitration could even commence in earnest.[231]

Where factual inequalities are manifest, a fair trial would require that, at the very least, each party bears their own legal costs. Otherwise, a claimant would potentially have such extensive exposure to the IO's legal costs that they may fear raising a claim at all.[232] What is more, the costs of the arbitration in general should be born by the IO for it is ultimately the IO's responsibility to provide for an appropriate DRM. If an IO refuses to incur such costs on its own accord, then the intervention of the arbitral tribunal may become necessary. Ultimately, without costs protections, several claimants will not be able to access justice equally and fairly for justice becomes simply unaffordable. In sum, the question of central importance considered is whether arbitration can in principle constitute an appropriate DRM to resolve claims against IOs. The answer to that question is to be given in the affirmative, but this conclusion must be qualified. Only if all aspects of independence, impartiality and fairness can be realised will an arbitral framework constitute an appropriate DRM to resolve claims against IOs.

3.3.3 *Assessing How IOs Use Arbitration: A Deficient Regime*

Arbitrations against IOs have tended to be ad hoc. Awards are difficult to source.[233] And when one takes into account the very limited number of arbitrations that IOs seem to be involved in, it is unwise to categorically make conclusions about the IO experience when using arbitration as

231 See the discussion of this particular arbitration in L Bergolla, 'More Rights for More People?: The Struggle of Independent Contractors to Arbitrate Employment Claims against International Organisations' (2020) 9 Indian Journal of Arbitration Law 1, 78–96, 95.

232 However, for indigent claimants, it may be the case that to ensure a fair trial, a respondent IO may be required to provide legal aid to ensure access to justice.

233 Not only are there very limited arbitrations between private claimants and IOs, but there are also few reported arbitral decisions concerning IOs and states: see *European Molecular Biology Laboratory v Germany*, Arbitration Award of 29 June 1990, 105 ILR (1997) 1050; *Tax Regime Governing Pensions Paid to Retired UNESCO Officials Residing in France* (France–UNESCO), Arbitration Award of 14 January 2003, XXV UNRIAA 231–6.

a DRM. But on the limited empirical evidence available, it may be said that international arbitration does not come close to providing a fair trial to the victims of IO conduct. From the very inception of the arbitration until the enforcement stage, the arbitral process is riddled with barriers to access to justice. It can be queried whether IOs engage with the arbitral process in good faith,[234] with (a) the process proving largely ineffective to resolve claims fairly and justly; (b) arbitration clauses being susceptible to misuse, creating uncertainty for litigants; and (c) the process being opaque.

3.3.3.1 International Arbitration and IOs: An Ineffective DRM

Experience has shown that international arbitration has not been effective in resolving claims against IOs fairly and justly. For example, in one case, the respondent IO, UNESCO, refused to appoint an arbitrator despite entering into an arbitration agreement with the claimant. Such an attitude demonstrates a manifest lack of good faith in upholding the sanctity of the arbitration clause. The French courts came to the rescue of the plaintiff by exercising jurisdiction over the IO, holding that the arbitration agreement amounted to a waiver of UNESCO's jurisdictional immunities.[235] Had French courts not taken jurisdiction, a denial of justice would have been the result. If national courts are unwilling to act, the outcome can be drastically different.

In another case that ultimately went to the European Court, a candidate was denied a job at the EPO based on his disability.[236] The aggrieved party approached the EPO's internal review mechanism to challenge his discriminatory treatment; however, the EPO dismissed his claims for lack of standing.[237] The EPO suggested to the complainant that he may approach the ILOAT even though it was clear that the complainant did not possess standing before that tribunal.[238] The complainant then approached German courts arguing that his right to access to a court had been breached for he could neither access

[234] The principle of good faith includes acting honestly, fairly and reasonably. It also prohibits the abuse of rights: 'International Law Association Berlin Conference (2004) Accountability of International Organizations' (2004) 1 International Organizations Law Review 221 236.

[235] *UNESCO v Boulois* (19 June 1998, Court of Appeal) Revue de l'arbitrage 343 (Paris, France).

[236] *Klausecker v Germany* (n 221), paras 4–8. The organisation stated that at some unknown time in the future, the applicant may not be able to perform his job due to his disability, and that purportedly justifies refusing the candidate the relevant job for which he was found to be otherwise suitable.

[237] Ibid, para 10.

[238] Ibid, para 11.

justice within the EPO nor at the ILOAT.[239] German courts refused to lift the EPO's immunities.[240]

The complainant then filed a claim before the ILOAT. Unsurprisingly, the tribunal determined that the complainant did not possess standing before it. However, it took a dim view of EPO's conduct, urging it to submit the dispute to arbitration given the legal vacuum that the complainant faced.[241] Following the ILOAT's decision, after two years of litigation, the EPO offered the complainant the possibility to arbitrate.[242] The claimant did not agree to arbitrate the dispute according to the terms offered by EPO, claiming that the process was unfair.[243] The arbitration never eventuated.

The applicant subsequently approached the European Court, arguing that his right to a fair trial enshrined in Article 6 of the European Convention had been contravened. Disregarding the significant delays that had already occurred – more than three years had passed since the claimant first approached the EPO's internal justice system before the offer of arbitration was made – the European Court dismissed the applicant's claims holding that the belated offer of arbitration constituted an appropriate or reasonable alternative DRM.[244] Over a period of ten years, the claimant approached four dispute resolution forums. These were the IO's internal justice system, the ILOAT, German courts and the European Court. On each occasion, his claim was rejected. It is somewhat surprising that the belated offer to arbitrate was considered as an appropriate or reasonable alternative DRM given the undue delays that the claimant faced before the offer of arbitration was actually made. Leaving to one side the arguable outcome of that case, the attitude demonstrated by IOs to implement arbitration as a DRM does not instil confidence that such procedures can effectively realise access to justice.

3.3.3.2 A Questionable Approach to Arbitration Clauses

Arbitration clauses entered into by IOs are susceptible to misuse and create uncertainties for claimants. Two specific points may be made. The first concerns the potential misuse of arbitration clauses as a device to oust another DRM's jurisdiction. The second involves the inclusion of contractual provisions that seek to protect IO immunities even where an arbitration clause is

239 Ibid, para 12.
240 Ibid, paras 14–16.
241 Ibid, paras 19–20.
242 Ibid, paras 21–2.
243 Ibid, para 25.
244 Ibid, para 76.

agreed upon, thereby creating uncertainty as to the enforceability of any award.

On the first issue, IOs may choose to agree on an arbitration clause simply to oust the jurisdiction of a court or tribunal. As we saw earlier, the approach of IATs to refuse jurisdiction where an arbitral clause is present without inquiring into its effectiveness makes it possible to include arbitration clauses for iniquitous reasons. An IO may agree to an arbitration clause simply attempting to exclude the possibility for the claimant to seek justice before another tribunal, as opposed to making a genuine attempt to provide access to justice. It is worth pointing out that in the context of employment claims, on the basis of two arbitrations, the UN had determined that arbitration is not financially viable.[245] Yet, it continues to include an arbitration clause in its general conditions of contracts.[246] Given this paradoxical attitude, one may question the efficacy of even including an arbitration clause in a contract at all.

Second, where IOs enter into arbitration clauses, more often than not, they seek to also maintain immunity from enforcement in their contractual arrangements.[247] As a result, the potential of international arbitration to provide an effective remedy through an enforceable decision is considerably weakened. It is well-known that through the mechanisms of the New York Convention the global enforceability of arbitration awards has been achieved. This is one of the most important reasons why arbitration has been a preferred forum to resolve international disputes. While the enforcement regime of the New York Convention should in principle apply to any arbitral award rendered in an arbitration to which an IO is a party as well,[248] the enforceability of awards is nevertheless thrown into some doubt due to any contractual provision that may aim to preserve an IO's immunity from enforcement.[249] That

[245] Report of the Secretary-General (n 100), paras 168 and 170–2.

[246] See the General Conditions of Contracts for the Services of Consultants and Individual Contractors (19 December 2013) UN Doc ST/AI/2013/4, section 16, (annex I) Administrative Instruction, Consultants and individual contractors (UN General Conditions).

[247] This is the case regardless of the subject matter of the dispute. For the purported applicability of UN immunities even where arbitration is entered into, see ibid, section 17; for other cases, a standard clause used by the UN in all its contracts was noted in the 1995 Secretary-General report – Report of the Secretary-General (n 108), para 6: 'Nothing in or relating to this Contract shall be deemed a waiver of any of the privileges and immunities of the United Nations, including, but not limited to, immunity from any form of legal process.'

[248] The New York Convention (n 8) provides both for the international recognition and enforcement of agreements to arbitrate (Article 2) and for the international recognition and enforcement of arbitral awards (Article 3): 'It is the foundation stone of modern international arbitration': Caron, Schill, Cohen Smutny and Triantafilou (n 215), 1.

[249] See H Fox and P Webb, *The Law of State Immunity* (3rd edn, Oxford University Press 2015), 394–400; also see Chapter 5, Section 5.6.

being said, there are indications that where an IO enters into an arbitration agreement, any resulting award may be enforced against it.[250] Still, a private party can have little confidence that arbitration will be an effective way to resolve claims against IOs given the lengths to which they may be required to seek enforcement. A way to avoid this predicament is for IOs to include express provisions waiving their immunities where an arbitration clause is agreed on. This however does not seem to be a common practice.

3.3.3.3 Assessing the Appropriateness of Arbitration in Resolving Claims against IOs

Ultimately, until such times that IOs take a significantly different approach to international arbitration, both in terms of how arbitration clauses are incorporated into an IO's legal relationships and how IOs treat an arbitration once the process is underway, it is hard to imagine how an arbitral framework can deliver effective justice. If international arbitration is to ever provide a sustainable dispute resolution framework to resolve claims against IOs, significant reform is necessary.

Like the ICSID Convention which sets the parameters for how investment disputes between private persons and states should be resolved through ISA, there is no equivalent instrument created to resolve disputes against IOs. The ICA framework to resolve claims against IOs is not always appropriate given the significant factual inequality that will often exist between a private claimant and a respondent IO. This means that the high costs associated with pursuing an arbitral procedure would be a real barrier to access justice for most claimants. Moreover, it is important to address the opaqueness of international arbitration involving IOs. In the absence of transparency, the legitimacy of any arbitral regime set up to resolve claims against IOs is undermined. As a comprehensive arbitral infrastructure to resolve claims against IOs has not been created, arbitrations involving IOs are not conducted as per modern standards of transparency which require the publication of awards.[251] In the final analysis, until a specialised arbitration framework is developed to resolve

[250] Relying on French jurisprudence, where an IO refused to honour an arbitration award against it and in relation to a dispute about rental payments, a Lebanese court categorically held that an agreement to arbitrate waived any IO immunities from enforcement: Obeid Law Firm, 'Arbitration and Immunity from Execution: A Bold Court Decision' (*International Law Office*, 10 April 2014) <https://www.lexology.com/commentary/arbitration-adr/lebanon/obeid-law-firm/arbitration-and-immunity-from-execution-a-bold-court-decision > accessed 25 September 2021.

[251] This is a topic that has raised much controversy: see Menon (n 217), 232–4; Sweet and Grisel (n 213), 4–5; and Kidane (n 210), 286. Treaty action has also recently sought to enhance transparency in investment arbitration: see United Nations Convention on Transparency in

disputes involving IOs, it is highly unlikely that international arbitration conducted on an ad hoc basis can provide for an appropriate DRM. How precisely an IO may develop an appropriate and effective arbitration scheme is an issue on which this author has commented elsewhere.[252]

3.4 OTHER TYPES OF NON-JUDICIALISED DRMS: A COMPLEMENT BUT NOT A SUBSTITUTE TO FORMAL JUSTICE MECHANISMS

Courts and tribunals, as well as arbitral processes, constitute judicialised modes of dispute resolution for they involve, or should involve, independent and impartial decision-makers making binding decisions. For the right to a fair trial to be complied with, IOs must provide private claimants access to a judicialised mode of dispute resolution. While IOs have established IATs to resolve employment claims, and international arbitration has played a more limited role in general, IOs have also established non-judicialised DRMs attempting to provide justice in other contexts. In non-judicialised DRMs, the decision-maker lacks the power to make a final and binding decision. As a result, such mechanisms cannot constitute a substitute to a full-fledged court or arbitral framework. Even though non-judicialised DRMs will not comply with modern standards of a fair trial, it is important to pass brief comment on such mechanisms given their prevalence today.

Non-judicialised DRMs at IOs often consist of ombudsman mechanisms. An ombudsman refers to 'an independent official overseeing the public sector'.[253] Nowadays, there are some divergences in the kinds of ombudsman review mechanisms implemented around the world. But some common themes can be gleaned. A comparative analysis of the concept in domestic jurisdictions shows that:

> [t]he concept of the ombudsman encompasses independent investigators who hear complaints from individuals ... without charge against the actions of the public sector. They may also launch their own investigations when appropriate. Each has some form of responsibility to Parliament and all rely primarily (or exclusively) upon 'alternative' non-judicial methods to resolve disputes. In addition, they are not limited by the specific legal rules to declare a complaint upheld but instead look at more substantive reasons such as

Treaty-based Investor-State Arbitration (adopted 10 December 2014, entered into force 18 October 2017) A/RES/69/116 (New York).

252 Gulati and John (n 110).

253 WJ Hopkins, 'Ombudsman' in Max Planck Encyclopedia of Comparative Constitutional Law (August 2016), para 6.

> unfairness, poor behaviour or breach of rights. Although many have a specific human rights focus, all have responsibility to ensure 'good administration'.[254]

While ombudsman review mechanisms were largely confined to the domestic sphere, increasingly, they are playing a role in the international order too. A good example is the European Ombudsman established in 1995.[255] The European Ombudsman was precisely created in an 'attempt to assuage concern that individuals had no right of redress against European institutional decisions' at the time.[256] No doubt the European Ombudsman plays an important oversight role within the EU and can assist in resolving individual complaints against EU institutions informally and cost-effectively.[257] It is, however, not a substitute to the judicial infrastructure present at the EU as typified by the CJEU, to which individual access now exists.[258] Hofmann has observed:

> [O]mbuds-review is always subordinate to judicial review. ... The [Ombudsman] Implementing Provisions ... obligate the [European Ombudsman or] EO, once he or she has found maladministration, to cooperate, as far as possible, with the institution or body concerned to find a 'friendly solution' to eliminate the maladministration and to satisfy the complainant. Friendly solution proposals typically identify shortcomings in institutional behaviour, which are often remedied in accordance with solutions proposed by the institution itself and may take the form of a sincere apology or some type of compensatory action offered to the complainant by the institution. In principle, the idea is that the EO facilitates finding such a friendly solution. But the fact remains that the measures available to the EO have no legally binding effect vis-à-vis the institutions

254 Ibid, para 42.

255 See Treaty on the Functioning of the EU (2012) and (ex) Article 195 (TEC), art 228, states that 'A European Ombudsman, elected by the European Parliament, shall be empowered to receive complaints from any citizen of the Union or any natural or legal person residing or having its registered office in a Member State concerning instances of maladministration in the activities of the Union institutions, bodies, offices or agencies, with the exception of the Court of Justice of the European Union acting in its judicial role. He or she shall examine such complaints and report on them.' Also see generally, European Ombudsman, 'Treaty on the Functioning of the European Union' <www.ombudsman.europa.eu/en/legal-basis/treaties/en> accessed 18 April 2021.

256 Hopkins (n 253), para 22.

257 See generally, HCH Hofmann, *The Developing Role of the European Ombudsman* (Edward Elgar 2017), 1–27.

258 Now, if a decision by an EU institution has affected a private person directly and individually, they may approach the CJEU: see 'Court of Justice of the European Union (CJEU)' (2020) <https://europa.eu/european-union/about-eu/institutions-bodies/court-justice_en> accessed 24 April 2021.

and bodies concerned and do not generate subjectively enforceable rights in individuals.[259]

Because an Ombudsman does not render binding decisions and does not constitute a judicial DRM, it can only act as a complement to a formal justice system as opposed to replacing it. In addition to the European Ombudsman, more and more IOs have created ombudsman processes to enhance their dispute resolution legal infrastructure. Where such DRMs act as a complement to a formal system of justice, the dispute resolution machinery greatly benefits from its existence. The Office of the UN Ombudsman and Mediation Services plays a significant role in informally resolving employment-related disputes (see Section 3.2.1). This particular ombudsman process is an informal mode of dispute resolution. It does not substitute recourse to the UN's two-tiered formal justice system but only adds to it.[260] For informal dispute resolution processes to work effectively, the presence of a strong formal dispute resolution machinery is crucial. If recourse to judicialised mechanisms is not provided, informal dispute resolution becomes ineffective as it becomes easier for authorities to ignore their findings and conclusions.[261]

Indeed, instances of IOs ignoring or failing to implement decisions made by DRMs lacking the power to make binding decisions are much too common. In respect of claims concerning the UNMIK's responsibility and liability for the lead poisoning of individuals in Kosovo, adverse findings against the UNMIK by the UN's own Human Rights Advisory Panel remain unenforced.[262] The disregard of that Panel's findings has been made possible because it does not constitute a judicial body that is appropriately resourced to make binding decisions. As Chinkin has said, '[l]ike the UN Treaty Bodies on which it is modelled, the Panel is not a Court; it is at best quasi-judicial, and

259 Hofmann (n 257), 14–15.

260 See Office of the United Nations Ombudsman and Mediation Services, 'The Ombudsman Is Here to Help!' (2021) <www.un.org/en/ombudsman/> accessed 24 April 2021.

261 Hopkins (n 253), para 45.

262 As Human Rights Watch noted in 2017: 'Despite the human rights panel's recommendations, the UN announced in May 2017 that it would create only a voluntary trust fund for community assistance projects to help "more broadly the Roma, Ashkali and Egyptian communities" – staying short of a public apology or acceptance of responsibility': K Rall, 'UN: Compensate Kosovo Lead Poisoning Victims' (*Human Rights Watch*, 7 June 2017) <www.hrw.org/news/2017/09/07/un-compensate-kosovo-lead-poisoning-victims> accessed 6 June 2018; for the findings of the Human Rights Advisory Panel, see *NM and Others v UNMIK* (Human Rights Advisory Panel, 26 February 2016) Case no 26/08; it does not seem that any effective remedy has been provided until today: see 'UN Must Urgently Provide Redress for Minorities Placed in Toxic Kosovo Camps, Says UN Rights Expert' (13 March 2019) <www.ohchr.org/EN/NewsEvents/Pages/DisplayNews.aspx?NewsID=24319&LangID=E> accessed 18 April 2021.

can only recommend compensation or other measures'.[263] If its recommendations are ignored, there is little the Panel can do.

The Kosovo Human Rights Advisory Panel was an experiment constituting 'the first international mechanism established to receive and consider individual complaints of violations of international human rights committed by an UN administration with respect to its operations in the field'.[264] As far as meaningful access to justice for the victims of IO conduct is concerned, that experiment has mostly failed in delivering a timely and effective remedy. Similarly, claims against World Bank institutions and other multilateral development banks concerning serious breaches of individual rights due to negligent implementation of development projects funded by such organisations cannot be advanced before fair trial compliant justice mechanisms. IOs such as the IDB, the IFC, the MIGA, the AfDB, the ADB and the EBRD have created international accountability mechanisms for project-affected individuals.[265] The services of these accountability mechanisms 'can include compliance reviews, dispute resolution services, monitoring ... and advisory services'.[266] Such DRMs do not constitute, and were not intended to constitute, substitutes to judicial mechanisms. Bradlow notes:

> While the IAM will make an effort to establish that there is a bona fide dispute between the parties and that it can contribute to its resolution, it makes no effort to determine who is to blame for the dispute. The IAM's role is to help the parties resolve their differences in a way that is mutually acceptable to them rather than to actively guide the parties to a particular outcome. It will also seek to ensure that the process is fair to all parties to the dispute. It is important to stress that dispute resolution is a voluntary process. It cannot succeed if either party is unwilling to engage in the dispute resolution process or does not accept any of the outcomes proposed by the other side.[267]

263 C Christine Chinkin, 'The Kosovo Human Rights Advisory Panel', Remarks delivered at Chattam House (26 January 2012), 5.

264 Ibid.

265 DD Bradlow, External Review of the Inspection Panel's Toolkit, Prepared for the Committee on Development Effectiveness (2018), para 8. These accountability mechanisms include AfDB's Independent Review Mechanism (AfDB/IRM), which consists of a Roster of Experts and the Compliance Review and Mediation Unit (AfDB/CRMU); the ADB's Accountability Mechanism (ADB/AM), which consists of the Office of the Special Project Facilitator (ADB/OSPF) and the Compliance Review Panel (ADB/CRP); the EBRDs Project Complaints Mechanism (EBRD/PCM), which consists of a Roster of Experts and a Projects Complaints Officer (EBRD/PCO); the EIB's Complaints Mechanism (EIB/CM); the IFC and MIGA's Compliance Advisor Ombudsman (IFC- MIGA/CAO); the IDB's Independent Consultation and Investigation Unit (IDB/MICI).

266 Ibid.

267 Ibid, para 48.

Findings in favour of any project-affected people made by such DRMs can thus be ignored or otherwise not acted on. There is no better example of such behaviour than the IFC's attitude demonstrated in the *Jam* litigation that went all the way up to the US Supreme Court in 2019 (see further Chapter 4). In that case, the complainants, a group of Indian nationals, who lived and worked within the proximity of a particular coal-fired plant built as part of an IFC-funded loan, alleged that the main legacy of the project has been environmental and social harm, damage to health and the destruction of the claimants' way of life.[268]

To seek a remedy, the claimants complained to the IFC's CAO, the IFC's 'independent recourse and accountability mechanism'. The CAO found that the IFC had failed adequately to consider the environmental and social risks to which the claimants would be exposed as a result of the plant's development, and that the IFC then compounded that error by failing to perform an environmental and social impact assessment 'commensurate with project risk' and by failing to 'address [subsequent] compliance issues during [project] supervision'.[269] The CAO remained dissatisfied with the steps taken by the IFC to address the claimants' grievances, and until today, the project-affected individuals have not received an effective remedy. The point of note being that the CAO was incapable of providing a fair trial and effective remedy to the claimants due to its limited competence. In fact, as an external review commissioned by the IFC itself found:

> [M]ost CAO non-compliance findings do not lead to effective remedy. The only aggregate evidence available on the effectiveness of remedial actions to correct stated non-compliances and related harm are outcome statistics provided by CAO on results of its monitoring ... in the vast majority of cases, IFC responses to address project-level compliance findings are insufficient and/or ineffective ... only 13 percent of monitored projects demonstrated satisfactory actions by IFC, 37 percent of projects were partly unsatisfactory, and 50 percent of projects were unsatisfactory. As of FY2019, 50 percent of the projects for which the CAO compliance monitoring process was closed remained in substantial non-compliance status.[270]

268 See *Jam et al. v International Finance Corporation* (D.D.C. 2016) No 15-612 (*Jam* First Instance); also see for a discussion of the Jam litigation, R Gulati, 'The Immunities of International Organisations: The End of Impunity?' (Opinio Juris, 2019) <http://opiniojuris.org/2019/03/01/the-immunities-of-international-organisations-the-end-of-impunity/> accessed 24 April 2021.

269 *Jam* First Instance (n 268), 4.

270 'External Review of IFC/MIGA E&S Accountability, including CAO's Role and Effectiveness Report and Recommendations' (June 2020), para 311.

DRMs such as the CAO cannot constitute substitutes to formal judicial processes as they cannot render binding decisions. While some MDBs are taking steps to reform accountability mechanisms, none of these reforms create or contemplate establishing fair trial compliant judicialised bodies.[271] This does not mean that alternative DRMs such as Ombudsman mechanisms should not be created, and where they exist, improved. The incremental improvements made to the ombudsman delisting process operating at the UN Security Council allowing individuals placed on UN Sanctions Lists to approach a relatively independent office to seek review of decisions that freeze their assets, or restrict movement, should be of course welcomed.[272] However, courts and commentators alike have pointed out that significant deficits continue to exist.[273] Fundamentally, as opposed to a judicialised mode of dispute resolution that can provide a fair trial to individuals placed on a UN sanctions list, the limited 'Ombudsperson procedure remains a diplomatic and intergovernmental process where the final decision to delist or not rests with the Security Council'.[274] Even though the ombudsman process has seen improvements following the much discussed *Kadi* litigation in European Courts, it does not constitute the type of DRM through which an IO may fully discharge its access to justice obligation.

In the final analysis, each of the DRMs mentioned earlier, while constituting useful accountability mechanisms, cannot substitute a full-fledged judicial or arbitral mechanism capable of delivering a fair trial and an effective remedy. Alarmingly, the predicament faced by a vast number of other private persons impacted by IO conduct is even worse. There are numerous instances where private parties harmed by IO conduct do not have access to any DRM whatsoever. This harm can arise in various contexts. For example, there are potentially thousands of instances where vulnerable individuals, including children, have been subjected to grave sexual offences and abuse at the hands

271 See, D Desierto et al., 'The "New" World Bank Accountability Mechanism: Observations from the ND Reparations Design and Compliance Lab' (EJIL Talk, 2020) <www.ejiltalk.org/the-new-world-bank-accountability-mechanism/> accessed 26 April 2021.

272 See, Resolution 2368 (2017) (adopted by the Security Council at its 8007th meeting, on 20 July 2017) UN Doc S/RES/2368, Annex 2; for a comprehensive discussion on the UN Security Council Sanctions regime and issues of due process in terms of access to justice for individuals impacted by UNSC sanctions, see generally, D Hovell, *The Power of Process: The Value of Due Process in Security Council Sanctions Decision-Making* (Oxford University Press 2016).

273 For recent jurisprudence on the topic, see *Al-Dulimi and Montana Management Inc. v Switzerland* App no 5809/08 (ECtHR, 21 June 2016), para 52.

274 JE Alvarez, 'The UN Charter Over Time: The Contemporary Security Council' in JE Alvarez, *The Impact of International Organizations on International Law* (Brill Nijhoff 2016), 112–13.

of UN Peacekeepers.[275] The UN accepts its responsibility where such harm is caused. Freedman points out:

> The UN itself has long accepted that the international responsibility of the United Nations for the activities of United Nations forces is an attribute of its international legal personality and its capacity to bear international rights and obligations. In 2004, the UN's legal counsel noted that '[a]s a subsidiary organ of the United Nations, an act of a peacekeeping force is, in principle, imputable to the Organization, and if committed in violation of an international obligation entails the international responsibility of the Organization and its liability in compensation'.[276]

Despite the UN's acceptance of its responsibility for sexual abuse perpetrated by peacekeepers and lofty rhetoric and promises of 'zero tolerance', justice for those victims continues to be unattainable.[277] Most SOFAs entered into between the organisation and a host state anticipate that third-party claims are to be settled by a standing claims commission. Such commissions can be created at the request of one party.[278] No such commission has been established thus far.[279] In spite of the express obligation to provide 'appropriate modes' of dispute resolution, on too many occasions, IOs simply fail to provide them at all. This grave justice deficit has devastating consequences for the most vulnerable of claimants. The plight of the victims of the genocide in Srebrenica and cholera in Haiti, for which the UN has itself assumed a degree of responsibility, has been subjected to much attention. It is unconscionable that thousands of those victims have been completely denied justice.[280] To sum up, one can hardly disagree with the observation that the 'greatest obstacle preventing parties from challenging acts of [international organisations] is the lack of a legal forum where such disputes may be brought'.[281]

[275] See generally, JK Westendorf and L Searle, 'Sexual Exploitation and Abuse in Peace Operations: Trends, Policy Responses and Future Directions' (2017) 93 International Affairs 2, 365–87.

[276] R Freedman, 'Unaccountable: A New Approach to Peacekeepers and Sexual Abuse' (2018) 29 European Journal of International Law 3, 273.

[277] Ibid; for the various internal UN rules in place and relevant reports, see 'Standards of Conduct Peacekeeping' (*United Nations*) <https://peacekeeping.un.org/en/standards-of-conduct> accessed 22 July 2018.

[278] F Megret, 'Beyond UN Accountability for Human Rights Violations: Host State Inertia and the Neglected Potential of Sovereign Protection' (2019) 16 International Organizations Law Review 68–104, 79.

[279] See M Zwanenburg, *Accountability of Peace Support Operations* (Martinus Nijhoff 2005), 102.

[280] See Chapter 4 for further discussion.

[281] J Wouters and J Odermatt, 'Assessing the Legality of Decisions' in J Katz Cogan, I Hurd and I Johnstone (eds), *The Oxford Handbook of International Organisations* (Oxford University Press 2016), 1009.

3.5 CONCLUSION

The central aim of this chapter has been to assess the compliance of DRMs set up by IOs with the fair trial criteria developed. Three types of DRMs were assessed. First, I assessed permanent judicial mechanisms. The two leading international administrative regimes, that is, the UN tribunals and the ILOAT, were selected for assessment. The UN tribunals lack the necessary institutional, decisional and individual independence expected from a modern international court or tribunal. As a result, until improvements are made, the UN's two-tiered justice system, based solely on the independence shortfall, cannot be said to be delivering justice consistently with fair trial standards in general. Moreover, fairness and equality are increasingly being undermined due to OSLA's chronic underfunding and the undue delays in the administration of justice. Serious concerns about the effectiveness of the remedies that the UN tribunals can grant also prevail. Even more concerning is the significant discord that has recently been evident amongst the UNDT's judges, bringing the internal justice machinery at the UN into disrepute. As things stand, even though the UN's internal justice system has witnessed much reform, from a structural perspective, the UN tribunals do not generally constitute an appropriate DRM. Similarly, the ILOAT is not rendering justice consistently with modern standards of a fair trial. Several deficits concerning its institutional, decisional and individual independence are manifest. Moreover, assuming access to the ILOAT is provided in the first place, the complete lack of oral hearings and the excessive delays in the delivery of justice on their own are egregious fair trial contraventions. Unless significant changes to the ILOAT's constituent arrangements and practice are made,[282] it is unlikely that individuals having access to the ILOAT can receive justice that is fair trial compliant.

Second, the role international arbitration plays in resolving claims against IOs was considered. In principle, international arbitration can provide for an appropriate DRM. But based on the experience with arbitration so far, as of now, arbitration does not provide for a just and fair mode of dispute resolution. A vast number of claimants pursuing claims against IOs will find international arbitration simply unaffordable. Moreover, little thought has been given to implement arbitration as a sustainable and viable option. Unless a specialised arbitral regime is created that takes into account the particularities of disputes

[282] Only limited reforms to the ILOAT have been pursued. Amendments proposed by the ILO's Governing Body to the ILOAT's Statute seek to strengthen judicial independence to some extent at the ILOAT: ILO Document (n 177).

involving IOs, the chances of arbitration providing for an appropriate DRM are dim. Finally, the chapter made a brief comment on non-judicialised DRMs. While such DRMs play an important complementing role, they cannot replace an independent and impartial forum empowered to render a binding judgment. Recommendations made by non-judicialised DRMs can be readily ignored. Until non-judicialised DRMs are transformed into judicialised mechanisms, or new judicialised DRMs are created, the access to justice deficit will continue to prevail for countless individuals harmed by IO conduct. Alarmingly, in too many situations, private parties cannot access any DRM at the international level at all. More and more victims approach national courts to seek justice as a last resort. Unfortunately, for the victims, as is demonstrated in Chapter 4, an approach to national courts has generally not yielded access to justice either.

4

The Nature of Institutional Immunities

A Conundrum Yet to Be Resolved

4.1 INTRODUCTION

Victims of IO conduct frequently approach national courts to seek justice against IOs because justice at the institutional level is absent. However, national courts have not yet proven to be adept at resolving such claims. In this chapter, I focus on how the application of an IO's jurisdictional immunities prevents victims from accessing justice at the national level too. There is no other aspect of international institutional law that has attracted more academic discussion than the topic of IO immunities.[1] The aim of this chapter is not to rehash that entire discussion. Instead, I focus on the almost insuperable challenges a claimant faces when suing an IO in a national court. The discussion first focuses on the basis of an IO's domestic legal personality which allows suits to be brought against them at all (Section 4.2). The chapter then identifies how IO immunities are applied today. Whereas IO immunities were intended to be functional (Section 4.3), they have become by and large de facto absolute (Section 4.4). This means that a claimant's case is procedurally

[1] For detailed studies, see A Reinisch (ed), *The Privileges and Immunities of International Organizations in Domestic Courts* (Oxford University Press 2013); for an early authoritative text, see CW Jenks, *International Immunities* (Stevens 1962); and for an analysis of comparative jurisprudence on IO immunities in national courts, see A Reinisch, *Challenging Acts of International Organizations before National Courts* (Oxford University Press 2010); also see N Blokker and N Schrijver, *Immunity of International Organizations* (Brill 2015); C Ryngaert, 'The Immunity of International Organizations before Domestic Courts: Recent Trends' (2010) 7 International Organizations Law Review 121, 125. For a functionalist perspective, see PHF Bekker, *The Legal Position of Intergovernmental Organizations: A Functional Necessity Analysis of Their Legal Status and Immunities* (Brill 1994); for a global constitutional perspective on IO immunities, see A Peters, E Lagrange, S Oeter and C Tomuschat, *Immunities in the Age of Global Constitutionalism* (Brill 2015), 285–354; for a recent discussion, see P Schmitt, *Access to Justice and International Organizations: The Case of Individual Victims of Human Rights Violations* (Edward Elgar 2017), 224–327.

defeated and the merits do not get a chance to be ventilated. There are some indications that the tide might be shifting in favour of the claimant. Still, the way in which claims against IOs are addressed at the national level is unsustainable and requires a fundamental reframing (Section 4.5).

4.2 THE IO IS THE PROPER RESPONDENT

A threshold question is why sue the IO at all? Why should victims of IO conduct not bring claims against member states that fund IOs and control the purse strings, thereby exercising significant practical control on an IO's behaviour. The answer is simple. While member states can be held responsible for their own breaches,[2] IOs are responsible for their own conduct internationally as well as nationally. In addition to having personality on the international plane, IOs are domestic legal persons too. As IOs are domestic legal persons in their own right, any claim at the national level alleging a breach committed by an IO must be brought against the organisation itself. Indeed, without domestic personality, an IO will not be able to function effectively.

Klabbers has identified that IOs need domestic legal personality as a matter of 'functional necessity'.[3] Schermers and Blokker note, without domestic personality, IOs would simply be unable to do their day-to-day work.[4] Unlike states, IOs do not possess their own territory, and as a matter of geographical compulsion are located on the territory of nation-states, coming into contact with national law. IOs need to carry out routine activities, such as entering into contracts, leasing premises, acquiring and disposing of movable and immovable property, buying and selling goods, registering patents and initiating legal action to protect their rights before national courts.[5] The ability to exercise all of the aforementioned capacities requires the existence of status at the domestic level.

[2] See, for example, *Mothers of Srebrenica Association et al. v The Netherlands* (19 July 2019, Supreme Court of the Netherlands) ECLI:NL:HR:2019:1223. For an analysis of this decision, see C Ryngaert and O Spijkers, 'The End of the Road: State Liability for Acts of UN Peacekeeping Contingents after the Dutch Supreme Court's Judgment in Mothers of Srebrenica' (2019) 66 Netherlands International Law Review 1.

[3] J Klabbers, *An Introduction to International Institutional Law* (2nd edn, Cambridge University Press 2012), 44.

[4] HG Schermers and NM Blokker, *International Institutional Law* (5th edn, Brill 2011), section 1599.

[5] Whether or not an organisation has the competence to exercise those capacities will depend on its internal law. Domestic personality means that the state may not limit the exercise of an organisation's legal capacities as a domestic legal person: Ibid.

Thus, most constituent instruments of IOs expressly require member states to grant them legal personality within their domestic legal orders.[6]

For example, Article 104 of the UN Charter[7] provides for domestic personality using a functional necessity rationale, stating that the UN 'shall enjoy in the territory of each of its Members such legal capacity as may be necessary for the exercise of its functions and the fulfilment of its purposes'. Other constituent instruments may use different formulations. The Articles of Agreement of the International Monetary Fund and the Articles of Agreement of the International Bank for Reconstruction and Development both state that the Fund and the Bank, respectively, 'shall possess full juridical personality, and, in particular, the capacity: (i) to contract; (ii) to acquire and dispose of immovable and movable property; (iii) to institute legal proceedings'.[8] Domestic personality thus entitles an IO to possess the capacities typically exercised by legal persons in the domestic order of the granting state. The granting state must not restrict the enjoyment of those capacities.[9] However, it is one thing for an international arrangement to require that IOs be granted domestic personality, and yet another for an international requirement to translate into legal reality at the national level. The basis on which personality is acquired under domestic law can differ somewhat. These distinctions are rooted in how international law is received in a particular national legal order. Because an IO's work will tend to be conducted across national jurisdictions, IOs will not only come into contact with the national laws of host and member states, but also non-member states. It is therefore important to set out the basis on which domestic personality will exist in both those contexts.

4.2.1 *How IOs Acquire Domestic Personality*

It may be assumed that member states must grant domestic personality to an IO under the constituent instruments of the concerned

6 Where express grant is absent, domestic personality will be implied: CF Amerasinghe, *Principles of the Institutional Law of International Organizations* (2nd edn, Cambridge University Press 2005), 69; as Reinisch points out, even where no explicit treaty provision on domestic personality exists, member states tend to recognise the organisation's domestic personality: A Reinisch, *International Organisations before National Courts* (Cambridge University Press 2000), 50.

7 Charter of the United Nations (opened for signature 26 June 1945, entered into force 24 October 1945) 1 UNTS XVI (UN Charter).

8 IMF, 'Articles of Agreement of the International Monetary Fund' (April 2016) < www.imf.org/External/Pubs/FT/AA/index.htm> accessed 22 April 2021 (IMF Articles of Agreement), Article IX, section 2; IBRD, 'IBRD Articles of Agreement' (16 February 1989) 2 UNTS 134 <http://siteresources.worldbank.org/EXTABOUTUS/Resources/ibrd-articlesofagreement.pdf> accessed 22 April 2021 (IBRD Articles of Agreement), Article VII, section 2.

9 Amerasinghe (n 6), 77; Schermers and Blokker (n 4), sections 1598–9.

organisation.[10] These include host state agreements (where applicable) as well as an IO's founding treaty arrangements. Several states, such as Germany, the Netherlands, Belgium, Austria and the United States, which allow for the direct effect of treaties within their national legal orders, recognise the legal personality of the organisation in their legal systems without the need for incorporation via domestic law.[11] Other states, such as the United Kingdom, and others belonging to the Commonwealth of Nations, require domestic incorporation before an organisation will be recognised as a legal person.[12] Vis-à-vis member states, the existence and recognition of domestic legal status is generally not a contentious issue.

But are non-member states required to treat an IO as a domestic legal person?[13] The answer is in the affirmative, although different bases can be used to ground personality. Some see domestic legal personality directly deriving from an organisation's international status. This view is taken by monist states, including Belgium, Switzerland and Italy, meaning that the international personhood of an entity directly translates into domestic personhood.[14] Although this view may be instinctively attractive for its simplicity, it is logically unsound. International and domestic personalities are established in distinct ways, can produce differing consequences and should not be conflated. Another way in which an IO's domestic personality may be upheld in a non-member state is by applying private international law rules. This approach recognises the personality of an IO as a matter of international comity. It was set out in the case of the *Arab Monetary Fund v Hashim and Others* (*AMF case*).[15] The AMF brought proceedings in the English courts to recover its funds allegedly misappropriated by its former Director-General. Arguing that the AMF could not bring the proceedings in England as they were not incorporated as a legal person in that jurisdiction, the defendants argued that the AMF's claims should be struck out.[16] Based on

10 Even where no explicit treaty provision on domestic personality exists, member states tend to recognise the organisation's domestic personality: Reinisch (n 6), 50.

11 Ibid, 48; Amerasinghe (n 6), 70; see, for example, *Balfour, Guthrie & Co. Ltd et al. v United States et al.* (1950) USDC ND Cal, 17 ILR 323, 324; a US court affirmed the UN's capacity to institute legal proceedings in the US based on Article 104 of the UN Charter (n 7), which – as a treaty ratified by the US – formed part of the supreme law of the land.

12 Amerasinghe (n 6), 70; Reinisch (n 6), 49.

13 Such issues may also arise for member states that may fail to incorporate through national law the domestic personality of IOs when such incorporation may be required.

14 Schermers and Blokker (n 4), section 1595, citing *Branno v Ministry of War* (1955, Giurisprudenza Italiana) 22 ILR 756, 904, where the Italian Court of Cassation derived the legal personality of the North Atlantic Treaty Organisation (NATO) under Italian law from its international personality.

15 *Arab Monetary Fund v Hashim and Others (No 3)* [1991] 1 AC 114, [1991] 6 Arab LQ 90.

16 See ibid.

international comity and the rules of private international law,[17] the House of Lords upheld the legal personality of the AMF. Lord Templeman stated that comity required that the status of an IO incorporated by a foreign state should be recognised by the Courts of the United Kingdom,[18] explaining:

> [W]hen sovereign states enter into an agreement by treaty to confer legal personality on an international organisation, the treaty does not create a corporate body. But when the AMF agreement was registered in the UAE by means of Federal Decree No. 35 that registration conferred on the international organisation legal personality and thus created a corporate body which the English courts can and should recognise.[19]

Based on the private international law norm that the status of an entity is to be determined by the law of the place where it is incorporated, the domestic personality of the AMF in the UAE meant that English courts were willing to recognise the organisation as a domestic legal person in the United Kingdom as well. Reinisch confirms that the 'technique of accepting the legal personality of foreign juridical persons is inspired by the provisions of the 1956 Hague Convention on the Recognition of the Legal Personality of Foreign Companies, Associations and Foundations and the 1968 Brussels Convention on the Mutual Recognition of Corporations and Juridical Persons, as well as by domestic private international law/conflict of laws principles'.[20] This approach is as much logical as it is sensible. As per the approach taken by Jenks on the issue, IOs do and can act and behave like international body corporates.[21] That is the very reason they are granted domestic personality. On questions of status, there is no functional distinction between IOs and other forms of corporate entities. Reliance on the well-recognised international rules to coordinate across national legal orders is thus perfectly warranted.

17 International comity is a doctrine that seeks to sustain mutual respect between distinct national legal orders and help mediate legal relationships between states – it is a somewhat contentious concept. For jurisprudence on the concept, see *Belhaj and Another v Straw and Others* [2017] UKSC 3, [2017] 2 WLR 456 and *Rahmatullah (No 1) v Ministry of Defence and Another* [2017] UKSC 1, [2017] UKSC 3, para 225 (per Lord Sumption); for an analysis of the concept generally, see WS Dodge, 'International Comity in American Law' (2015) 115 Columbia Law Review 2071.

18 See *Arab Monetary Fund v Hashim and Others (No 3)* (n 15) (per Lord Templeman), 92.

19 Ibid, 7. In a related proceeding, taking a similar position, a US court said: 'the AMF is a juridical person (a corporation, a persona ficta, an entity capable of legal battle) under United Arab Emirates law. . . . Once this has been decided, capacity follows under American law as a matter of "customary law"': *Re Hashim* 188 B.R. 633 (D. Arizona 1995), 649.

20 Reinisch (n 6), 50.

21 CW Jenks, *The Proper Law of International Organisations* (Stevens 1962), 4, where Jenks treats IOs as a form of an international body corporate.

In the end, to resolve which particular approach should be used to base an IO's domestic status is currently unnecessary. Different states adopt different approaches based on the underlying relationship between international and national law relevant to their particular jurisdictions. Regardless of the specific approach taken, one way or another, an organisation's domestic personality has been upheld and recognised in member and non-member states alike. As to what flows from such personality is the issue of real significance.

4.2.2 *Consequences of Domestic Personality*

As has been said, one of the main reasons why IOs are granted domestic personality is to ensure that they can exercise the capacity to approach national courts to protect their legal rights. The corollary being that it is the IO that should be the proper respondent when its conduct is impugned at the national level too. As Schermers and Blokker state, 'international organizations are responsible for violations of their obligations and liable for their debts. This is as simple as it is logical: otherwise, the separate legal personality of the organization, distinct from its member states, would be little more than a fiction'.[22]

The much discussed House of Lords decision in *Maclaine Watson & Co. Ltd v International Tin Council*[23] neatly demonstrates the principle of member non-responsibility.[24] The ITC was an IO mandated to regulate the worldwide production and marketing of tin.[25] Following the 1980s collapse in the price of tin, the ITC became insolvent, accepted that it could not pay its debts[26] and its creditors sought to recover debts owed by the organisation from its member states, arguing that the ITC was tantamount to an unincorporated association and its members were liable for its debts.[27] For the ITC's creditors to succeed in their primary argument, they needed to establish that the ITC was not a distinct legal person and that damages from the ITC's member states could be recovered, even though it was the organisation that had entered into the relevant agreements with the creditors.

22 Schermers and Blokker (n 4), section 1583.

23 *Maclaine Watson & Co. Ltd v International Tin Council* [1989] 81 ILR 670, [1990] 29 ILM 670 (*ITC case*).

24 For the significance of this decision, see P Palchetti, 'Maclaine Watson & Co. Ltd v International Tin Council 26 October 1989, United Kingdom House of Lords, 81 ILR 670' in C Ryngaert, IF Dekker, RA Wessel and J Wouters (eds), *Judicial Decisions on the Law of International Organizations* (Oxford University Press 2016), 37.

25 *ITC case* (n 23), 672.

26 Ibid, 673 and 691.

27 Ibid.

To determine the ITC's domestic personality, of relevance was the ITC (Immunity and Privileges) Order 1972 made pursuant to the International Organisations Act 1968 of the United Kingdom, which provided that 'the Council shall have the legal capacities of a body corporate'.[28] While that order granted the ITC legal capacities, it did not expressly state that the organisation possessed legal personality. Relying on the absence of an express grant, the creditors argued that

> the Order of 1972 did not incorporate the I.T.C. but only conferred on the I.T.C. the legal capacities of a body corporate. Therefore, it is said, under the laws of the United Kingdom the I.T.C. has no separate existence as a legal entity apart from its members; the contracts concluded in the name of the I.T.C. were contracts by the member states.[29]

Rejecting this submission, the House of Lords concluded that the ITC was a legal person in UK law as the capacities bestowed on it presumed the existence of domestic personality. Lord Templeman stated that the ITC 'cannot exercise the capacities of a body corporate and at the same time be treated as if it were an unincorporated association'.[30] Of course, had the ITC's legal personality been precisely incorporated into domestic law, certainly it would have been enhanced, and the need for legal acrobatics avoided. Still, once the domestic personality of the ITC was upheld by the House of Lords, the primary argument put forward by the creditors was bound to fail.

Interestingly, assuming that the organisation was found to be a legal person, the ITC's creditors put forward two further arguments in support of their claims. It was argued that the ITC was not a typical corporation, and was analogous to a Scottish partnership, or a *societe en nom collectif* in the law of France, where the members may be held secondarily liable for the acts of the entity.[31] Avoiding the same error at the national level as was made by the ICJ at the international one, emphasising that legal personality did not exist in 'gradations',[32] the House of Lords rejected the argument that the member states could be held secondarily liable.[33] Yet another argument put forward by the ITC's creditors was that there existed a rule of international law that the member states were responsible for the debts of the organisation absent any treaty provision to the contrary. This argument was readily rejected. The court

[28] Ibid, 673; International Organisations Act 1968 c48.
[29] *ITC case* (n 23).
[30] Ibid, 674 (per Lord Templeman); also see Lord Oliver, ibid, 696–9.
[31] Ibid, 675–6 (per Lord Templeman).
[32] Ibid, 702 (per Lord Oliver).
[33] Ibid, 701 (per Lord Oliver).

found that no such rule of international law existed and that the ITC's constituent instruments did not provide for any such provision in any event.[34]

Ultimately, the consequences of legal personality of an IO at the national level are no different from the situation at the international level, although those consequences are manifest in the domestic legal order. At its core, an IO is responsible for its own actions at the domestic level too. The fact that as domestic legal persons IOs are liable for their own conduct is now well-established. This position has not only been taken by English courts, but by other courts too.[35] Consequently, a complainant who seeks to impugn the actions of an IO must raise a claim directly against it. Whether or not a complainant can actually do so is a matter substantially impacted by the procedural bar of jurisdictional immunities.[36]

4.3 THE FUNCTIONAL IMMUNITIES OF IOS

The possession of legal personality means that, in principle, IOs can be sued in national courts when it is the IO's conduct that is impugned. But an explicit structural bias in the regulatory regimes governing IOs has so far prevented private persons from successfully doing so in most situations. How IO immunities are presently applied constitutes the key reason for why so many genuine claimants continue to be denied justice. Before considering how national courts apply IO immunities, it is first important to understand why IOs are granted functional immunities in the first place. Section 4.3.1 briefly outlines what 'functionalism' in the international institutional context means in general, and Section 4.3.2 outlines how it informs, or should inform, the nature and scope of an IO's immunities.

4.3.1 *The Concept of 'Functionalism' Generally*

To understand what functional immunities were intended to mean, it is necessary to briefly comprehend the concept of 'functionalism'. States

34 Ibid, 707 (per Lord Oliver).

35 Also see the decision of the Swiss Federal Tribunal in *Westland Helicopters* (Arbitral Award) (1988) 28 ILM 687, 691, where it was said that the organisation possessed 'total juridical independence' and its members could not be secondarily liable (discussed in Amerasinghe (n 6), 276).

36 C Wickremasinghe, 'Immunity from Jurisdiction, International Organizations – Relationship between International and Domestic Law' in Rudiger Wolfrum (ed), *Max Planck Encyclopedia of Public International Law* (Oxford University Press 2013), para 4: 'The immunities of international organizations required under relevant treaty provisions usually operate as a simple bar to the jurisdiction of the national courts, which may in other respects be competent to hear the complaint.'

establish IOs to secure international cooperation to resolve and pursue various purposes for which such cooperation is considered necessary. The underpinning of IOs is the theory of 'functionalism'. Klabbers traced the origin and development of the concept as follows:

> [T]he term 'function' [can be traced] back to the late 19th century writings of Georg Jellinek who ... attributed a [in German] Verwaltungszweck to some kinds of cooperation between states. This was picked up by several others, most notably by Paul Reinsch. For Reinsch, the outstanding characteristic of organizations was that they were assigned a function and, employing a fairly narrow definition of organization, he could confidently view those functions as emanations of the common good. Hence, function and moral appeal went hand in hand, culminating in Nagendra Singh's classic 1950s claim that international organizations were considered to contribute to the 'salvation of mankind'.[37]

Similarly, the ILC Special Rapporteur on the topic of relations between states and international organisations observed:

> The 'functional' sector of international organization is that part of the mass of organized international activities which relates directly to economic, social, technical, and humanitarian matters. ... Functional activities are immediately and explicitly concerned with such values as prosperity, welfare, social justice and the 'good life'.[38]

'Functionalism' may thus reflect both legal and moral aspects. While a discussion about its non-legal dimension remains outside the scope of this work, in its legal sense, 'functionalism' can be concretised. When understanding 'functionalism', it is useful to start with the assumption that every IO is created on a 'functional' basis. Without a functional imperative, there would be no need for IOs. Given the breadth of functions that IOs now perform, from the highly general to the very specific, it comes as no surprise that the concept of functionalism can cause confusion and controversy. As was noted by Leonardo Diaz Gonzalez, the ILC Special Rapporteur on the relationship between states and IOs, it is not possible to enumerate a neat list of the functions engaged in by IOs generally, as different organisations are set up

37 J Klabbers, 'The Transformation of International Organizations Law' (EJIL Talk, 2015) <www.ejiltalk.org/the-transformation-of-international-organizations-law/> accessed 3 June 2018; see also for a detailed discussion, J Klabbers, 'The EJIL Foreword: The Transformation of International Organizations Law' (2015) 26 European Journal of International Law 1 (EJIL Foreword), 9–83.

38 ILC, 'Second Report of the Special Rapporteur, Mr Abdullah El-Erian' (1978) (30th session) 277, [104].

to achieve differing goals and possess correspondingly distinct functions.[39] However, the challenge of neatly prescribing the functions of all organisations does not mean that the concept of 'functionalism' has no work to do. What is often of concern in practice is not a determination of the aggregate functions of all the IOs combined, which is an impossible undertaking, but a focus on the overall competence or specific functions of individual organisations in a given context. It is moreover important not to conflate between the purposes, functions and powers of an IO. These are different concepts, although they can interrelate.

In particular, all international institutions are set up to achieve certain purposes or goals and have been assigned functions or tasks to help achieve them.[40] To perform their assigned functions, IOs need powers,[41] being 'the ability to alter legal rights and duties of other persons'.[42] These powers may be express or implied and must be exercised according to legal limits placed by the IO's constituent instruments or any other international or domestic legal obligations imposed or assumed by an IO.[43] When assessing an IO's functions, it is therefore important to distinguish between an IO's purposes and goals, which can be very broad, its functions, which will be more precise, and the limits placed on an IO in terms of how it may carry out its functions. Of course, different organisations are ascribed different functions. For instance, the UN's functions are broadly defined, allowing it to perform tasks aiming to maintain international peace and security, and on occasions even to perform state-like functions.[44] Other organisations may be set up to undertake highly technical or specialised work, as is the case with the mandate of several Specialized Agencies of the UN.[45] Further,

39 LD Gonzalez, 'Fourth Report on Relations between States and International Organizations' (1989) UN Doc A/CN.4/424 and Corr.1, para 35.

40 G Verdirame, *The UN and Human Rights: Who Guards the Guardians?* (Cambridge University Press 2011), 68–9.

41 For a description of the nature of an IO's powers, see generally Klabbers (n 3), 53–71.

42 Verdirame (n 40), 68–89.

43 *Legality of the Use by a State of Nuclear Weapons in Armed Conflict* (Advisory Opinion) [1996] ICJ Rep 66 (*Nuclear Weapons Advisory Opinion*), 78, para 25.

44 See UN Charter (n 7), arts 1 (1–4), 7, 10, 11, 13, 14, 16, 17, 22, 24, 41 and 42.

45 Examples of UN Specialized Agencies include the International Labour Organization, Food and Agriculture Organization, World Health Organization, World Bank, International Monetary Fund, International Telecommunication Union, World Meteorological Organization, World Intellectual Property Organization, International Atomic Energy Agency and the International Criminal Court. For a list of the Specialized Agencies of the UN, see 'UN Specialized Agencies' (2021) <https://ask.un.org/faq/140935> accessed 25 September 2021. Note, Multilateral Financial Institution and MDBs can also constitute a Specialized Agency. While the UN Specialized Agencies have been brought into relationship with the UN through special arrangements, hundreds of other organisations performing work in discrete subject matters exist today.

MDBs,[46] such as the World Bank institutions,[47] pursue broad development goals. However, their functions are much more precise. A good example is provided by Article 2 of the ADB's founding agreement,[48] which provides:

> To fulfil its *purpose*, the Bank shall have the following *functions*: (i) to promote investment in the region of public and private capital for development purposes; (ii) to utilize the resources at its disposal for financing development of the developing member countries in the region; (iii) to meet requests from members in the region to assist them in the coordination of their development policies and plans with a view to achieving better utilization of their resources, making their economies more complementary, and promoting the orderly expansion of their foreign trade; (iv) to provide technical assistance for the preparation, financing and execution of development projects; (v) to co-operate, in such manner as the Bank may deem appropriate, within the terms of this Agreement, with the United Nations, its organs and subsidiary bodies ... and with public international organizations and other international institutions, as well as national entities whether public or private, which are concerned with the investment of development funds in the region, and to interest such institutions and entities in new opportunities for investment and assistance; and (vi) to undertake such other activities and provide such other services as may advance its *purpose* (emphasis added).[49]

It is apparent that the 'functions' of an IO equate to the specific activities it is mandated to perform. The tasks an IO performs would naturally differ from organisation to organisation. Ultimately, to determine an organisation's functions, a close analysis of an IO's constituent instruments and its practice must be undertaken. Such an undertaking may be arduous, but must be embarked

46 Some prominent regional MDBs include the European Investment Bank, European Bank for Reconstruction and Development, Inter-American Development Bank, Central American Bank for Economic Integration, African Development Bank, Asian Development Bank, Asian Infrastructure Investment Bank, the New Development Bank and the Islamic Development Bank.

47 The World Bank Group consists of five distinct institutions, with each performing a specified mandate. In addition to the ones already stated, the World Bank Group also includes the International Centre for the Settlement of Investment Disputes, commonly known as ICSID: see World Bank Group, 'Who We Are' (*World Bank*) (2021) <www.worldbank.org/en/who-we-are> accessed 3 June 2018.

48 ADB, 'Agreement Establishing the Asian Development Bank' (opened for signature 4 December 1965, entered into force 22 August 1966).

49 For an overview of how the MDBs operate in the market place, see R Faure, A Prizzon and A Rogerson, 'Multilateral Development Banks: A Short Guide' (*Overseas Development Institute*, 12 December 2015) <www.odi.org/publications/10160-multilateral-development-banks-short-guide> accessed 3 June 2018.

upon when questions about the functional scope of an IO's activity arise. Determining such functionality is especially relevant for questions of IO immunities for such immunities are also grounded in the concept of 'functionalism'.[50]

4.3.2 *The Functional Nature of IO Immunities*

If an IO is to be effective, it must have autonomy to pursue its functions, that is, without undue interference from its member states, including its host state where the organisation may be headquartered or otherwise located. It is to exclude the possibility of such interference that IOs are granted jurisdictional immunities before national courts. Jenks has said that 'international immunities are the legal device through which international action escapes national control',[51] and goes on to say that:

> [I]nternational institutions should have a status which protects them against control or interference by any one government in the performance of functions for the effective discharge of which they are responsible to democratically constituted international bodies in which all the nations concerned are represented.[52]

To protect an IO's 'functional independence', IOs are thus granted jurisdictional immunities through their constituent arrangements before national courts. According to this functional standard, IOs should only possess immunities to the extent that is strictly necessary for the performance of their functions.[53] Clarifying an IO's immunity underpinned by this very 'functionalist' rationale,[54] the Supreme Court of Canada stated:

> International organizations derive their existence from treaties, and the same holds true for their rights to immunities. … [An international] organization must operate on the territory of a foreign state and through individuals who have nationality and is therefore vulnerable to interference, since it possesses neither territory nor a population of its own. This reality makes immunity essential to the efficient and independent functioning of international

[50] R Higgins, P Webb, D Akande, S Sivakumaran and J Sloan, *Oppenheim's International Law – United Nations*, vol 1 (Oxford University Press 2017), section 16.20.

[51] Jenks (n 1), 13.

[52] Ibid, citing, 'General Note: Third Item on the Agenda: The Status, Immunities and Other Facilities to be Accorded to the International Labour Organization' (10 December 1945) Vol XXVII No 2 ILO Official Bulletin, 197–223.

[53] Gonzalez (n 39), paras 26–7.

[54] M Wood, 'Do International Organizations Enjoy Immunity Under Customary International Law?' (2013) 10 International Organizations Law Review 2, 287–316, 315.

organizations. It also shapes the immunities and privileges that are granted to international organizations.[55]

As such, IO immunities are clearly shaped through the lens of 'functionalism'. But some commentators have said that what is actually within the scope of 'functionality' is left without specific guidance, rendering the concept vague. Reinisch notes that '[m]ost constituent instruments of international organizations generally provide for "functional immunities". Hardly any such instrument explains what is meant by the term immunity "necessary for the functioning" of an international organization'.[56] This criticism is misplaced. The logical way to determine the scope of functional immunities is to refer to the functions of an organisation provided for in its constituent instruments, or look at an IO's subsequent practice, and then to assess whether the performance of those function(s) will be impeded if a national court adjudicates the claim at hand.

Klabbers however casts doubt on whether the functions of an IO can even be gleaned. He observes that '[o]ften enough, constituent documents may refer to a variety of goals or purposes (some of them perhaps conflicting), and there might be a discrepancy between the formal task of an institution and the reasons for its creation'. That view disregards the conceptual distinction between the goals or purposes of an organisation and its assigned functions. As has been alluded to, those are different things. What should be relevant to determine the functional scope of an organisation's activity is not its broad goals, aims or purposes but an analysis of the particular functions it has been tasked with. Identifying the nature of the assigned functions of an organisation, such as the UN's peacekeeping activity, the lending activity of MDBs, or specialised functions undertaken by other organisations, by no means should constitute an indeterminate exercise.[57] Ultimately, when determining the functions of an IO, the search is for what IOs do, or are meant to do, as opposed to the often nebulous exercise of why they do something. Once the correct question is asked, and the nature of an IO's function(s) established, determining the scope of functional immunities becomes possible.

Questions on the scope of IO immunities then ought to turn on an assessment of whether adjudication of a claim at the national level undermines the

55 *Amaratunga v North Atlantic Fisheries Organisation* [2013] SCC 66, [2013] 3 SCR 866, para 29.

56 A Reinisch, 'Immunity of Property, Funds, and Assets' in A Reinisch and P Bachmayer (eds), *The Conventions on the Privileges and Immunities of the United Nations and Its Specialized Agencies: A Commentary* (Oxford University Press 2016), 73.

57 N Blokker, 'International Organizations: The Untouchables?' (2013) 10 International Organizations Law Review 2, 259–75, 275; as Blokker argues: 'ultimately, "functional necessity" is not only the raison d'etre of the immunity rules of international organizations, but also the rationale of an adequate accountability regime'.

IO's ability to perform its assigned activity/activities. If the answer is in the negative, then immunities have no work to do. However, what should be a relatively straightforward inquiry has proven to constitute one of the most difficult questions in international law today. As the remainder of this chapter demonstrates, significant confusion persists on how IO immunities should be applied. This has resulted in diverging approaches to IO immunities across jurisdictions, with most courts leaning towards upholding immunities even if the result is a grave denial of justice.

4.4 THE FLAWED APPLICATION OF IO IMMUNITIES AT THE NATIONAL LEVEL

IO immunities were meant to be functional, but they have become mostly de facto absolute. As a result, claimants are denied justice at multiple levels. The failure to provide justice to private persons impacted by IO action at the international level has already been stated in Chapter 3. The refusal of national courts to adjudicate claims against IOs thus blocks the final opportunity for claimants to access justice. This section discusses why national courts generally refuse to adjudicate claims against IOs based on their alleged immunities. There are three crucial matters warranting attention. First, the word 'functional' has played little role in delimiting IO immunities, thereby wrongly expanding their application considerably (Section 4.4.1). Some jurisdictions even conflate IO immunities with state immunity further complicating the regulatory regime governing IOs (Section 4.4.2). Moreover, access to justice concerns do not in any meaningful way impact the existence or non-existence of IO immunities (Section 4.4.3). Ultimately, due to a fundamental misunderstanding of what IO immunities are meant to achieve, they are mostly applied incorrectly.

4.4.1 *'Functionalism' Ignored*

For most part, the concept of 'functionalism' has not been material to determine the scope of IO immunities. This assertion is backed up by reference to the UN's highly influential immunities regime provided for in the UN Charter and the General Convention. This regime has formed a blueprint for numerous other immunities regimes, including that of the UN Specialized Agencies.[58] Moreover, there have been perhaps more suits brought against the

[58] The Convention on the Privileges and Immunities of the United Nations (opened for signature 13 February 1946, entered into force 17 September 1946) 1 UNTS 15 (General Convention) establishes the immunity regime for the United Nations, being a treaty that is

UN than any other IO, making an understanding of the UN's immunity regime even more crucial for practical reasons.

The first thing to note is the manifest inconsistency between the UN Charter and the specific treaty providing for the UN's immunities regime, that is, the General Convention. Enshrining immunities on a 'functional' basis, Article 105(1) of the UN Charter states that '[t]he Organization shall enjoy in the territory of each of its Members such privileges and immunities as are necessary for the fulfilment of its purposes'.[59] For reasons explained in Section 4.3.2, the use of the word 'purposes' is unfortunate. The provision is best understood as providing for immunities to allow the UN to independently perform its functions or activities. In other words, to ensure the UN's functional independence. But the General Convention provides in its Article II, section 2, that '[t]he United Nations, its property and assets wherever located and by whomsoever held, shall enjoy immunity from every form of legal process except insofar as in any particular case it has expressly waived its immunity'.[60] There is an obvious tension between those two provisions. While the UN Charter provision grants immunities to the UN in 'functional' terms, on its face, Article 2, section 2, of the General Convention grants

widely ratified: as of the date of writing, the General Convention has 162 State Parties, see United Nations Treaty Collection, 'UN, United Nations, UN Treaties, Treaties' (*United Nations*) <https://treaties.un.org/Pages/ViewDetails.aspx?src=TREATY&mtdsg_no=III-1&chapter=3&clang=_en> accessed 25 September 2021. The General Convention not only contains provisions that form the core international law rules governing the immunity regime for several other organisations, but also forms the basis for other significant treaty regimes, chief amongst them being the Specialized Agencies Convention (opened for signature 21 November 1947, entered into force 2 December 1948) 33 UNTS 261 (Specialized Agencies Convention). The Specialized Agencies Convention has 129 State Parties, and applies to several IOs such as the ILO, Food and Agriculture Organization, UNESCO, International Monetary Fund and so on: see United Nations Treaty Collection, 'UN, United Nations, UN Treaties, Treaties' (*United Nations*) <https://treaties.un.org/Pages/ViewDetails.aspx?src=TREATY&mtdsg_no=III-2&chapter=3&clang=_en> accessed 25 September 2021; for an early work on this convention, see K Ahluwalia, *The Legal Status, Privileges and Immunities of the Specialized Agencies of the United Nations and Certain Other International Organizations* (Martinus Nijhoff 1964); also see R Gulati, 'Convention on the Privileges and Immunities of the United Nations, 13th February 1946' (1 UNTS 15, 1 UST 1418) OXIO 73 <http://opil.ouplaw.com/view/10.1093/law-oxio/e28.013.1/law-oxio-e28?rskey=4tJ2gf&result=9&prd=OXIO> accessed 28 May 2018; A Reinisch, 'Introduction' in A Reinisch and P Bachmayer (eds), *The Conventions on the Privileges and Immunities of the United Nations and Its Specialized Agencies: A Commentary* (Oxford University Press 2016), 3, paras 5–6, where it is noted that '[m]ost other international organizations have followed the UN's … immunities paradigm. The constituent agreements of the World Health Organization, the Organization of American States, the World Trade Organization are just some examples'.

59 UN Charter (n 7), art 105(1).

60 General Convention (n 58), art II, section 2.

immunity in absolute terms.[61] This inconsistency creates legal loopholes, allowing courts to ignore the concept of 'functionalism' when determining the scope of the organisation's immunities.[62]

A prominent example is provided by the challenge to the UN's immunities before Dutch courts arising out of the genocide in Srebrenica which constituted a manifest failure of the international community to collectively prevent one of the gravest violations of human rights since World War II.[63] Through its Resolution 743 of 21 February 1992, the UN Security Council established the UNPROFOR 'to create the conditions of peace and security required for the negotiation of an overall settlement of the Yugoslav crisis'.[64] On 16 April 1993, the Security Council adopted Resolution 819, mandating that 'all parties and others concerned treat Srebrenica and its surroundings as a safe area which should be free from any armed attack or any other hostile act'.[65] On 10 July 1995, the VRS, a Serb force,[66] attacked the Srebrenica 'safe area' with overwhelming force. Despite requests made by the Dutch commander on the ground asking 'his United Nations superiors for air support' no such support was forthcoming.[67] Consequently,

> Bosniac men who had fallen into the hands of the VRS were separated from the women and children and killed. Some succeeded in reaching safety. . . . It is now generally accepted as fact that upwards of 7,000, perhaps as many as 8,000 Bosniac men and boys died in this operation at the hands of the VRS and of Serb paramilitary forces.[68]

Several women whose family members were killed as well as a Dutch association representing 6,000 survivors filed a civil action before the District Court of The Hague, seeking compensation from the UN.[69] The civil claims against the

61 No substantial discussion was undertaken regarding Article II Section 2 of the General Convention (n 58) at the time of its negotiation. Instead, the prefatory discussions focused mostly on the immunities of officials. For a background, see AJ Miller, 'The Privileges and Immunities of the United Nations' (2009) 6 International Organizations Law Review 7, 17–18.

62 Reinisch (n 56), 73.

63 See, *Stichting Mothers of Srebrenica v The Netherlands* App no 65542/12 (ECtHR, 11 June 2013) (*Srebrenica case*), para 20.

64 Ibid, para 7.

65 Ibid, para 15.

66 Also known as the Army of the Republika Srpska or the Bosnian Serb Army. The VRS was mostly comprised of Serbs: Ibid, para 8.

67 Ibid, para 17.

68 Ibid, para 19. Also see *Application of the Convention on the Prevention and Punishment of the Crime of Genocide (Bosnia and Herzegovina v Serbia and Montenegro)* [2007] ICJ Rep <www.icj-cij.org/files/case-related/91/091-20070226-JUD-01-00-EN.pdf> accessed 20 June 2018, 43.

69 Claims against the UN were defeated at every level: see ibid; *Mothers of Srebrenica Association et al. v The Netherlands and the United Nations* (10 July 2008, The Hague District Court) ECLI:NL:RBSGR:2008:BD6795; *Mothers of Srebrenica Association et al. v The Netherlands*

UN were based on the contention that the UN, which bore overall responsibility for UNPROFOR, 'despite earlier promises and despite their awareness of the imminence of an attack by the VRS, had failed to act appropriately and effectively to defend the Srebrenica "safe area" and, after the enclave had fallen to the VRS, to protect the non combatants present'.[70] Particularly, the civil aspects of the claims were founded in contract and tort, with the plaintiffs alleging that:

> [F]irstly, that the United Nations . . . had entered into an agreement with the inhabitants of the Srebrenica enclave (including the applicants) to protect them inside the Srebrenica 'safe area' in exchange for the disarmament of the ARBH forces present, which agreement the United Nations and the State of the Netherlands had failed to honour; and secondly, that the Netherlands State, with the connivance of the United Nations, had committed a tort (onrechtmatige daad) against them by sending insufficiently armed, poorly trained and ill-prepared troops to Bosnia and Herzegovina and failing to provide them with the necessary air support.[71]

A significant obstacle before the claimants concerned the UN's immunities before national courts. But they argued the UN's functional immunity could not override the international law prohibition of genocide. The claimants specifically argued that the immunity of the United Nations was always intended to be functional only. This was 'reflected by the wording of Article 105 of the United Nations Charter. Although Article II, section 2 of the Convention on the Privileges and Immunities of the United Nations suggested otherwise, it was subordinate to the Charter'.[72] Without conducting a detailed analysis on the scope of the UN's immunities, deferring uncritically to the broad wording of Article 2, section 2, of the General Convention, Dutch courts found that the organisation's immunities were far-reaching. Effectively, the organisation was found to be absolutely immune.[73]

The claimants then approached the European Court, which also did not engage with the concept of 'functionalism' in any meaningful way, accept to say that:

> [S]ince operations established by United Nations Security Council resolutions under Chapter VII of the United Nations Charter are fundamental to

and the United Nations (30 March 2010, The Hague Court of Appeal) ECLI:NL:GHSGR:2010:BL8979; *Mothers of Srebrenica Association et al. v The Netherlands and the United Nations* (13 April 2012, Supreme Court of the Netherlands) ECLI:NL:HR:2012:BW1999.

70 *Srebrenica case* (n 63), para 54.

71 Ibid, para 55.

72 Ibid, para 90.

73 Ibid, para 79.

> the mission of the United Nations to secure international peace and security, the Convention cannot be interpreted in a manner which would subject the acts and omissions of the Security Council to domestic jurisdiction without the accord of the United Nations. To bring such operations within the scope of domestic jurisdiction would be to allow individual States, through their courts, to interfere with the fulfilment of the key mission of the United Nations in this field, including with the effective conduct of its operations.[74]

The claimants were not impugning any decision of the Security Council taken under Chapter VII of the UN Charter at all. The correct question should have been whether a national court adjudicating a claim against the UN for alleged breaches of privately held rights, where there was a good basis for the claim,[75] impeded the UN from carrying out its peacekeeping function. Where the Dutch Supreme Court has been willing to assign liability to the Dutch state in precisely the same set of circumstances,[76] it is hardly convincing that holding an IO liable for its own errors, which it in fact accepts,[77] and where no other forum is established to deliver justice to the victims, impedes the UN's ability to engage in its peacekeeping activities. After all, Dutch peacekeepers still participate in peacekeeping missions.[78] There is no reason to think that if a competent national court, after providing a fair hearing, upholds the UN's responsibility in a particular case, the organisation cannot also continue to perform its peacekeeping activities. Putting to one side the correctness of the conclusions reached in the *Srebrenica case*, the point of note is that functionalism has had little impact on delimiting immunities. Either it is completely dismissed as irrelevant due to the absolute wording of Article 2, section 2, of the General Convention or it has been interpreted so broadly that functional immunities tend to amount to de facto absolute immunities.[79] This is the case concerning claims not only against the UN but also other IOs.[80]

74 Ibid, paras 152–4.

75 For an analysis of relevant case law, see Ryngaert and Spijkers (n 2).

76 See, *Mothers of Srebrenica Association et al. v The Netherlands* (n 2).

77 *Srebrenica case* (n 63), para 127, citing Report of the Secretary-General pursuant to General Assembly Resolution 53/35 (15 November 1999) UN Doc A/54/549, para 501.

78 See, 'Netherlands' (*United Nations Peacekeeping*) <https://peacekeeping.un.org/en/netherlands> accessed 26 April 2021.

79 See, for example, *Manderlier v Belgium State and UN* (15 September 1969, Brussels Appeal Court) 69 ILR 139; (1969) UN Juridical Yearbook, 236–7; where certain individuals brought claims against the UN in Belgian courts for damage to persons and property caused by the UN Force in the Congo, an appeals court upheld the UN's immunities in absolute terms; those claims were ultimately settled through a lump sum payment. See also *Brzak v United Nations* (2d Cir 2010) 597 F.3d 107 (*Brzak v UN*).

80 See, for example, *Brzak v UN* (n 79); *Mendaro v World Bank* (D.C. Cir. 1983) 717 F.2d 610, 618; *Atkinson v IADB* (D.C. Cir. 1998) 156 F.3d 1335; *Broadbent v OAS* (D.C. Cir. 1980) 628

Nonetheless, it should be acknowledged that in a limited set of circumstances, primarily in employment cases, 'functionalism' has performed its intended role to delimit the scope of immunities. In the following situations, national courts have been willing to pierce institutional immunities on the basis that taking jurisdiction would not interfere with the organisation's functional independence. First, where the claim is lodged by individuals in an organisation's employment who are only incidentally connected to the work of that organisation, certain national courts have indicated that immunities cannot be upheld in such cases.[81] Second, some courts have shown a willingness to take jurisdiction over claims that only concern pecuniary disputes.[82] For example, in an employment dispute regarding a senior staff member of the North Atlantic Fisheries Organisation headquartered in Canada, while immunities were maintained with respect to the substance of the claim of unlawful dismissal, the Supreme Court of Canada nevertheless decided that the aspects of the plaintiff's claims relating to his pecuniary entitlements under the organisation's rules could be subjected to the jurisdiction of Canadian courts for such matters did not impinge on the defendant organisation's functional independence.[83] The third category of cases where 'functionalism' has played some role is that where criminal conduct is alleged. In a case concerning the scope of the immunities possessed by certain officials of the ADB accused of criminally defaming the complainant, disregarding the former's immunities, the Supreme Court of the Philippines held that '[S] landering a person could not possibly be covered by the immunity agreement

F.2d 27; 63 ILR 337; *Trempe v Assoc du personnel de l'OACI* (2003) CanLII 44121 (QCCS); *Trempe v Canada* (2005) CanLII 1031 (QCCA); *World Bank Group v Wallace* [2016] SCC 15; *Amaratunga v North Atlantic Fisheries Organisation* (n 55); *Mukoro v European Bank for Reconstruction and Development and Another* [1994] ICR 897; 107 ILR 604; *Entico Corp. Ltd v United Nations Educational, Scientific and Cultural Organization and Another* [2008] 1 CLC 524 (United Kingdom); Cour de Cassation (30 September 2003, Chambre sociale) JCP 2004 II 10102 (note Jean-Gregoire Mahinga); *G Bassi Reddy v International Crops Research Inst.* (14 February 2003, Appeal) 2399 of 1986; *PS Ochani v World Health Organization* (4 December 2001, India) 95 (2002) DLT 680; *Shigeko Ui v United Nations University* (1980, Japan) 23 Japanese Annual of International Law 196–200; and several others.

81 *Intergovernmental Committee for European Migration (ICEM) v Di Banella Schirone* (1978) RDI 575, 77 ILR 572 (8 April 1975, Court of Cassation, No 1266). See also *Spaans v Iran-US Claims Tribunal* (20 December 1985, Supreme Court) NJ 1986/438; ILDC 1759 (NL 1985), para 3.1, cited in R van Alebeek and A Nollkaemper, 'The Netherlands' in A Reinisch (ed), *The Privileges and Immunities of International Organizations in Domestic Courts* (Oxford University Press 2013), 180–206; see also, for example, *Claimant v European Patent Office* (23 October 2009, Hoge Raad) No 08/00118.

82 *Chirico v ICAMAS* (1991, Corte di Cassazione) Judgment No 4968/1989 (rivista di diritto inter nazionale privat e processuale).

83 *Amaratunga v North Atlantic Fisheries Organisation* (n 55), para 66–7.

because our laws do not allow the commission of a crime.'[84] While this case concerned criminal conduct and involved the immunities of an official, what is of significance is that it gave effect to the functional basis of immunities, although the immunity was of an organisation's official as opposed to the institution itself.

Overall, even though the concept of functionalism has occasionally played a role in determining the scope of IO immunities, it has not played any significant role in delimiting them in general. The UN's immunities regime, forming a blueprint for so many IOs, is inherently inconsistent and creates legal loopholes through which victims continue to slip. What were always envisaged to be limited 'functional' immunities are in practice de facto absolute. The result being that even in cases of grave violations where the organisation accepts its significant failures, domestic courts readily uphold the UN's immunities without meaningfully inquiring whether simply adjudicating a particular claim would actually obstruct the performance of its functions.

4.4.2 *Conflation of IO Immunity with State Immunity*

Further complicating the immunities regime governing IOs is the conflation between IO and state immunity in some jurisdictions. Of course, IOs are geographically dispersed and are subject to a varied network of regulatory schemes, the content of which can only be determined by reference to the specific treaty regimes, underpinned by how that regime may be domestically implemented.[85] Nevertheless, jurisprudence from certain jurisdictions tends to have more impact than from others due to the sheer number of IOs that are based there. For instance, the United States hosts the UN Headquarters, but also several MDBs, including the World Bank Group. It is recent US jurisprudence involving certain MDBs that has significantly changed the landscape of IO immunities, at least for institutions whose immunities regimes equate IO immunities with state immunity. This is the case in the United States for those IOs whose immunities are translated into domestic law through the US International Organisations Immunities Act 1945 (IOIA).[86]

84 See *Liang v People* (28 January 2000) GR No 125865; but see, *Greenpeace Nederland and Procurator General (Intervening) v EURATOM* (13 November 2007, Supreme Court of the Netherlands) Decision No LJN: BA9173, RvdW (2007) No 992, where the organisation's scope of functional immunities extended even where certain alleged environmental criminal offences were committed, decision discussed in C Brolmann, *International Law in Domestic Courts* (Oxford University Press 2007), 838, H.1.

85 Jenks (n 1), 3–4; Higgins, Webb, Akande, Sivakumaran and Sloan (n 50), section 16.1.

86 US International Organisations Immunities Act 1945 (IOIA).

The IOIA grants IOs subject to the legislative regime immunities similar to those enjoyed by states. In 1945, states enjoyed virtually absolute immunity,[87] and thus, IOs enjoyed similar immunities too.[88] However, the evolution of the restrictive doctrine of state immunity now widely accepted,[89] and culminating in the introduction of the US Foreign Sovereign Immunities Act 1976 (FSIA), provided that states were only entitled to immunities in respect of their sovereign or governmental functions, not their commercial acts.[90] The question then became whether this restricted view of state immunity was transposable to the immunities of IOs subject to the IOIA regime. For decades, US courts had decided that the IOIA froze IO immunities as they existed in 1945. So, even though state immunity had been significantly narrowed, IO immunities continued to be absolute.[91] This changed in 2019. In *Jam et al. v International Finance Corporation*, No. 17–1011, 27 February 2019 ('*Jam*'), the US Supreme Court decided that IOs subject to the IOIA enjoyed immunities consistently with the FSIA standard; that is, IOs possess immunities only concerning their non-commercial activity. However, equating IO immunity with state immunity creates more problems than it actually solves. As *Jam* highlights, the concept of functionalism does not neatly fit into the commercial versus non-commercial distinction relevant to determine state immunity.

87 For the leading work on the evolution of the law of state immunities, and a discussion of the move from the absolute to the restrictive doctrine, see H Fox and P Webb, *The Law of State Immunity* (3rd edn, Oxford University Press 2015), 2572.

88 See AI Young, 'Deconstructing International Organization Immunity' (2012) 44 Georgetown Journal of International Law 311–59, 311.

89 Over the decades, State immunity has increasingly been restricted, where states cannot benefit from immunities in respect of their 'private' (also referred to as 'commercial' or '*jure gestionis*' acts), but enjoy immunities only in respect of their 'public' (also referred to as 'sovereign' or 'governmental' or '*jure imperii*' acts: see Fox and Webb (n 87); R Van Alebeek, *Immunity of States and Their Officials in International Criminal Law and International Human Rights Law* (Oxford University Press 2008), 11–102; such developments are manifested in Art 10(1) United Nations Convention on Jurisdictional Immunities of States and Their Property (opened for signature 2 December 2004, not yet in force) UNGA Res 59/38.

90 Foreign Sovereign Immunities Act (2006) 28 USC (FSIA), para 1602.

91 *Jam et al. v International Finance Corporation* (D.D.C. 2016) No 15-612 (*Jam* First Instance); *Jam et al. v International Finance Corporation* (D.C. Cir. 2017) No 16-7051 (*Jam* Appeal); also see the brief analysis of US jurisprudence in R Gulati, 'The Conundrum of International Organisations Immunities: Jam et al. v International Finance Corporation (Part 1 of 2)' (*Opinio Juris*, 10 July 2017) <http://opiniojuris.org/2017/07/10/the-conundrum-of-international-organisations-immunities-jam-et-al-v-international-finance-corporation-part-1-of-2/> accessed 29 June 2018; R Gulati, 'The Conundrum of International Organisations Immunities: Jam et al. v International Finance Corporation (Part 2 of 2)' (*Opinio Juris*, 11 July 2017) <http://opiniojuris.org/2017/07/11/the-conundrum-of-international-organisations-immunities-jam-et-al-v-international-finance-corporation-part-2-of-2/> accessed 29 June 2018.

4.4.2.1 Squaring the Circle between Functionalism and the Commercial versus Non-Commercial Distinction: An Unresolvable Puzzle

The facts giving rise to *Jam* have already been stated in Chapter 3. It is presently important to set out the main reason behind the US Supreme Court's reasoning in that case. At stake were the immunities of the IFC, an MDB that is a World Bank institution. MDBs tend to perform inherently commercial functions, lending funds to states or private enterprise to build infrastructure projects, such as roads, bridges, dams, hospitals and power plants.[92] The IFC specifically provides loans to private corporations to build infrastructure in developing countries.[93] When errors are made in implementing such large-scale projects, private parties can suffer significant harm. If the victims are unable to access justice at the institutional level, as was the case in *Jam* (recall the Indian victims first approached the CAO), recourse to national courts becomes the only other viable option left. But again, IO immunities present a significant hurdle.

Like most MDBs, the IFC's immunities regime is provided for in international and domestic legal provisions together. As far as international agreement is concerned, Article VI, section 1, of the IFC's Articles of Agreement[94] grants immunities in classical functional terms stating that '[t]o enable the Corporation to fulfil the functions with which it is entrusted, the status, immunities and privileges set forth in this Article shall be accorded to the Corporation in the territories of each member'. As MDBs in general, and the IFC in particular, perform typically commercial activity, it was considered necessary that not only immunity be provided in 'functional' terms, but there also be included an express provision to allow private claimants to sue the organisation.[95] The idea is that if private persons cannot sue the IO to recover

[92] For a recent study on the work of the various MDBs, especially of the newly created Asian Infrastructure Investment Bank, see generally, P Quayle and X Gao (eds), *Good Governance and Modern International Financial Institutions: AIIB Yearbook of International Law 2018* (2018) (Brill Nijhoff, Leiden, 2018).

[93] See IFC, 'IFC – International Financial Corporation' (2021) <www.ifc.org/wps/wcm/connect/corp_ext_content/ifc_external_corporate_site/home> accessed 28 June 2018.

[94] World Bank Group, International Finance Corporation Articles of Agreement (opened for signature 25 May 1955, amended as of 27 June 2012) (Washington DC) (IFC Articles of Agreement).

[95] See, for example, the IBRD Articles of Agreement (n 8), which state in Article VII Section 3 that 'actions may be brought against the Bank only in a court of competent jurisdiction in the territories of a member in which the Bank has an office, has appointed an agent for the purpose of accepting service or notice of process, or has issued or guaranteed securities. No actions shall, however, be brought by members or persons acting for or deriving claims from members. The property and assets of the Bank shall, wheresoever located and by whomsoever

for any alleged harm caused by the latter, the former would be unlikely to do business with MDBs, and this would impede the functioning of the concerned institution.[96] Therefore, MDB immunity regimes tend to contain broad express waiver provisions. In the case of the IFC, Article VI, section 3, of its constituent agreement states:

> Actions may be brought against the Corporation only in a court of competent jurisdiction in the territories of a member in which the Corporation has an office, has appointed an agent for the purpose of accepting service of process, or has issued or guaranteed securities.

In principle, the IFC (and other similarly situated IOs) should thus be amenable to suit at a national court at the place where the IO is located or does its core business with relative ease given the broad language of express waiver provisions of the aforementioned kind. As will be soon clarified, this is not the case. For the moment, it is necessary to complete the picture as to the regulatory regime governing the IFC. In addition to the applicable treaty rules, the IFC is also subject to the provisions of the IOIA. According to its pre-*Jam* understanding, the IFC would have been absolutely immune from suit,[97] subject to the application of the express waiver provision. This entrenched position however recently changed when the US Supreme Court delivered its judgment in *Jam*. It said:

> In granting international organizations the 'same immunity' from suit 'as is enjoyed by foreign governments', the Act seems to continuously link the immunity of international organizations to that of foreign governments, so as to ensure ongoing parity between the two. The statute could otherwise have simply stated that international organizations 'shall enjoy absolute immunity from suit', or specified some other fixed level of immunity. Other provisions of the IOIA, such as the one making the property and assets of international organizations 'immune from search', use such noncomparative language to define immunities in a static way. . . . Or the statute could have specified that it was incorporating the law of foreign sovereign immunity as it existed on

held, be immune from all forms of seizure, attachment or execution before the delivery of final judgment against the Bank'.

96 *Mendaro v World Bank* (n 80); also see *Osseiran v Int'l Fin Corp* (D.C. Cir. 2009) 552 F.3d 836, where the court in holding that the IFC's immunities were waived, said: 'Both Mendaro and Atkinson stated that immunity from suits based on commercial transactions with the outside world can hinder an organization's ability to do business in the market place.'

97 *Atkinson v IADB* (n 80). But see the historically inconsistent approaches on the issue within the US legal system: Young (n 88), 329, citing amongst others, *OSS Nokalva v European Space Agency* (3d Cir 2010) 617 F.3d 756, 758 (where the 3rd circuit determined that IOs under the IOIA regime only possessed restrictive immunities).

a particular date. ... Because the IOIA does neither of those things, we think the 'same as' formulation is best understood to make international organization immunity and foreign sovereign immunity continuously equivalent.[98]

As a result, if a claimant can establish that the particular conduct impugned is of a commercial nature, then immunities will have no work to do. The concern that imposing the state immunity standard on IOs would result in a floodgate of litigation given the vast amount of commercial work MDBs perform was readily dismissed. A majority of the US Supreme Court stated:

The IFC's concerns are inflated. To begin, the privileges and immunities accorded by the IOIA are only default rules. If the work of a given international organization would be impaired by restrictive immunity, the organization's charter can always specify a different level of immunity. The charters of many international organizations do just that. ... Notably, the IFC's own charter does not state that the IFC is absolutely immune from suit.[99]

In reality, absent treaty reform, significant uncertainty on the scope of IO immunities now exists. One must not underestimate the difficulty in distinguishing between commercial and non-commercial activity. Just like the distinction has given significant challenges in the state immunity context (whether the focus should be on the nature of the transaction or its purpose),[100] the difficulty is even greater in the IO context. Dissenting from the majority in *Jam*, Breyer J said:

As a result of the majority's interpretation, many of the international organizations to which the United States belongs will discover that they are now exposed to civil lawsuits based on their (U.S.-law-defined) commercial activity. And because 'commercial activity' may well have a broad definition, today's holding will at the very least create uncertainty for organizations involved in finance, such as the World Bank, the Inter-American Development Bank, and the Multilateral Investment Guarantee Agency. The core functions of these organizations are at least arguably 'commercial' in nature; the organizations exist to promote international development by investing in foreign companies and projects across the world. ... The World Bank, for example, encourages development either by guaranteeing private

98 *Jam et al. v International Finance Corporation* (27 February 2019) No 17-1011 (*Jam* SC), 9–10. For an analysis, see R Gulati, 'The Immunities of International Organisations: The End of Impunity?' (*Opinio Juris*, 1 March 2019) <http://opiniojuris.org/2019/03/01/the-immunities-of-international-organisations-the-end-of-impunity/> accessed 27 April 2021.

99 Ibid, 17–18.

100 See generally, Fox and Webb (n 87), 17-8.

loans or by providing financing from its own funds if private capital is not available.[101]

Although there is a growing consensus that the characterisation of an IO's activity as commercial or non-commercial depends on the nature of the transaction and not its purpose,[102] in the hard cases, uncertainty will continue to prevail. Indeed, following the US Supreme Court's decision in *Jam*, the case was returned to the US District Court for the District of Colombia for reassessment. In February 2020, that court decided that the core of the IFC's impugned activity did not constitute commercial activity carried out in the United States so the organisation continued to enjoy immunities even on the restricted standard.[103] At the date of writing, this case is still being litigated. It is thus unwise to make any categorical statements, save to note that distinguishing between what constitutes an IO's commercial and non-commercial activity will continue to present difficulties.[104]

Crucially, the conflation of IO and state immunity is conceptually problematic. It is incorrect to equate immunities founded in the sovereign equality

101 *Jam* SC (n 98), 29 (per Breyer J).

102 See, for example, *Francisco S. v Aetna Life Insurance Co.* (D Utah 2020), where a claim concerning breaches of a health insurance plan applicable at the World Bank was considered to be commercial in nature. It was said: 'The question then becomes whether providing health insurance to one's employees constitutes a commercial act. Section 1605(a)(2) "reflects Congress's intent to restrict a foreign state's immunity 'to cases involving acts . . . which are sovereign or governmental in nature, as opposed to acts which are either commercial in nature or those which private persons normally perform". . . . The commercial character of an activity shall be determined by reference to the nature of the course of conduct or particular transaction or act, rather than by reference to its purpose."'; also see *Shape v Supreme* (3 September 2020) Case C-186/19, paras 56 and 69, where the CJEU found that legal 'proceedings concerning a claim arising from alleged non-payment for fuel supplied for the purposes of a peacekeeping operation carried out by that organisation, is covered by the concept of "civil and commercial matters"', with the purpose of the transaction not affecting the characterisation of a typical private transaction freely entered into between the parties. Contrast this with *Noah J. Rosenkrantz et al. v Inter-American Development Bank* (5 April 2021) Civil Action No 20-3670 (BAH), 19, where the United States District Court for the District of Columbia decided that an IO's alleged failure to comply with internal Sanctions Procedures, said to breach IDB-financed contracts, did not constitute commercial activity, with the court stating: 'plaintiffs' suit is based upon alleged violations of the Sanctions Procedures by the IDB in the course of its investigation and prosecution of Prohibited Practices charges against plaintiffs. The process by which IDB undertakes and prosecutes such charges, pursuant to its Sanctions Procedures, is the type of activity by which government entities defend against fraud and corruption in the use of public funds. Plaintiffs therefore have not established that the gravamen of the Complaint – IDB's alleged violations of its own Sanctions Procedures – constitutes commercial activity'.

103 See *Jam et al. v International Finance Corporation* (14 February 2020) Civil Action No 15-612 (JDB) (*Jam v IFC*). More on this in Chapter 5.

104 Of course, sometimes there will be no issue whether a transaction is commercial or not.

of states, being the basis of state immunity, with IO immunities, the latter strictly treaty-based and 'functional' in nature.[105] The sovereign versus non-sovereign distinction, also referred to as commercial versus non-commercial or private versus public, a distinction now relevant to establish whether state immunity can exist,[106] is irrelevant in the context of institutional immunities.

The activity of IOs cannot be divided into sovereign or non-sovereign. The pitfall of particularly using that distinction in the context of MDBs was pointed out by the Court of Appeal in *Jam*. Judge Silberman (with Judge Edwards agreeing) said that 'if that exception applied to the IFC, the organization would never retain immunity since its operations are solely "commercial," i.e., the IFC does not undertake any "sovereign" activities'.[107] This is an absurd outcome. An equally absurd position is reached if we try to square the circle on how the concept of functionalism fits within the rubric of the commercial versus non-commercial distinction. Where the very function of an IO is to perform commercial activity, perversely, functional immunity could amount to virtually absolute immunity. This could not have possibly been the intention behind the MDB immunities regime as is evident by the nature of broadly drafted express waiver provisions whose utility may now be questioned.

4.4.2.2 The Express Waiver Provisions in MDB Immunities

As was said, to allow MDBs to effectively function, their immunities are subject to express waiver provisions. Such provisions allow third parties to bring actions against an MDB before a competent court located in the territory of a member state in which the organisation may be based or does its core business. On its face, such provisions are very broad, even incorporating a waiver from execution. According to the plain meaning of the words, the immunities of MDBs seem to have little work to do for any claimant could pursue a claim against it. Indeed, such treaty language has been referred to as 'somewhat clumsy and inartfully drafted'.[108] To deal with this problem, courts have developed imaginative ways of addressing the issue.

In particular, US courts have developed the so-called corresponding benefit test, which requires close scrutiny of an organisation's functions and the underlying purpose of immunities.[109] In *Mendaro v the World*

105 Wood (n 54).
106 This in itself is a difficult distinction.
107 *Jam* Appeal (n 91), 8.
108 *Mendaro v World Bank* (n 80).
109 For a recent example, see *Noah J. Rosenkrantz et al. v Inter-American Development Bank* (n 102), especially jurisprudence cited at 34–7.

Bank,[110] it was said that 'most organizations would be unwilling to relinquish their immunity without receiving a corresponding benefit which would further the organization's goals'.[111] The express waiver provision has been interpreted narrowly. Immunities are only inapplicable concerning 'actions arising out of [an organization's] external commercial contracts and activities'.[112] The rationale is that if third parties do not have an option to seek legal redress against an IO, they might not be minded to do business with it. Hence, the benefit to the IO would demand a waiver in such circumstances. Ultimately, the corresponding benefit test is nothing but a manifestation of the functionalist concept of immunities, although the concept of functionalism is understood overly broadly.

For instance, in *Jam*, another line of argument pursued by the plaintiffs was that as the claims arose out of the IFC's external activity, the express waiver was applicable. This argument was rejected, with the first instance court saying '[p]laintiffs' own complaint characterizes the suit as one that "arises out of" IFC's "irresponsible and negligent conduct ... in appraising, financing, advising, supervising and monitoring its significant loan" to CGPL. ... By focusing on IFC's internal decision-making processes, the suit invites – indeed, demands – "judicial scrutiny of the [IFC's] discretion to select and administer its programs"'.[113] Thus, the more the Court is required to scrutinise the internal working of an organisation, the less likely the waiver would apply for this would allegedly intrude into the organisation's functional autonomy. This is even so where the possibility of allowing a claim to proceed could provide some incentive for an IO to 'adhere more scrupulously to its policies'.[114] Some judges have criticised this approach. In *Jam* itself, Judge Pillard of the Court of Appeal said:

> It is not entirely clear why we have drawn the particular line we have. ... Why are suits by a consultant, a potential investor, and a corporate borrower in an international organization's interest, but suits by employees and their dependents not? Entities doing regular business with international organizations can write waivers of immunity into their contracts with the organizations. ... Sophisticated commercial actors that fail to bargain for such terms are surely less entitled to benefit from broad immunity waivers than victims of torts or takings who lacked any bargaining opportunity.[115]

110 *Mendaro v World Bank* (n 80).
111 Ibid, 617.
112 Ibid, 620.
113 *Jam* First Instance (n 91), 9.
114 Ibid, 10–11; *Jam* Appeal (n 91), 1.
115 Decision of Judge Pillard in *Jam* Appeal (n 91), 7.

Even though its application has been subjected to justified criticism, the corresponding benefit test gave US courts an opportunity to introduce functional considerations into delimiting IO immunities.[116] With the US Supreme Court not engaging with the concept of functionalism in *Jam*,[117] and homing in on the commercial versus non-commercial distinction for determining questions of IO immunities, MDB immunities have been plunged into a deep confusion. IO immunities are wrongly conflated with state immunity. Countless hours and dollars will be spent on pursuing litigation before courts trying to resolve the unresolvable conundrum as to how functional immunities fit into the commercial versus non-commercial dichotomy. What is more, the role that functionalism could play in determining the scope of immunities through the operation of the corresponding benefit test may be sidelined significantly. If immunity on the commercial versus non-commercial distinction is upheld, with the impugned activity being classified as 'public', it is difficult to comprehend when exactly the express waiver provision could actually apply to limit immunities. Thus, considerable uncertainty now exists on whether the express waiver provision has any meaningful work to do at all. In the final analysis, victims of IO conduct will continue to confront the immunities conundrum when seeking justice against IOs in general, and MDBs in particular. With victims of IO conduct unable to successfully argue against limiting IO immunities based on 'functionalism' in general, attempts have been made to make immunities contingent on the provision of access to justice at the institutional level. Despite signs of progress, it cannot be said that access to justice considerations have in any meaningful way limited immunities either.

4.4.3 *IO Immunities and Access to Justice*

Due to the operation of IO immunities, a structural bias is built into the regulatory regimes governing IOs. Whereas an IO is free to approach a national court to realise its legal rights, a person wishing to raise a claim against an IO cannot readily do so. This entrenched structural inequality, while not impermissible under international law as such,[118]

[116] For a detailed discussion on the history of the US IO immunities regime and relevant jurisprudence, see Young (n 88); also see the discussion in CH Brower, 'United States' in A Reinisch (ed), *The Privileges and Immunities of International Organizations in Domestic Courts* (Oxford University Press 2013), 303–27.

[117] *Jam* SC (n 98).

[118] HRC, 'General Comment No 32: Right to Equality before Courts and Tribunals and to a Fair Trial' (23 August 2007) UN Doc CCPR/C/GC/32 (General Comment No 32), para 18; *Waite*

embeds a bias in favour of the organisation by rendering it immune from suit. To counter this structural bias, a key regulatory demand on the exercise of institutional power is that IOs must provide access to justice to individuals who are harmed by their actions (see Chapter 1). With the jurisdictional immunities accorded to IOs preventing claimants from successfully approaching national courts, compliance with an organisation's access to justice obligations assumes even greater significance. It has aptly been said that the access to justice obligations on IOs cushions the impact of jurisdictional immunities.[119] Reinisch observes that this obligation to provide for alternative dispute settlement mechanisms in case of an IO's immunity from legal process can be regarded 'as an acknowledgment of the right of access to court as contained in all major human rights instruments'.[120]

Often, the same instrument that provides for an IO's immunities also creates an access to justice obligation binding on the IO. The UN's regulatory regime is a good example. As was observed earlier in this chapter, the General Convention grants the UN immunities from the jurisdiction of domestic courts to preserve its functional independence. The General Convention also imposes an access to justice obligation on the organisation seeking to blunt the harsh impact of immunities on third parties.[121] Article VIII, Section 29, of the General Convention provides that the 'United Nations shall make provisions for appropriate modes of settlement of: Disputes arising out of contracts or other disputes of a private law character to which the United Nations is a party.'[122] When justice is denied at the institutional level (see Chapter 3), claimants have increasingly tried to argue that immunities cannot exist. In other words, immunities are contingent on the provision of appropriate modes of dispute resolution. Different approaches are evident. At one end of the scale, access to justice is completely irrelevant to determine IO immunities.

and Kennedy v Germany App no 26083/94 (ECtHR, 18 February 1999) (*Waite and Kennedy*), para 63.

119 K Schmalenbach, 'Dispute Settlement (Article VIII Sections 29–30 General Convention)' in A Reinisch and P Bachmayer (eds), *The Conventions on the Privileges and Immunities of the United Nations and Its Specialized Agencies: A Commentary* (Oxford University Press 2016), 530.

120 A Reinisch, 'Convention on the Privileges and Immunities of the Specialized Agencies New York, 21 November 1947' (*Introductory Note*, United Nations Audiovisual Library of International Law) <http://legal.un.org/avl/ha/cpiun-cpisa/cpiun-cpisa.html> accessed 20 June 2018.

121 See, Schmalenbach (n 119), 529.

122 General Convention (n 58), art VIII, section 29, para (a).

4.4.3.1 Access to Justice Ignored

Some national courts, including US courts, have decided that the existence of immunity is not dependent on whether the IO has complied with its access to justice obligation. As the outcome of the Haiti cholera litigation shows, this approach results in grave denials of justice. In October 2010, cholera broke out in the Artibonite region of Haiti. The disease caused severe devastation in that country, infecting over 7 per cent of the population and killing more than 9,000 people.[123] The victims' accounts detail how cholera caused a 'violent onset of sickness, rapid death, psychological trauma, and total loss of livelihood'.[124] There are countless stories of hardship. The following being just one example:

> The Petitioners include the daughter of a man who was the sole provider for her family. The father fell sick in the middle of the night with continuous diarrhoea. His family rushed him to the Cholera Treatment Center in Mirebalais. After three days, his condition worsened and he was transferred to the hospital. There, the daughter watched as her father lay still for hours until he died. The daughter and her family are now struggling to survive without any financial support.[125]

The victims alleged that the cholera outbreak was directly attributable to the UN because of its gross negligence and deliberate indifference for the health and lives of Haiti's citizens by the UN and its subsidiary, the MINUSTAH, amounting to the commission of a tort under Haitian law.[126] It was claimed that cholera was introduced in Haiti by UN Peacekeepers and that the UN was responsible because it 'failed to screen troops for cholera infection prior to deployment from Nepal'.[127] The link between cholera in Haiti and UN Peacekeepers from Nepal is now undeniable. This much has been concluded by the Independent Panel established by the UN Secretary-General to investigate the source of cholera in Haiti.[128] Consistent with the UN's internal procedures, the plaintiffs first filed administrative claims at the UN in November 2011, seeking compensation pursuant to the UN's obligations under Section 29 of the General Convention, as well as the 2005 SOFA

[123] See 'Cholera Litigation' (*Institute for Justice and Democracy in Haiti*) (2018) <www.ijdh.org/cholera/cholera-litigation/> accessed 3 June 2016.

[124] BAI/IJDH petition submitted to the UN on behalf of 5,000 clients on 3 November 2011: 'Petition for Relief', available at 'Cholera Accountability' (*Institute for Justice and Democracy in Haiti*) <www.ijdh.org/choleraaccountability/> accessed 3 June 2016, para 61.

[125] Ibid.

[126] Ibid.

[127] Ibid.

[128] Ibid.

between the UN and Haiti.[129] The UN did not respond until February 2013. Once it belatedly responded, the UN said that the claims were not receivable because consideration of the claims would involve 'a review of political and policy matters'.[130] That response should be seen for what it is: an evasive tactic to wash the organisation's hands of liability in what plainly is a typical claim in negligence where privately held rights are manifestly contravened. Until recently, the UN continued to deny its responsibility despite 'overwhelming evidence of its wrongdoing and mounting public pressure for accountability and action'.[131]

In October 2013, the plaintiffs filed a class action in negligence against the UN in the US District Court for the Southern District of New York.[132] For the plaintiffs to succeed, they needed to overcome UN immunities provided for in the General Convention. The plaintiffs argued that UN immunity under Section 2 of the General Convention did not apply given the mandatory nature of the UN's access to justice obligation contained in Section 29 of the General Convention which the UN had breached.[133] However, on 9 January 2015, the court said that 'nothing in the text of the CPIUN suggests that the absolute immunity of section 2 is conditioned on the UN's providing the alternative modes of settlement contemplated by section 29'.[134] This view was upheld on appeal.[135] As a result, despite compelling evidence of fault on the UN's part and no appropriate modes of dispute resolution provided at all, liability has been avoided and the well-accepted principles of tort law flagrantly contravened. As Boon notes, 'under ordinary principles of tort law the maxim ubi jus, ibi remedium applies: "Where there is a right, there is a remedy."'[136] This 'principle holds true when an individual or entity causes harm, even when acting with the best of intentions'.[137] As

[129] Pursuant to Art 55 of the Status of Forces Agreement (SOFA), the UN must establish a Standing Claims Commission to resolve disputes of a 'private law character'. In the case at hand, the UN did not do so. Accordingly, consistent with UN procedures, the claims were filed at the UN Claims Unit on 3 November 2011.

[130] UN's response to BAI/IJDH challenge on July 2013 <www.ijdh.org/cholera/cholera-litigation/> accessed 3 June 2016.

[131] See, Cholera Litigation (n 123).

[132] See, 'Complaint by D. Georges and Others ("plaintiffs") against Secretary-General Ban Ki-moon, the United Nations and Others' (9 October 2013) <www.ijdh.org/cholera/cholera-litigation/> accessed 3 June 2016, 534.

[133] *Delama Georges et al. v United Nations* No 1:2013cv07146 Doc 62 (SDNY 2015), 2–3.

[134] Ibid, 5.

[135] *Georges v United Nations* (US 2nd Cir, August 2016) No 15-455-cv; for related litigation, see information contained at <www.ijdh.org/cholera-litigation/> accessed 25 April 2021.

[136] KE Boon, 'The United Nations as Good Samaritan: Immunity and Responsibility' (2016) 16 Chicago Journal of International Law 2, 349.

[137] Ibid.

much as the outcome of the Haiti cholera litigation is unsatisfactory, the reality is that in many jurisdictions access to justice considerations have no bearing on limiting IO immunities whatsoever. However, certain other jurisdictions have allowed access to justice concerns impact IO immunities to a limited extent.

4.4.3.2 Access to Justice: A Factor in Limiting IO Immunities?

A key way in which private persons have sought to impugn the actions of IOs is by suing host states for the breach of the right to a fair trial found in human rights treaties. IOs are not parties to human rights treaties in general. Thus, this particular method to bring an IO to account is somewhat indirect as the international responsibility directly invoked is that of the host state. The idea is that where a host state's courts refuse to adjudicate a claim against an IO, and where that IO fails to provide appropriate modes of dispute resolution, the host state is itself in breach of its obligations to guarantee the right to access to court to the claimant. If a violation against the host state is found, as Olson points out in the European context:

> A court order to an ECHR member state forbidding it to honor [the organization's] immunities on grounds that [the organization's] internal procedures do not conform to the standards set forth in the Convention thus has the identical effect in the real world as would direct application of the Convention's terms to [the organization].[138]

Thus, in principle, ensuring compliance with the right to a fair trial at the national level could require piercing IO immunities. The European Court's decision in the case of *Waite and Kennedy v Germany* (*Waite and Kennedy*)[139] constitutes landmark jurisprudence propagating this principle, although national courts in South American jurisdictions had already adopted it in the 1980s based on fair trial rights contained in domestic constitutions.[140] *Waite and Kennedy* involved certain IO contractors raising a claim against the territorial state, Germany, for contraventions of their right to a fair trial due

138 P Olson, 'Immunities of International Organizations: A NATO View' (2013) 10 International Organizations Law Review 2, 419–32, 427.

139 *Waite and Kennedy* (n 118); *Beer and Regan v Germany* App no 28934/95 (ECtHR, 18 February 1999).

140 See, for example, *Washington Julio Efrain Cabrera v Comision Tecnica Mixta de Salto Grande* (CSJN, 5 December 1983) CSJN Fallos 305:2150, discussed in RE Vinuesa, 'Argentina' in A Reinisch (ed), *The Privileges and Immunities of International Organizations in Domestic Courts* (Oxford University Press 2013), 19–21 (see for an analysis of Argentinian jurisprudence).

to the application of IO immunities.[141] Mr Waite and Mr Kennedy, the applicants, provided services to the ESA pursuant to contractual arrangements. After those contractual arrangements ended, the applicants argued that under German labour law, ESA was obliged to deem the applicants as its employees independent of any contractual relationship.[142] ESA did not do so and the applicants sued the organisation for alleged breaches of their employment rights before German courts.[143] ESA successfully relied on its immunity before the German courts.[144] The applicants approached the European Court, arguing that their inability to argue the merits of the case before German courts was in contravention of the right to access a court in Article 6 of the European Convention.[145] The central question concerned was whether the ESA could rely on its immunities before German courts.

The European Court made two critical findings. First, it said that the right to access a court and a fair trial, while subject to restrictions, could not be limited in a way so as to 'reduce the access left to the individual in such a way or to such an extent that the very essence of the right is impaired'.[146] It went on to hold:

> 'The Court is of the opinion that where States establish international organisations in order to pursue or strengthen their cooperation in certain fields of activities, and where they attribute to these organisations certain competences and accord them immunities, there may be implications as to the protection of fundamental rights. It would be incompatible with the purpose and object of the Convention, however, if the Contracting States were thereby absolved from their responsibility under the Convention in relation to the field of activity covered by such attribution. It should be recalled that the Convention is intended to guarantee not theoretical or illusory rights, but rights that are practical and effective. This is particularly true for the right of access to the courts in view of the prominent place held in a democratic society by the right to a fair trial.[147]

Second, it was also stated:

> For the Court, a material factor in determining whether granting ESA immunity from jurisdiction is permissible under the Convention is whether

[141] *Waite and Kennedy* (n 118), para 11.
[142] Ibid, para 15.
[143] Ibid, para 15.
[144] Ibid, paras 22–24.
[145] Ibid, para 43.
[146] Ibid, para 59.
[147] Ibid, para 67.

> the applicants had available to them reasonable alternative means to protect effectively their rights under the Convention.[148]

Consequently, if IOs do not create 'reasonable alternative means' to settle claims against them, a 'material factor' indicating that immunities should be breached will be present. The words 'reasonable alternative means' have now become part of the folklore of IO immunities and are often repeated in European Court judgments formulaically.[149] However, *Waite and Kennedy* has not had a meaningful impact on promoting access to justice for victims so far. There are two principal reasons for this state of affairs. First, for no rational reason, the *Waite and Kennedy* jurisprudence is limited to the employment sphere, thereby diminishing its utility. For instance, in the *Srebrenica case*, one of the questions before the European Court concerned whether the immunity enjoyed by the UN is subject to a test of its compatibility with the right of access to a court. It was contended that the UN's failure to set up an alternative mechanism to provide redress meant that its immunities were inapplicable.[150] Without meaningfully engaging with this issue, the European Court simply concluded '[i]t does not follow ... that in the absence of an alternative remedy the recognition of immunity is *ipso facto* constitutive of a violation of the right of access to a court'.[151] As to why such a conclusion was reached, and the *Waite and Kennedy* rationale not applied, remains a mystery.

Second, even where the *Waite and Kennedy* jurisprudence applies, its impact has been inconsistent and underwhelming. On the one hand, occasionally, courts have breached IO immunities not only where alternative means are completely absent, but even where alternative means are not considered to be 'reasonable' or 'appropriate'. For example, Belgian courts have pierced an organisation's immunity for want of 'reasonable alternative means' where an internal justice system lacked independence.[152] Similarly, in a French case concerning a labour dispute against the AfDB,[153] the social chamber of the

148 Ibid, para 68.

149 See, for example, *Klausecker v Germany* App no 415/07 (ECtHR, 29 January 2015), para 64; *Srebrenica case* (n 63), para 139; to name just a few examples.

150 *Srebrenica case* (n 63), paras 73–4.

151 Ibid, para 164.

152 *Siedler v Western European Union* (17 September 2003, Appeal judgment) JT 2004, 617, ILDC 53, paras 63–6; also see *Western European Union v Siedler* (December 2009, Appeal judgment) Cass no S 04 0129 F, ILDC 1625 (BE 2009), 21; *General Secretariat of the ACP Group v Lutchmaya* (21 December 2009, Final Appeal judgment) Cass no C 03 0328 F, ILDC 1573 (BE 2009); *General Secretariat of the ACP Group v BD* (21 December 2009, final Appeal judgment) Cass no C 07 0407 F, ILDC 1576 (BE 2009).

153 *African Development Bank v X* (25 January 2005, Court of Cassation) Appeal no 04-41012, ILDC 778, 477.

Cour de Cassation decided to render the bank's immunity inapplicable because of the absence of any internal tribunal accessible to the complaining staff member, on the basis that such a denial was contrary to the French international public order and a denial of justice.[154] After analysing French jurisprudence, a French expert in the field, Burdeau, concludes that when making immunities determinations, French courts not only check that alternative means exist, but they also ensure that the alternative forum accords the plaintiff a fair trial.[155] This sensible approach giving content to the word 'reasonable' in the phrase 'reasonable alternative means' is also taken in the recently promulgated Guidelines of the Inter-American Juridical Committee in its Practical Application Guide on the Jurisdictional Immunities of International Organizations (the IAJC Guidelines).[156]

The IAJC Guidelines provide that IO immunities can only be upheld where dispute resolution mechanisms established by IOs to resolve 'private law disputes are adequate and effective'.[157] The Rapporteur's notes to those Guidelines state that:

> In the case of *Waite and Kennedy v. Germany*, the European Court of Human Rights held that immunity depends on the availability of adequate and effective remedies. The European Court has specified three requirements for maintaining immunity: (i) immunity must not restrict or diminish the right to due process; (ii) the limitations to immunity must pursue a legitimate aim; (iii) there must be a reasonable relationship of proportionality between the means used and the aim accomplished. The functional nature of immunities requires that individuals' right of access to justice be preserved. *Therefore, the mere obligation to establish dispute resolution mechanisms is insufficient; these mechanisms should be adequate and effective. Those mechanisms should also be governed by the principles of independence, transparency, professionalism, decentralization, legality, and due process* (emphasis added).[158]

By making compliance with the right to a fair trial practical and not illusory, the IAJC Guidelines seem to better translate the *Waite and Kennedy* intent into reality

[154] Ibid.

[155] G Bastid Burdeau, 'France' in A Reinisch (ed), *The Privileges and Immunities of International Organizations in Domestic Courts* (Oxford University Press 2013), 118–19; Although national courts have taken inconsistent approaches to immunities, see M Steinbruck Platise, 'The Development of the Immunities of International Organisations in Response to Domestic Contestations' in M Kanetake and A Nollkaemper (eds), *The Rule of Law at the National and International Level* (Hart 2016), 67–96, 70.

[156] 'Inter-American Juridical Committee Report. Immunities of International Organizations' (16 August 2018) CJI/doc.554/18 rev.2 (IAJC Guidelines).

[157] Ibid, 6.

[158] *Waite and Kennedy* (n 118).

than the very court that rendered that decision. The European Court adopts a low threshold of what an IO internal justice system ought to provide to be compliant with fair trial standards. It has held that an IO's internal justice system only needs to provide 'Equivalent protection' when compared with domestic tribunals.[159] But the conception of 'equivalent protection' presents a low bar and is established where the alternative means are not 'manifestly deficient'.[160] As a result, the word 'reasonable' in the 'reasonable alternative means' test is empty of any content. Unsurprisingly, *Waite and Kennedy* has failed to live up to its potential to ensure that access to justice does not become victim to the blunt instrument of IO immunities. So far, the European Court has granted broad deference to IOs in meeting their obligation to create reasonable alternative means.[161] To this author's knowledge, there does not appear to be any case, including *Waite and Kennedy*,[162] where the European Court has found an IO's internal justice system to be lacking.[163] As was demonstrated in Chapter 3, this is not because the alternative means were necessarily 'reasonable' or 'appropriate', but due to the court's unwillingness to scrutinise the 'alternative means' with the nuance that is warranted.

4.5 CONCLUSION

IO immunities were always intended to be functional, but the term 'functional' has been made redundant when delimiting IO immunities. Whether it be the immunities of the UN, MDBs or any other IO, the term 'functional' is interpreted so broadly that IO immunities have become mostly absolute. Even though *Jam*

159 C Ryngaert, 'Belgium' in A Reinisch (ed), *The Privileges and Immunities of International Organizations in Domestic Courts* (Oxford University Press 2013), 65.

160 See *Bosphorus Hava Yollari Turizm ve Ticaret Anonim Pirketi v Ireland* App no 45036/98 (ECtHR, 30 June 2005), paras 152–7; as was pointed out in the concurring opinion of Judge Keller in the case of *Al-Dulimi and Montana Management Inc. v Switzerland* App no 5809/08 (ECtHR, 21 June 2016), para 13, the European Court has developed a presumption of immunity and equal protection in respect of several IOs, including the EU, UN and NATO; particularly in the context of staff disputes, see AM Thevenot-Werner, 'The Right of Staff Members to a Tribunal as a Limit to the Jurisdictional Immunity of International Organisations in Europe' in A Peters, M Devers, AM Thevenot-Werner and P Zbinden (eds), *Les acteurs dans l'ere du constitutionnalisme Global / Actors in the Age of Global Constitutionalism* (Societe de legislation comparee 2014), 111–39.

161 *Gasparini v Italy and Belgium* App no 10750/03 (ECtHR, 12 May 2009); and *Klausecker v Germany* (n 149); *Perez v Germany* App no 15521/08 (ECtHR, 6 January 2015).

162 In this case, the European Court said that the contractors could have accessed alternative remedies without considering whether those remedies would have proven effective: *Waite and Kennedy* (n 118), paras 69–70.

163 See, for example, the discussion by Schmitt (n 1), 264–8, where the author considers European jurisprudence showing that the European Court has never breached the immunities of an IO for lack of reasonable alternative means yet.

has seemingly curtailed IO immunities, at least vis-à-vis MDBs, its logic of equating state and IO immunity is flawed. It does little to clarify how functional immunities ought to be applied in practice. Much energy and resources will be continually spent on determining procedural questions before national courts, effort that would be better spent on resolving the actual merits of a claim. Moreover, when it comes to a contest between the right to a fair trial and IO immunities, the latter generally prevail.[164] Courts have lamented this state of affairs where denials of justice have become much too common.[165] In both the *Haiti* and *Srebrenica cases*, despite compelling fault on the UN's part, responsibility has been evaded. It is worth recalling the rhetoric of the then UN Secretary-General who said that the survivors of the Srebrenica massacre were absolutely right to demand justice for 'the most heinous crimes committed on European soil since World War II'.[166] Such statements have proven to be nothing but empty words. The principle that IOs must provide reasonable alternative means of dispute resolution if immunity is to be retained is gaining broad acceptance. Still, most courts, in most countries, and in most cases, deny claims against IOs without the merits ever being ventilated. Instead of checking whether the alternative forum is actually 'reasonable' and delivers justice consistently with fair trial standards, close scrutiny on the quality of justice provided is absent. Immunities are regularly upheld even where the quality of justice delivered is poor. As a result, access to justice does not play a meaningful role in delimiting IO immunities. Ultimately, real or perceived concerns about IO independence, which justifies the grant of jurisdictional immunities to international institutions, tend to trump the right to a fair trial. The following chapter will show that it is however possible to uphold IO independence and at the same time ensure access to justice if better coordination between the national and institutional legal orders is achieved.

164 IO immunities and access to justice are treated in terms of a conflict of norms. Some commentators have argued that an interpretative approach is well-suited and is able to resolve the access to justice deficit resultant from the manner in which the rules on IO immunities are presently interpreted and applied by avoiding the conflict altogether: see R Pavoni, 'Human Rights and the Immunities of Foreign States and International Organizations' in E De Wet and J Vidmar (eds), *Hierarchy in International Law: The Place of Human Rights* (Oxford University Press 2012), 72. The reality remains that immunities bar access to justice for all practical purposes, and a conflict between the concepts does exist in practice.

165 For example, in one prominent early case, *Manderlier v Belgium State and UN* (n 79), 236–7, where certain individuals brought claims against the UN in Belgian courts for damage to persons and property caused by the UN Force in the Congo, an appeals court upheld the UN's immunities in absolute terms while criticising 'the present state of international institutions [being that] there is no court to which the appellant can submit his dispute with the United Nations' as being a situation that 'does not seem to be in keeping with the principles proclaimed in the Universal Declaration of Human Rights'.

166 *Srebrenica case* (n 63), para 129.

5

Realising Access to Justice in Claims against International Organisations

Coordinating Regulatory Authority between the National and Institutional Legal Orders

5.1 INTRODUCTION

How to ensure access to justice does not become victim to the blunt instrument of IO immunities has proven to be a conundrum. Ultimately, both access to justice and IO immunities embed equally important values that need to be reflected appropriately in any solution that resolves this conundrum. On the one hand, access to justice values manifesting themselves as the right to a fair trial and effective remedy in IHRL is a cardinal feature of the rule of law. And on the other hand, IO immunities are said to promote an IO's functional autonomy. With IOs helping the world fight international terrorism, combat climate change, facilitate global trade and commerce, promote development, resolve disputes peacefully, deal with global health emergencies and ensure international cooperation in countless other spheres, we need effective and independent IOs more than ever before. In the quest to realise a fair trial, IO independence should of course not be compromised. This chapter demonstrates that it is indeed possible to uphold IO independence and at the same time ensure access to justice if better coordination between the national and institutional legal orders is achieved.

In this chapter, I argue that a PIL framework to resolve claims against IOs can guarantee victims' access to justice without compromising on IO independence. PIL concerns itself with three things, namely, adjudicative jurisdiction, applicable law and the recognition and enforcement of foreign judgments.[1] It has great potential to play a coordinating role between distinct legal orders and help appropriately allocate regulatory authority (Section 5.2).

[1] For a brief description of PIL's three elements, especially in the transnational setting, see H Muir Watt, 'The Relevance of Private International Law to the Global Governance Debate' in H Muir Watt and DP Fernandez Arroyo (eds), *Private International Law and Global*

This potential can be harnessed to mediate between the national and institutional orders (Section 5.3). Without better coordination between the national and institutional orders, there is little hope of developing a regulatory framework that neatly slices regulatory authority between them. Such a framework is presently absent and is needed to provide a theoretical justification for national courts to exercise their authority over an IO in the right circumstances.

Once the justification for PIL to mediate the relationship between the national and institutional order is provided, the chapter discusses the specific coordinating role PIL rules can play in practice to ensure victims' access to justice without compromising on IO independence. Concerning the rules on adjudicative jurisdiction (Section 5.4), I suggest that DRMs located in the IO legal order should constitute the primary forum where a private person's fair trial rights should be realised. A competent national court must nevertheless play a secondary role where a DRM based at the institutional level is either absent or not 'reasonable' or 'appropriate'. In the present sense, the terms 'reasonable' and 'appropriate' both mean the same thing, namely, the DRM must deliver justice consistent with fair trial standards found in IHRL.

Giving the institutional legal order the first opportunity to deliver justice provides IOs with a ready opportunity to significantly reduce the risk of a national court taking jurisdiction over them. All that IOs need to do is to create fair trial compliant modes of dispute resolution, which they are required to do by international law in any event.

But if national courts are asked to exercise jurisdiction due to institutional failures, I argue that a conventional PIL approach to adjudicative jurisdiction should be taken. This approach requires that jurisdiction is exercised if the parties to the dispute, or its subject matter, have close connections to the forum. Taking such an approach would ensure that victims can access a fair trial at the national level where justice is denied at the international one and IOs are not required to defend claims before distant forums. Where a national court takes jurisdiction over an IO in this circumscribed way, the rules on

Governance (Oxford University Press 2014), 1. All texts on PIL would have a focus on these main components. See, for example, R Mortensen, R Garnett and M Keyes, *Private International Law in Australia* (2nd edn, LexisNexis Australia 2011), 3; for a leading and comprehensive discussion on PIL (especially in the UK context), see generally, P Torremans, U Grusic, C Heinze, L Merrett, A Mills, C Otero Garcia-Castrillon, ZS Tang, K Trimmings and L Walker (eds), *Cheshire, North & Fawcett: Private International Law* (15th edn, Oxford University Press 2017); for a comparative discussion, see J Basedow, G Ruhl, F Ferrari and PA de Miguel Asensio (eds), *Encyclopedia of Private International Law* (Edward Elgar 2017), also see CW Jenks, *The Proper Law of International Organisations* (Stevens 1962) for an early work specifically in the context of IOs.

applicable law (Section 5.5) and the recognition and enforcement of judgments (Section 5.6) can further be calibrated to coordinate between the national and IO legal orders in such a nuanced manner that the chance of intrusion into an IO's independence is eliminated. In the end, this book proposes that a carefully crafted PIL regime allocates regulatory authority between the national and institutional orders so as to allow maintaining IO independence without contravening the individual right to access a fair trial.

5.2 PIL'S COORDINATING FUNCTION

PIL allows authorities in different legal orders to readily interact where such interaction is necessary due to the international nature of a particular dispute. PIL rules are especially triggered when a civil dispute cross-cuts legal orders and has connections with more than one legal system.[2] In such situations, a dispute is said to possess a 'foreign element'.[3] A foreign element can arise when a dispute has links to more than one legal order due to the location of the parties or the subject matter of the dispute.[4] When a dispute has a foreign element, PIL concerns itself with three main things. First, it regulates which court can adjudicate the dispute (competent court or adjudicative jurisdiction).[5] Second, it provides rules on whether the merits of the dispute will be resolved under the substantive law of the state of adjudication (*lex fori*) or under the law of another state having a connection to the dispute (choice of law or applicable law).[6] And third, PIL sets out the requirements under which the courts of one legal order will recognise and enforce a judgment rendered in another (recognition and enforcement).[7]

At the micro-level, PIL rules seek to reduce the risk of inconsistent treatment of the same dispute by different courts.[8] Such an inconsistency of treatment is anathema to the effective administration of

2 PIL is also known as conflict of laws in some jurisdictions, such as in the United States: see M Davies, A Bell and P le Gay Brereton, *Nygh's Conflict of Laws in Australia* (8th edn, LexisNexis 2010), 4. The term PIL is used in this work as I adopt an internationalist perspective on the subject. For an excellent discussion on the evolution of PIL, and for an understanding of the theoretical perspectives, see A Mills, *The Confluence of Public and Private International Law: Justice, Pluralism and Subsidiarity in the International Constitutional Ordering of Private Law* (Cambridge University Press 2009), 26–73.

3 See Mortensen, Garnett and Keyes (n 1), 3.

4 R Michaels, 'Jurisdiction, Foundations' (2016) Duke Law School Public Law & Legal Theory Series No 201653, 19–22. These concepts are further discussed in Section 5.4.1.

5 For a good description of these three elements, see SC Symeonides, *Choice of Law* (Oxford University Press 2016), 1–2.

6 Ibid.

7 Ibid.

8 Mills (n 2), 22–3.

justice.[9] It can result in parallel proceedings, conflicting judgments and the re-litigation of claims.[10] Through its three components, PIL seeks to ensure that disputes with a foreign element are adjudicated efficiently and in line with party expectations.[11] It thus aims to ensure that legal disputes cross-cutting legal boundaries are resolved justly and fairly.[12]

PIL also plays a much broader systemic role in the international order. Although PIL is still seen as part of a state's domestic law, it plays a significant role by mediating between state-based legal orders hand in hand with public international law.[13] It provides a stable, pragmatic and workable regime to help allocate regulatory authority across legal orders transnationally. Indeed, it has performed this function for centuries. As has been said, '[t]he Conflict of Laws approach to international regulatory coordination has a long and established pedigree. It was developed and legitimized over centuries into a universally recognized body of law in the context of the need for stable trade relations'.[14] When compared to public international law, PIL pursues relatively modest goals. Instead of seeking uniformity in substantive law, it aims to allocate regulatory authority across legal orders. Riles has observed:

> [PIL] rejects at the outset full international substantive legal harmonization as a utopian pipe dream. Rather, it accepts that regulatory pluralism, and even regulatory nationalism are facts of life, and sets for itself the more modest goal of coordination among different national regimes. In other words, the approach of this body of law is not to define one set of rules that apply for all, as in the case of public international law, but rather to define under what circumstances a particular dispute or problem shall be subject to one regulatory authority or another.[15]

9 The fact that parallel proceedings are to be avoided as a matter of comity is now accepted wisdom, making the *forum non conveniens* doctrine an aspect of international comity: see *472900 BC Ltd v Thrifty Can Ltd* [1998] 168 DLR 4th 602, para 32.

10 See T Schultz and N Ridi, 'Comity and International Courts and Tribunals' (2017) 50 Cornell International Law Journal 3, 578–608, 586; for early jurisprudence, see *Belgenland* (1885) 114 US 355, 363 (where the doctrine of *forum non conveniens* was used to show respect to foreign states in admiralty cases).

11 Mills (n 2), 3–4.

12 Ibid.

13 The debate whether PIL is a part of domestic or international law continues. The dogmatic view is that PIL is an aspect of domestic law. However, both public and private international laws together regulate international legal relationships: see generally, ibid; also see V Ruiz Abou-Nigm, K McCall-Smith and D French, *Linkages and Boundaries in Private and Public International Law* (Oxford University Press 2018).

14 A Riles, 'Managing Regulatory Arbitrage: A Conflict of Laws Approach' (2014) 47 Cornell International Law Journal 63, 89.

15 Ibid, 89.

PIL allocates regulatory authority by undertaking issue-by-issue determinations pertaining to a dispute in terms of who may adjudicate a claim and which legal order ought to supply the rules relevant to determine it.[16] What drives PIL is not just doing justice in individual cases, but allocating regulatory authority systemically. This is done based on what are referred to as 'connecting factors'. Mills explains:

> Private international law rules do not merely address the problem of reducing the potential for inconsistent legal treatment of disputes. They are not just concerned with achieving a rational or orderly division of regulatory authority. They also involve the normative question of how that ordering of regulatory authority should be achieved. The selection of a particular rule of jurisdiction or choice of law rule is not just a recognition that ... other legal orders may be more justly applied to a dispute. It is also a determination of which legal order should govern; it implies that the *connecting factor* adopted in that choice of law rule should be the foundation of the division of the regulatory authority of states (emphasis added).[17]

It is thus the connecting factor that eventually determines how PIL's three components are calibrated, and consequently, how regulatory authority across jurisdictions is ultimately allocated. The so-called connecting factors in PIL pay due regard to public international law limits. Public international law conceives of the world as divided into states. Each state possesses the freedom to legislate, adjudicate and enforce laws in relation to persons, things or subject matters having a territorial connection to it.[18] As will be observed in Sections 5.4–5.6 in greater detail, in respect of all of PIL's three key concerns – competent court, applicable law or recognition and enforcement – 'territoriality' still constitutes a principal connecting factor too.[19] Even though territoriality constitutes the chief connecting

[16] Ibid, 90.

[17] Mills (n 2), 22–3.

[18] See H Fox and P Webb, *The Law of State Immunity* (3rd edn, Oxford University Press 2015), 73–4. In addition to territoriality, a state's jurisdiction may be based on certain other grounds, that is, nationality, protective and universal jurisdiction. As the authors explain, 'nationality as a basis may be active or passive; the first relates to jurisdiction based on acts performed by the nationals of a State and the second to acts suffered as victims by nationals of a State'. The protective principle allows a state to exercise jurisdiction over foreigners outside its territory 'to protect its own governmental functions'. Universal jurisdiction, by far the most controversial, is said to entitle a state to exercise jurisdiction over a limited number of acts, such as piracy on the high seas.

[19] A Mills, 'Rethinking Jurisdiction in International Law' (2014) 84 British Yearbook of International Law 1, 187239, 195.

factor in international law, may it be of the private or public kind,[20] PIL has the advantage of being able to divide regulatory authority with much greater precision compared to public international law.

By dividing questions of jurisdiction and applicable law, PIL makes it possible for a court to adjudicate a claim, but still decide the merits based on the law of a different legal order given the particular connecting factors at play.[21] In such a case, regulatory authority is neatly divided. While the courts of one legal order are considered competent to adjudicate the case, the prescriptive authority of another legal order is also recognised through the choice of law determination. As a result, private rights are enforced in one jurisdiction, but this is done without compromising the prescriptive autonomy of another. PIL can thus provide for a powerful tool to address overlapping or conflicting claims to regulatory authority in a methodical and nuanced way. It has been aptly said that the law of conflicts is a central piece of the global law governance regime because 'it is the switchboard that routes agreements and rights for interpretation and enforcement'.[22] This so-called switchboard has not been put to good use in mediating between the national and institutional legal orders.

As is evident from the discussion in the previous chapters, there is little to no focused interaction between national and institutional DRMs. We find ourselves in an ecosystem of diverse regimes that coexist without speaking to each other. This results in blind spots and overlaps between pieces of regulatory authority.[23] The net result is that victims of institutional conduct are regularly denied justice, and IOs remain uncertain as to when a national court may decide to exercise its authority over them. By playing their coordinating and allocative roles, PIL techniques are ideally suited to manage the relationship between the national and institutional legal orders by appropriately allocating regulatory authority to each of them.

20 Although, in both public and private international law, territoriality is coming under stress.

21 As has been said, '[o]ne of the fundamental starting insights of Private International Law is that questions of jurisdiction and questions of choice of law are divisible inquiries. What this means is that simply because a given regime has the power to govern a certain issue (just because it has jurisdiction) does not mean that it should do so (choice of law). In certain circumstances, it might be more appropriate for it to defer to another regulatory authority and to apply that authority's rules if, for example, the parties have stipulated among themselves that a different law should apply to their transaction and it is appropriate to defer to the will of the parties, or again if another regulatory authority has a greater interest in the matter': see Riles (n 14), 90.

22 Ibid, 88.

23 Ibid, 72.

5.3 THE ABILITY OF PIL TO COORDINATE BETWEEN INSTITUTIONAL AND NATIONAL LEGAL ORDERS

PIL rules have traditionally coordinated the relationship between legal systems with reference to state-based legal orders.[24] Some may argue that legal orders that are governed by distinct normative frameworks are not comparable so PIL should not mediate in such situations.[25] I argue that from a conceptual point of view, PIL techniques are perfectly capable of mediating between institutional and national legal orders. IOs are subjects of international law and have their own distinct legal orders which must be recognised in a pluralist global space (Section 5.3.1). Moreover, it is demonstrated that PIL rules already apply to mediate between the national and institutional order, although their potential is not fully realised (Section 5.3.2). I conclude that for PIL to play a mediating role between the national and institutional legal orders effectively, it must take into account the peculiarities of the latter (Section 5.3.3).

5.3.1 *Institutional and National Legal Orders: Coexisting in a Pluralist Legal Space*

How PIL may coordinate regulatory authority between IOs and states is an important conceptual question. This is because IOs and states are seemingly unequal legal entities and PIL conventionally is used to coordinate between equals. Of course, states are 'sovereign' and the national legal order possesses a vast regulatory competence. As a matter of comity, one state must thus give due recognition to the regulatory authority of another.[26] But for present purposes, a threshold question concerns whether IOs are the type of entity that makes it worthy of recognition at the national level too. In other words, are national and IO legal orders co-equal for PIL's purposes? The answer is in the affirmative. Two points are important to make: (a) the IO and national legal orders must recognise each other, and (b) this recognition occurs between co-equals for PIL's purposes.

[24] P Schiff Berman, 'Global Legal Pluralism' (2007) 80 Southern California Law Review 1155, 1228.

[25] H Kelsen, 'The Concept of the Legal Order' (1982) 27 American Journal of Jurisprudence 1, 73–6.

[26] See especially, the discussion in FA Mann, *Foreign Affairs in English Courts* (Oxford University Press 1986), chapter 7.

5.3.1.1 Mutual Recognition between the IO and National Legal Order

First and foremost, as was discussed in Chapter 1, IOs are 'subjects' of international law and constitute independent actors on the international plane.[27] In public international law, IOs are legal subjects as much as states. As subjects of international law, IOs possess their own independent legal order distinct from any other, including the general international one. If the bodies of law between which the coordination is to take place are of the same nature, there are – from this perspective – no conceptual obstacles to coordination between them. As in the conventional setting between domestic legal orders, coordination would then occur between two similar legal entities, that is, between two subjects of international law having their own distinct legal orders. Indeed, the fact that IOs possess their own legal orders underpinned by their constituent treaties is well-accepted. Treves has noted:

> The existence of internal legal systems of international organizations, distinct from the domestic legal systems of member States, as well as from the international legal system, has been recognized for some decades. These legal systems are based on the constitutive instruments of the organization. Such instruments do not function only as treaties establishing obligations for the member States. The implementation of these obligations creates the factual conditions for applying the constitutive treaty as the constitution of the organization, which is to say the basic rule upon which the internal legal system of the organization is built. . . . This system of rules should, nonetheless, be seen as separate from general international law . . . one could say, because this system has a specific social basis distinct from that of the international legal system.[28]

Once brought into existence, the IO legal order forms its own autonomous order and possesses the regulatory authority based on the terms of its constituent instruments.[29] For example, the UN's order is created by the UN Charter,[30] the World Trade Organisation's legal system is based on the

[27] See the discussion in Chapter 1, Section 1.2.

[28] See T Treves, 'International Organisations as Parties to Contentious Cases: Selected Aspects' in L Boisson de Chazournes, CPR Romano and R Mackenzie (eds), *International Organizations and International Dispute Settlement: Trends and Prospects* (Brill 2002), 44.

[29] As HG Schermers and NM Blokker, *International Institutional Law* (5th edn, Brill 2011), section 1145, explains: 'The constitution sets the pattern for the legal order of the international organization. Further rules develop from the operation of its organs. The power of these organs to take decisions stems from the constitution. From this common source, a hierarchy of the various legal rules is developed, and a single legal order thus created.'

[30] It was pointed out in *Villamoran v Secretary-General of the United Nations* (12 July 2011) UNDT/2011/126, para 29 that the UN legal order consists of constitutional characteristics. At

constituent instruments of that organisation,[31] and so on. One could refer to an IO's legal order as its domestic legal order, containing organs roughly comparable to states, for example, a law-making and executive organ.[32] This does not mean that the overall competences of IOs and states are the same. Although many scholars have noted that IOs increasingly exercise 'conferred sovereign powers' that are in some respects analogous to states,[33] by and large, the regulatory autonomy of IOs and the powers that flow from it are delimited by reference to the concept of 'functionalism'. Mosler points out that the legal order of IOs is 'limited to the exercise of the functions entrusted to the organization by its constituent treaty'.[34] And Schermers and Blokker posit that '[c]onstitutions of international organizations are partial and functional'.[35]

Whatever the scope of their regulatory autonomy may be, the fact remains that IOs possess their own legal orders worthy of recognition by other legal orders.[36] An IO's constituent arrangements would thus tend to expressly require that the national legal order gives due recognition to the institutional one.[37] Conversely, just like states are to recognise the IO legal order, the

the top of the hierarchy of the organisation's internal legislation is the Charter of the United Nations (opened for signature 26 June 1945, entered into force 24 October 1945) 1 UNTS XVI (UN Charter), followed by resolutions of the General Assembly, staff regulations, staff rules, Secretary-General's bulletins and administrative instructions.

31 See generally, DZ Cass, *The Constitutionalization of the World Trade Organization: Legitimacy, Democracy, and Community in the International Trading System* (Oxford University Press 2005).

32 'As is suggested by their charters, a tripartite structure is common to many IOs. Many have a plenary body consisting of the full membership, charged with broad powers to discuss policy . . . ; an organ of more reduced membership capable of exercising some select powers, particularly of implementation; and a staff or secretariat of ostensibly "independent" international civil servants drawn from, and broadly representative of, member states and headed by a "Secretary" or "Director" general': see JE Alvarez, *International Organizations as Law-Makers* (Oxford University Press 2006), 9.

33 D Sarooshi, *International Organizations and Their Exercise of Sovereign Powers* (Oxford University Press 2007), 15; also see Jenks (n 1), 25; for more recent work on the public authority exercised by IOs, see A von Bogdandy, R Wolfrum, J von Bernstorff, P Dann and M Goldmann (eds), *The Exercise of Public Authority by International Institutions: Advancing International Institutional Law* (Springer 2010).

34 Cf H Mosler, 'The International Society as a Legal Community' (1974) 140 RdC, 191.

35 Schermers and Blokker (n 29), section 1341.

36 C Tomuschat, 'International Organizations as Third Parties under the Law of International Treaties' in E Cannizzaro (ed), *The Law of Treaties Beyond the Vienna Convention* (Oxford University Press 2011), 210–11; also see C Brolmann, *The Institutional Veil in Public International Law: International Organisations and the Law of Treaties* (Hart 2007), 253.

37 See, for example, Section 8 of the United Nations and United States of America Agreement regarding the Headquarters of the United Nations (opened for signature 26 June 1947, entered into force 21 November 1947) No 147 (UN-US Headquarters Agreement).

organisation itself is under obligation to respect the laws and regulations of the host state, or any other state where it may perform its work. The grant of privileges and immunities in no way implies that IOs are able to ignore national laws and undermine the regulatory authority of the national legal order.[38] Privileges and immunities are not meant to create a state of lawlessness. All they do is give IOs a degree of procedural protection from being sued before national courts (immunities), and exempt IOs and their officials from the application of a very small category of national laws, such as a state's taxation laws (privileges).[39]

Clearly, national and institutional legal orders are required to grant each other mutual respect, and recognise them within their own legal orders. What is more, such a mutual recognition between the national and IO legal orders is to be seen as occurring between orders that exist as equals, thus making a PIL-based coordination conceptually possible between them. Adopting a legal pluralist stance,[40] both legal orders can be said to coexist in a heterarchical manner. The IO legal order is not to be perceived as hierarchically linked to other legal orders. Competing claims to regulatory authority between IO law and state law are thus to be resolved via PIL as opposed to some sort of a 'primacy clause' – which makes a different kind of coordination necessary.

5.3.1.2 IOs and States Are Co-equal for PIL's Purposes: A Legal Pluralist Stance

The term 'legal pluralism expresses the idea that a society often has a number of legal orders, of which state law is just one – an important one but not the only one'.[41] In today's globalised world where law-making, adjudicating and, to a more limited extent, enforcement occur in both state- and non-state-based legal orders, differing legal orders exist side by side and without a ranking relationship.[42] As Michaels puts it, 'the irreducible plurality of legal orders, the coexistence of domestic state law with other legal orders, the absence of

38 See, ibid, sections 7(b), 7(c) and 9(b).

39 For an outline of the privileges normally provided for, see R Gulati 'Convention on the Privileges and Immunities of the United Nations, 13th February 1946' (1 UNTS 15, 1 UST 1418) OXIO 73 <http://opil.ouplaw.com/view/10.1093/law-oxio/e28.013.1/law-oxio-e28?rskey=4tJ2gf&result=9&prd=OXIO> accessed 28 May 2018.

40 For an overview of this approach, see A Bianchi, *International Law Theories: An Inquiry into Different Ways of Thinking* (Oxford University Press 2016), 228–45.

41 See DJ Galligan, *Law in Modern Society* (Oxford University Press 2006), 162.

42 Berman (n 24), 1160–1.

a hierarchically superior position transcending the differences' is a reality today.[43] Along the same lines, Berman has said:

> [I]t is now clear that the global legal system is an interlocking web of jurisdictional assertions by state, international, and non-state normative communities. And each type of overlapping jurisdictional assertion (state versus state; state versus international body; state versus non-state entity) creates a potentially hybrid legal space that is not easily eliminated.[44]

Indeed, as subjects of international law, IOs and national legal orders coexist, living together in a pluralist and hybridised legal space.[45] Unsurprisingly, as cohabitants in such a space, conflicting claims to authority between IOs and states can arise from time to time. These conflicts must be resolved by reference to PIL. This is because the mutual recognition that IOs and national legal orders are already required to grant each other occurs between equal orders.[46] As has been said, 'the three classic legal doctrines often grouped together under the rubric of conflict of laws – jurisdiction, choice of law, and judgment recognition – are specifically meant to manage hybrid legal spaces'.[47] The application of PIL to coordinate the relationship between IO and national legal orders was in fact already envisaged in 1962. Jenks had said:

> [W]e may have to broaden the concept of the conflict of laws as generally understood. . . . As international law evolves from a law among States towards the common law of mankind, the conflict of laws will increasingly embrace conflicts between legal systems some of which are not the law of particular States but other types of legal system falling within the general framework of a world legal order.[48]

Seyersted went one step further simply asserting that 'formally, the internal law is a separate legal system for each organization, as national law is for each State. And it is via its rules on conflict of laws, not via incorporation in national law, that the internal law of an IGO is [to be] applied by national courts'.[49]

43 See R Michaels, 'Global Legal Pluralism' (2009) 5 Annual Review of Law & Social Science; Duke Law School Public Law & Legal Theory Research Paper No 259 <https://ssrn.com/abstract=1430395>, 1.

44 Berman (n 24), 1159.

45 Ibid, 1163; Michaels (n 43).

46 For a PIL approach to public international law fragmentation, see R Michaels and J Pauwelyn, 'Conflict of Norms or Conflict of Laws?: Different Techniques in the Fragmentation of Public International Law' (2012) 22 Duke Journal of Comparative & International Law 349.

47 Berman (n 24), 1228.

48 Jenks (n 1), 27.

49 See F Seyersted, *Common Law of International Organizations* (Martinus Nijhoff 2008), 55.

Although Jenks or Seyersted did not provide a conceptual basis for their views, one may readily glean a legal pluralist understanding which drove them. The theoretical foundation for the application of PIL to coordinate the relationship between the institutional and national orders is best understood through the lens of legal pluralism. Where multiple legal orders now heterarchically coexist, PIL can indeed play a powerful role in coordinating regulatory authority between the institutional and national order. To an extent, such coordination is already occurring.

5.3.2 *IOs Are Already Subjected to PIL*

IOs regularly enter into relationships where they impact privately held rights and PIL rules apply in their usual way. Recall that the very reason IOs are granted personality is to allow them to enter into private relationships in their own right.[50] It is impossible to create an exhaustive list of each and every private law right or obligation an IO may possess or assume, save to say that these may be of varying types. IOs may employ staff members; enter into contracts for services; purchase and lease real property; contract for public utilities; take out insurance policies for the protection of their property and to cover liabilities towards third parties; possess rights in intellectual property; charter ships and aircraft; enter into financial transactions, including taking out and granting loans, investing reserve funds and holding bonds, shares, treasury bills or negotiable instruments; and may be also vulnerable to tortious liability where negligence is alleged.[51] All of these types of transactions or activities are demonstrably of a private law character.

Actually, characterising an IO's activity as private or non-private should not be as controversial as some make it out to be. To assess whether a particular transaction or legal relationship of an IO is of a private law character, it is important to focus on the nature of the transaction or legal relationship and not its purpose. If regard is had to the purpose of an activity, then possibly every transaction of an IO could be non-private. Almost all things that an IO would do, for instance, even buying stationary, in a very small way helps the IO in its functioning. This position is plainly absurd.[52] This is why the characterisation of a transaction or activity as private should depend on its inherent nature. This point was well made in a case that concerned alleged breaches of contract in connection with the purchase of oil by certain NATO entities, where that

50 See the discussion in Chapter 4.
51 Jenks (n 1), 36.
52 See the discussion relating to the Haiti cholera litigation against the UN in Chapter 4.

oil was to be used for a peacekeeping mission in Afghanistan.[53] The CJEU held that the transaction at issue constitutes a civil and commercial one to which PIL would apply.[54] In doing so, it clarified how IO activity is to be characterised, stating:

> [The aim of the proceeding] was to ensure the protection of the claims arising from a legal relationship of a contractual nature, namely the [Basic Ordering Agreements] concluded between SHAPE and the Supreme companies. The BOAs, although they concern the supply of fuel to SHAPE for a military operation directed by NATO for the purposes of peace-keeping and security in Afghanistan, are the basis, between the parties to the main proceedings, of a legal relationship governed by private law under which those parties freely took on rights and obligations. How SHAPE subsequently used the fuel supplied in execution of the BOAs is not ... such as to have an effect on the nature of such a legal relationship. The public purpose of certain activities does not, in itself, constitute sufficient evidence to classify them as being carried out iure imperii, in so far as they do not entail the exercise of any powers falling outside the scope of the ordinary legal rules applicable to relationships between private individuals.[55]

Accordingly, where IOs freely assume rights and obligations by entering into contracts, it can hardly be denied that such transactions or relationships should not be characterised as belonging to the private law realm regardless of the purpose that transaction is meant to serve. Similarly, where IOs harm third parties and negligence is alleged against them, IOs are subject to the rules of tort law regardless of the underlying purpose of the activity being pursued.[56] In the end, whenever an IO impacts privately held rights, a civil dispute of a private law character may arise even if that dispute is susceptible to multiple forms of classification.[57] What is more, when IOs impact privately held rights, how PIL would treat an IO is no different to how it would treat any other legal entity involved in a civil dispute having a foreign element.[58] Thus, when an IO sues or is being sued in a transnational civil dispute, a likely occurrence given that IOs tend to operate across state boundaries and their actions have effects in multiple legal orders, its status as an international

53 *Shape v Supreme* (3 September 2020) Case C-186/19.

54 If conduct was characterised as public or non-private, the transaction would have not attracted the application of the PIL framework applicable in the EU: Ibid, paras 68–9.

55 *Shape v Supreme* (n 53), paras 65–6.

56 See further Section 5.5.

57 Ibid.

58 Seyersted (n 49), 449.

public authority does not impact how PIL should allocate regulatory authority in its usual way. Schermers and Blokker note:

> In many legal relations, private international law designates a particular national legal system (for example the law of the place where immovable property is situated or where a contract has been concluded), which can be applied to international organizations as well as to any other subjects of law.[59]

In a civil claim involving an IO, PIL rules can thus help determine whether a court has jurisdiction, whether that jurisdiction should be exercised, what law applies and whether judgments sought in one jurisdiction can be enforced in another. In fact, PIL has already played its coordinative and allocative role in some instances. For example, Chapter 1 showed how PIL rules were applied to recognise an IO's domestic legal personality in one legal order (the United Kingdom) based on the IO's status in the law of another (UAE).[60] This gave effect to the well-accepted rule of PIL that the status of a body corporate is to be derived from the law of the place of its incorporation. In that case, had the House of Lords not used PIL tools to recognise the IO's personality in the United Kingdom, the organisation would have been unable to access judicial protection to recover the proceeds of corruption from its former Director-General.[61] Clearly, in this case, the IO was subjected to the regulatory authority of one national jurisdiction that was then recognised by another.

One may conclude that PIL can, and to an extent already does, mediate between distinct legal orders in respect of transnational civil disputes involving IOs. Although steadily rising, the dearth of jurisprudence focusing on PIL in claims involving IOs is not because of its irrelevance. It is because most claims against IOs in national courts are dismissed based on a blunt application of IO immunities, meaning that PIL is often not considered in any detail. This has meant that PIL's coordinative and allocative ability has not so far been properly harnessed to allocate regulatory authority between the national and institutional legal orders. I argue that PIL should play a greater role in achieving such coordination. In doing so, it is important that PIL accounts for the particularities of the institutional order.

5.3.3 *The Need for a Tailored Regime*

As has already been stated, for PIL's purposes, IOs and states are equals. They are both subjects of international law possessing distinct legal orders. The

59 See Schermers and Blokker (n 29), section 1601.

60 *Arab Monetary Fund v Hashim and Others (No 3)* [1991] 1 AC 114, [1991] 6 Arab LQ 90, discussed in Chapter 4, Section 4.2.1

61 Ibid.

national order will often need to defer to the regulatory authority of the institutional legal order, and vice versa. Whether or not one order should defer to another's authority ultimately depends on the applicable connecting factors. How these connecting factors operate in mediating between state-based legal orders cannot be directly transposed to manage the relationship between the national and institutional orders. Unlike states, IOs do not have their own territory. With territoriality still constituting the key connecting factor in international law, if PIL is to play a coordinative and allocative role to manage the relationship between the national and institutional legal order, it must accommodate the peculiarities of the latter. Those peculiarities principally involve the grant of jurisdictional immunities to IOs impacting the circumstances in which national courts should exercise jurisdiction over IOs. As the remainder of this chapter demonstrates, by calibrating the three PIL components that properly reflect the division of regulatory authority between states and IOs, we can achieve effective coordination between the national and institutional order. Ultimately, through well-tailored rules on jurisdiction (Section 5.4), applicable law (Section 5.5) and recognition and enforcement (Section 5.6), access to justice for the victims of IO conduct can be secured without compromising on IO independence.

5.4 ADJUDICATIVE JURISDICTION IN CLAIMS AGAINST IOS

This section shows how carefully calibrated rules on adjudicative jurisdiction allow for a victim's right to a fair trial to be realised, but without adversely impacting an IO's independence. The first step is to state what the term 'jurisdiction' in the present sense means, and when a court's jurisdiction exists (Section 5.4.1). Second, just because jurisdiction exists, it does not have to always be exercised.[62] It is argued that IO immunities only impact whether jurisdiction should be exercised as opposed to whether it exists. Both national courts and institutional DRMs may thus possess concurrent jurisdiction over an IO. IO immunities create a presumption that it is the institutional DRM that ought to be given the first opportunity to adjudicate a claim against an IO (Section 5.4.2). But where an IO fails to deliver justice consistently with fair trial standards found in IHRL, a competent national court having a basis of jurisdiction must exercise it. This would ensure that justice to the victims of IO

[62] While this is the position in common law states, civil law states may take a different approach. Such comparisons are outside the scope of this work, which particularly focuses on the relationship between the institutional and national legal orders.

conduct is realised, and at the same time, IOs are not required to defend claims before distant forums (Section 5.4.3).

5.4.1 *Adjudicative Jurisdiction: Some General Observations*

Which court possesses the regulatory authority to adjudicate the merits of a claim is a crucial question for claimants and respondents alike. In the absence of adjudicative jurisdiction, a court will lack the power to adjudicate. In other words, it is not a competent court. In any proceeding, a claimant must establish the jurisdiction of a court before it will agree to decide the merits of a case. Accordingly, the existence of at least one DRM capable of providing a claimant against an IO a fair trial is indispensable to realise justice. Obviously, if there is no DRM competent to adjudicate a claim whatsoever, then access to justice is completely denied. With courts of general jurisdiction in the international legal order not providing direct access to individual claimants against IOs,[63] realistically, victims of IO conduct can either approach a DRM located in the institutional legal order or they may raise a claim before a national court.

Recall that the scope of a DRM's jurisdiction based within the institutional legal order is determined by the statute creating it.[64] If DRMs at the institutional level are capable of providing victims of IO conduct a fair trial, then the role of national courts becomes less relevant. But for access to justice to be realised at the institutional level, competent DRMs must exist in the first place. As was said in Chapter 3, more often than not, such DRMs do not exist, or where they do, institutional DRMs are not 'appropriate' or 'reasonable'.[65] Left with no other choice, victims try to invoke the jurisdiction of national courts to resolve their claims fairly and justly. To examine when adjudicative jurisdiction at the national level can exist is therefore a threshold question and must be addressed.

63 See M Steinbruck Platise, 'The Development of the Immunities of International Organisations in Response to Domestic Contestations' in M Kanetake and A Nollkaemper (eds), *The Rule of Law at the National and International Level* (Hart 2016), 67–96, 72, where the author observes: 'organisations are generally not subject to compulsory jurisdiction of any international tribunal that could compensate for the lack of jurisdiction by domestic courts over claims against international organisations. While victims of human rights violations can, as a rule, bring their claims against the offending state before domestic courts of that state, such "domestic" remedies are rarely available within international organisations. Their internal dispute settlement mechanisms are, for the most part, still in their nascent stage, if they are available all'.

64 See, Chapter 2, Section 2.2.

65 See the discussion in Chapter 3.

The rules on the existence of jurisdiction governing claims against IOs are no different from how they operate with respect to any other legal entity, although immunities can have an impact when jurisdiction should be exercised, an issue discussed in Section 5.4.2. For the moment, the discussion focuses on the international rules governing the existence of adjudicative jurisdiction at the national level. These international rules are found both in public and private international law. But as we will see, PIL rules are much more nuanced compared to public international law. The analysis commences by briefly outlining jurisdiction in public international law (Section 5.4.1.1), the outer limits of which PIL pays due regard to (Section 5.4.1.2). It is preferable that jurisdiction is founded on strong connecting factors to ensure fairness for the defendant (Section 5.4.1.3).

5.4.1.1 Jurisdiction in Public International Law

Jurisdiction in public international law is divided into prescriptive or legislative jurisdiction, enforcement jurisdiction and adjudicative jurisdiction (which in reality is a combination of prescriptive and enforcement jurisdiction).[66]

Prescriptive jurisdiction refers to 'the limits on the law-making powers of [a state] – the permissible scope of application of the laws of each state'.[67] Enforcement jurisdiction concerns the coercive ability of state institutions to engage in enforcement action. Such action may involve the seizure of persons or assets.[68] Adjudicative jurisdiction delimits the regulatory authority of national courts to determine a given claim.[69] It can involve aspects of both prescriptive and enforcement jurisdictions. Interpreting the law, and even judge-made law, are aspects of prescriptive jurisdiction,[70] and enforcement action by the judiciary is an exercise of a state's enforcement jurisdiction through the courts.[71] All those types of jurisdiction can only exist if a basis of jurisdiction can be established.

Public international law provides for various bases of jurisdiction, with territorial jurisdiction being the primary one. Conventionally, such a basis

66 Fox and Webb (n 18). For a discussion of jurisdiction in international law, see generally, Michael Akehurst, 'Jurisdiction in International Law' (1974) 46 British Yearbook of International Law 145, 258.

67 Mills (n 19), 194.

68 Ibid.

69 Ibid.

70 Ibid.

71 Ibid.

of jurisdiction gives a state broad regulatory authority, recognising a nearly plenary jurisdiction within its own territory.[72] The scope of territorial jurisdiction has been described in the following way:

> A state has jurisdiction to regulate within its territory, including in respect of events, persons or things in its territory (including cross-border events which are only partially in its territory), and, more controversially, external acts which have 'effects' within its territory.[73]

Thus, as far as adjudicative jurisdiction is concerned, public international law would consider it permissible for a national court to take jurisdiction over claims where the parties to that claim, or its subject matter, are somehow territorially connected to the state in which that court is located. While prescriptive jurisdiction, and by extension the prescriptive aspects of adjudicative jurisdiction, can be extraterritorial in character, the jurisdiction to enforce is strictly territorial.[74] Taking enforcement action without a foreign state's consent would be inconsistent with public international law notions of 'jurisdiction', which are rooted in the concept of sovereignty.[75] Overall, territoriality still provides for the primary basis of jurisdiction in public international law. But other bases of jurisdiction also exist. These are jurisdiction grounded in nationality,[76] the protective principle,[77] and in a limited number of cases, universal jurisdiction may be exercised, although this remains controversial.[78]

Providing a list of the types and grounds of jurisdiction in public international law is relatively straightforward. Translating them into how they are operationalised in particular situations is not. This is especially the case concerning adjudicative jurisdiction in civil cases, with the public international law notion of jurisdiction largely developed in the context of criminal law. So, when it comes to the factors that establish jurisdiction in civil cases, public international law is rather silent. As Fox and Webb note:

> There is . . . a surprising lack of certainty about the limitations which international law imposes on the exercise of jurisdiction by municipal courts in relation to civil proceedings; an uncertainty which exists with regard to the limits of civil jurisdiction over private parties, as well as over States [and equally IOs]. There is no general agreement as to the requirements of public

72 *France v Turkey* (1927) PCIJ Ser A, No 10 (*Lotus* case), para 46.
73 Mills (n 19), 195.
74 Ibid.
75 Fox and Webb (n 18).
76 Ibid.
77 Ibid.
78 Ibid.

> international law with regard to the bases for the exercise of civil jurisdiction … by States, although it seems likely that a court may not exercise jurisdiction where there is no significant connection with the forum.[79]

With public international law of little practical assistance in determining the scope of adjudicative jurisdiction in a civil case, it is PIL that provides nuanced rules concerning the basis of adjudicative jurisdiction in such instances.[80] As we see later in the chapter, PIL allocates regulatory authority across legal orders in the civil sphere with reference to connecting factors that are also rooted in territoriality. This must not come as a surprise. When PIL calibrates the connecting factors that apply to adjudicative jurisdiction in transnational civil disputes, it does not do so in a vacuum. PIL has developed its own connecting factors applicable to determine adjudicative jurisdiction taking into account the outer limits of public international law,[81] even though it tries to continually push those limits.

5.4.1.2 Adjudicative Jurisdiction in PIL

As was said, the rules on adjudicative jurisdiction in PIL become relevant in the resolution of civil claims that have a foreign element and transcend one legal order. In claims against IOs, a foreign element will always be present as the dispute in question is likely to have connections with one or more national legal orders, as well as the institutional legal order. When a dispute has connections with multiple orders, how PIL allocates regulatory authority to each order has attracted slightly different approaches,[82] although the goal is always to create jurisdiction for the court which is most closely connected to

79 Ibid, 86.

80 Ibid.

81 Mills (n 19), 195.

82 As Lord Goff observed in *Airbus Industrie v Patel* [1999] 1 AC 119, 131–2: 'On the continent of Europe, in the early days of the European Community, the essential need was seen to be to avoid any such clash between member States of the same community. A system, developed by distinguished scholars, was embodied in the Brussels Convention, under which jurisdiction is allocated on the basis of well-defined rules. This system achieves its purpose, but at a price. The price is rigidity, and rigidity can be productive of injustice. … In the common law world, the situation is precisely the opposite. There is, so to speak, a jungle of separate, broadly based, jurisdictions all over the world. In England, for example, jurisdiction is founded on the presence of the defendant within the jurisdiction, and in certain specified (but widely drawn) circumstances on a power to serve the defendant with process outside the jurisdiction. But the potential excesses of common law jurisdictions are generally curtailed by the adoption of the principle of forum non conveniens – a self-denying ordinance under which the court will stay (or dismiss) proceedings in favour of another clearly more appropriate forum.'

the dispute at hand. Not too dissimilar from the public international law basis of jurisdiction, the well-accepted connecting factors in PIL hone in on (a) consent or submission to jurisdiction as well as (b) territoriality. The latter is founded on the presence of the defendant on the territory of the legal order of the adjudicating forum, or the existence of a territorial connection between the subject matter of the dispute and the legal order in which the adjudicating court is based. Consent-based jurisdiction and jurisdiction based on territoriality form the strongest connecting factors in PIL. However, PIL can also allow for the presence of jurisdiction based on proximity through (c) state interests, and (d) exorbitant jurisdiction (which is controversial).[83]

(A) CONSENT 'Consent' is a well-recognised basis of jurisdiction in PIL. Where a respondent to a claim submits to the jurisdiction of a national court, there is little controversy that the court would possess adjudicative jurisdiction to determine the claim in question. As Michaels observes:

> [C]onsent is least problematical when the defendant submits to the jurisdiction during litigation. A defendant can consent to the jurisdiction either explicitly or implicitly, by pleading on the merits. ... Prior consent, through a choice-of-court agreement, is in principle no different. A defendant who consents to the jurisdiction of a court cannot complain that the exercise of that jurisdiction violates its rights and interests, whether vis-à-vis the court or vis-à-vis the plaintiff.[84]

If an IO submits to the jurisdiction of a national court by initiating proceedings itself, arguing the merits or entering into a choice of forum clause, consent-based jurisdiction would exist at the court where the submission has been made or before the selected forum, as the case may be. Obviously, jurisdiction based on submission can arise regardless of the subject matter of the dispute, except that choice of forum clauses would create jurisdiction specifically in contractual cases. Indeed, the international community has agreed on giving parties significant autonomy in choosing a court that may be approached to resolve a transnational civil or commercial dispute between

83 Indeed, exercise of extraterritorial civil jurisdiction has given rise to much controversy and debate. For a comprehensive analysis, see International Bar Association, 'Report of the Task Force on Extraterritorial Jurisdiction' (IBA, Legal Practice Division, 2008); the trend in jurisdictions such as the United States (a significant centre for transnational litigation) is a presumption against extraterritorial civil jurisdiction: see, for example, *Kiobel v Royal Dutch Petroleum Co.* (2013) 569 US 108, No 10-1491; *Morrison v National Australia Bank* (2010) 561 US 247, No 08-1191; and for a claim raised by an IO, see *RJR Nabisco Inc. v European Community* (2016) 579 US, No 15-138.

84 Michaels (n 4), 18.

them. For example, the provisions of the 2005 Hague Choice of Court Convention[85] (Choice of Court Convention) implements a robust jurisdiction and recognition and enforcement regime where parties have entered into an exclusive choice of forum clause in their contracts.[86] Where such a forum selection clause exists, the selected court is to take jurisdiction regardless of whether the dispute has a territorial connection, and the resulting judgment must be enforced by the courts of a contracting state.[87] The Choice of Court Convention aims to realise party expectations, and in doing so promotes the principle of 'party autonomy', being a concept that has perhaps assumed the character of a connecting factor in its own right.[88]

Where consent-based jurisdiction can be established, how IO immunities impact the exercise of adjudicative jurisdiction already deserves a comment. Where IO immunities do not exist because the impugned activity is commercial in nature, or taking jurisdiction does not impede the independence of an IO, consent-based jurisdiction should operate in its normal way and IO immunities are irrelevant.[89] However, where IO immunities are engaged, the issue becomes somewhat complex and it must be determined whether consent-based jurisdiction amounts to a waiver of immunities. On one approach, consent to jurisdiction should not be considered to automatically waive immunities unless an IO expressly says so. However, this approach brings about undesirable outcomes. It would be highly unfair to a claimant if an IO freely submits to jurisdiction, putting the claimant through the expense of pursuing their claim, and only to later raise immunities as a procedural bar. This approach would undermine party expectations.

If consent to jurisdiction is established, the sensible course is thus to consider IO immunities waived.[90] Thus, if an IO initiates a proceeding in

85 Convention on Choice of Court Agreements (opened for signature 30 June 2005, entered into force 1 October 2015) 44 ILM 1294 (Choice of Court Convention).

86 See, ibid, art 1(1). Articles 1(2) and (3) of the Choice of Court Convention create a broad scope. However, as a sign of protection of the weaker party, it does not apply in employment cases: Article 2(1)(b).

87 See, ibid, Article 5 of the Choice of Court Convention (the taking of jurisdiction); and Article 8 (on recognition and enforcement).

88 For a discussion on party autonomy in PIL and how it should be seen as consistent with the rise of the individual in public international law, see generally, R Gulati, 'Resolving Dual and Multiple Nationality Disputes in a Globalized World' (2014) 28 Journal of Immigration, Asylum and Nationality 1, 27–45, 41–2; for a recent work on the issue, see A Mills, *Party Autonomy in Private International Law* (Cambridge University Press 2018).

89 See Chapter 4 for a discussion on IO immunities.

90 For a discussion of waiver and submission to jurisdiction by IOs, see E Chukwuemeke Okeke, *Jurisdictional Immunities of States and International Organizations* (Oxford University Press 2018), 313–18.

the courts of a particular state, submission is readily established, and the IO cannot later seek to undermine the jurisdiction of the courts of that state.[91] If an IO submits to jurisdiction by arguing on the merits, IO immunities should be deemed waived.[92] Similarly, where an IO enters into a choice of forum agreement, consent-based jurisdiction is established, with immunities inoperable.[93] And where an arbitration clause exists, a relevant national court ought to possess supervisory jurisdiction over the conduct of the arbitration or else the arbitration clause can be rendered ineffective.[94]

In sum, consent-based jurisdiction at the national level exists and ought to be exercised where an IO initiates proceedings; contests the merits; enters into a choice of forum clause; or otherwise expressly waives its immunities. In practice, consent-based jurisdiction can be difficult to establish because courts tend to require an IO's unequivocal submission to jurisdiction, making it difficult to establish waiver.[95] Moreover, it does not appear that IOs tend to select national courts as a forum of choice in their contractual arrangements. Even though national courts can take jurisdiction over an IO on the basis of consent, other bases of jurisdiction may be of more relevance in practice.

(B) TERRITORIALITY Territoriality is the principal connecting factor in PIL, just like it is in public international law. The location of the parties, the subject matter of a dispute or both of these can create a territorial link for jurisdiction to exist.[96] How territoriality manifests in PIL is neatly surmised by Michaels in the following terms:

> Territoriality is an important – for many, the dominant – basis of jurisdiction. The most important territorial connection in the law of jurisdiction is a party's domicile ... or its habitual residence. In the common law, mere presence in the jurisdiction is sufficient as a ground for jurisdiction. Many

91 Ibid, 314.

92 However, appearance before a court just to contest jurisdiction does not amount to a waiver: see *United States Lines Inc v World Health Organization* (30 September 1983, Intermediate Appellate Court, Fourth Civil Cases Division) 107 ILR 182.

93 See *Standard Chartered Bank v International Tin Council* [1986] 3 ALL ER 257, 25 Int'L Leg Mat 650.

94 The limited number of cases on point support the conclusion that an arbitration clause amounts to submission in any related proceeding before a court: see *French Court of Appeal* (19 June 1998, Paris) Revue de l'Arbitrage 343; and *International Tin Council v Amalgamet* (1988, Supreme Court of New York) 138 Misc 2d 383; 524 NYS 2d 971; but see *Groupement d'Enterprises Fougerolle v CERN* (21 December 1992, Swiss Federal Tribunal) [1996] 102 ILR 209 (where a Swiss court did not imply a waiver based on the presence of an arbitration clause).

95 See, *World Bank Group v Wallace* [2016] SCC 15, paras 90–1.

96 Michaels (n 4), 19.

bases of specific jurisdiction are also based on a certain place – the place of conduct or of injury for torts, the place of entering into a contract or of performance for contracts, and so on.[97]

Territorial jurisdiction in PIL may accordingly be divided into general or personal jurisdiction, and specific or subject matter jurisdiction. General jurisdiction is 'party-related and is comprehensive – it exists, untechnically spoken, at the defendant's home'.[98] Different legal systems take somewhat distinct approaches to determine the defendant's 'home' for jurisdictional purposes. It may be based on the presence of the defendant on the territory of the concerned state, even where such presence is fleeting,[99] based on the defendant's domicile,[100] or another criteria such as habitual residence.[101] On the other hand, subject matter jurisdiction exists where the substance of the dispute is territorially connected to the legal order of the court whose jurisdiction is invoked. For example, jurisdiction in tort would usually exist at the place of injury, or place where damage was sustained; in respect of contract, the place where the contract was made, the breach of contract occurred or the place of performance of the obligation allegedly not performed;[102] in respect of property, the place where moveable or immovable property is located; and so on.[103]

The most solid basis of civil jurisdiction exists when suit is brought at the defendant's home.[104] Not only does this rule respect the territorial limitations to jurisdiction in general, but it also ensures that the respondent to a claim does not have to defend claims in distant forums. Accordingly, if an IO is sued

97 Ibid, 19. There is some controversy whether mere 'presence' on the territory can be a sufficient basis to constitute an adequate territorial nexus. However, 'presence' is a well-accepted basis for the existence of adjudicative jurisdiction (in common law states). Nonetheless, any excesses may be dealt with at the stage where a court uses discretionary criteria relevant to determine whether jurisdiction should be exercised in a given case: Mills (n 19), 201.

98 Michaels (n 4), 19.

99 Manifestations of 'presence' include 'resident', or 'at home' in the territory: Mills (n 19), 202; however, personal jurisdiction established just based on the defendant's fleeting presence on the forum's territory is criticised: for an interesting perspective, see generally, Andrea D Coles-Bjerre, 'A Linguistic Critique of Tag Jurisdiction: Justice Scalia and the Zombie Metonymy' (2018) 68 American University Law Review 1, 2–66.

100 This approach is taken within the EU. See, 'Jurisdiction' (*European Justice*) (2020) <https://e-justice.europa.eu/content_jurisdiction-85-en> accessed 1 May 2021.

101 See generally, P Rogerson, 'Habitual Residence: The New Domicile?' (2000) 49 International and Comparative Law Quarterly 1, 86–107.

102 See European Parliament and Council Regulation (EU) 1215/2012 of 12 December 2012 on Jurisdiction and the Recognition and Enforcement of Judgments in Civil and Commercial Matters (Recast Brussels I Regulation), art 7(1)(a).

103 Michaels (n 4), 19; Mills (n 19), 202.

104 Mills (n 19), 202.

at its home, it can hardly claim unfairness. Locating an IO's home is thus important for jurisdictional purposes. However, IOs do not have their own territory. As Judge Ago pointed out:

> [An] international organization is like a State, a subject of international law, but it is one which enjoys limited international legal capacity, and in particular, unlike a State, it is a subject of law which lacks all territorial basis. Its 'establishment' in the territory of a given State is therefore a condition sine qua non of its actually functioning as an organization, carrying on its activities and fulfilling its objects and purposes.[105]

To determine an IO's presence for the purposes of establishing general jurisdiction, they are best treated as analogous to body corporates. An IO's presence may thus be determined with reference to factors such as where an IO has its statutory seat, is incorporated, has its central administration or has its principal place of business.[106] Adapting this list to IOs, the headquarters of an IO would clearly be an IO's place of central administration and principal place of business for that is where it is geographically located and primarily conducts its work. Thus, if an IO is sued at the place where it is headquartered, or even where it has a substantial operation, a court located in that place would plainly possess general jurisdiction over the IO.[107]

It is also important to observe that PIL calibrates its rules on jurisdiction with considerable nuance. In some instances, to protect the weaker party in a particular relationship, PIL allows for enhanced jurisdictional choice to the claimant. For example, in employment claims, an employee may be permitted to commence proceedings against the employer at the place where they actually perform their work as well.[108] This should not be considered as an undermining of the territorial principle, but evidence of PIL's flexibility to calibrate its rules to ensure access to justice for the weaker party.[109] Conversely, choice can be restricted where the connection between the subject matter of the dispute and a given jurisdiction is especially strong.

105 *Interpretation of the Agreement of 25 March 1951 between the World Health Organization and Egypt* (Advisory Opinion) [1980] ICJ Rep 73, 155 (separate opinion Judge Ago); also see F Morgenstern, *Legal Problems of International Organizations* (Grotius 1986), 5.

106 See, Choice of Court Convention (n 85), art 4(2).

107 See, for example, *Steinberg* (D.C. Cir. 1981) 217 US App DC, 672 F2d 927.

108 See Recast Brussels I Regulation (n 102), arts 21 and 22.

109 L Merrett, *Employment Contracts in Private International Law* (Oxford University Press 2011), 69, 87–91. As the author notes, the definition of an employee is to be understood broadly, focusing on the substance of the relationship, public and private sector distinctions are now largely irrelevant to the applicability of PIL, and finally, almost all employment disputes are classified as civil disputes to which PIL would apply.

For instance, generally speaking, where a dispute is in respect of property, the courts of the place where that property is located would possess exclusive jurisdiction regardless of where the parties are located.[110] What is more, there will be circumstances where jurisdiction can be founded both on general and specific grounds. In a tort case, the claimant may commence proceedings at the home of the defendant, or the place where the harmful event occurred.[111] And in a contract case, absent a choice of forum clause, a claimant may sue at the defendant's home, or the place where the contractual obligation alleged to have been breached was to be performed.[112]

The aforementioned rules on adjudicative jurisdiction should apply in claims against IOs in their usual way. If an IO is sued where it is headquartered, has a substantial operation or at a place where a court's subject matter jurisdiction is established, a strong basis of civil jurisdiction would exist. However, one technical issue of much practical significance concerns the mechanics of how an IO is notified of proceedings against it. In some jurisdictions, the service of documents on a defendant actually preconditions personal jurisdiction.[113] Even if effective service does not precondition jurisdiction, it is an important procedural step for it ensures due process.[114] While the preferred approach should be that service ought not to impact the existence of jurisdiction as this results in a victory of form over substance,[115] the reality is that the lack of effective service can result in a claim being procedurally quelled.[116] These procedural challenges are brought into sharp focus in claims against IOs.

For example, US courts vacated a proceeding against OPEC, which successfully argued that service of process via international mail should be set aside as it was not undertaken consistently with the relevant Austrian law as it applied to OPEC, with those rules requiring that service either be undertaken through diplomatic channels or based on

110 Recast Brussels I Regulation (n 102), art 24.

111 Ibid, arts 4(1) and 7(2).

112 Ibid, arts 4(1) and 7(1).

113 See SW Teppler, 'The Continuing Relevance of Process Servers in the 21st Century' (2011) 11 National Law Review 121 <www.natlawreview.com/article/continuing-relevance-personal-service-process> accessed 1 May 2021.

114 See Convention of 15 November 1965 on the Service Abroad of Judicial and Extrajudicial Documents in Civil or Commercial Matters (HCCH Service Convention), art 15, which highlights that the purpose of service is to notify the defendant of a claim against them as opposed to a precondition to jurisdiction.

115 Ibid.

116 C Ryngaert, 'Domestic Legal Remedies against OPEC' in A Reinisch (ed), *Challenging Acts of International Organizations Before National Courts* (Oxford University Press 2010), 249.

OPEC's consent.[117] More recently, in an employment claim against the Caribbean Development Bank, where the IO first accepted service of documents at its premises, seemingly without any protest, but later returned them to the claimant's counsel, the High Court of Barbados decided that service was not effected lawfully because it contravened the inviolability of the organisation's premises provided for in the applicable headquarters agreement.[118] Such findings, if more widely adopted, may create an incentive for IOs to avoid service of judicial process using whatever means possible. This would result in a sorry state of affairs and undermines the dignity of the international system. Fortunately, recent jurisprudence from UK courts indicates that mere service of process in a materially similar circumstance did not violate international law. Holding that service by post did not violate the terms of the Vienna Convention[119] concerning the inviolability of diplomatic premises, Lord Sumption stated:

> The present question is whether there is an immunity from service, or from certain modes of service, implicit in the inviolability of a diplomat's Personal and private residence. This immunity is distinct from and additional to his immunity from jurisdiction. If it applies, then articles 29 and 30 of the [Vienna] Convention, being unqualified, must prevent service by post in all proceedings whether or not there is any jurisdictional immunity in respect of them. … The person of a diplomatic agent is violated if an agent of the receiving state detains him, impedes his movement or subjects him to any personal restriction or indignity. It is arguable that personal service on a diplomatic agent would do that, although it is not an argument that needs to be considered here. Premises are violated if an agent of the state enters them without consent or impedes access to or from the premises or normal use of them. … The delivery by post of a claim form does not do any of these things. It simply serves to give notice to the defendant that proceedings have been brought against him, so that he can defend his interests, for example by raising his immunity if he has any. The mere conveying of information, however unwelcome, by post to the defendant, is not a violation of the premises to which the letter is delivered. It is not a trespass. It does not affront his dignity or affect his right to enter or leave or use his home. It does of course

117 See, *Prewitt Enters Inc v Organization of Petroleum Exporting Countries* (11th Cir 2003) 353 F3d 916, 927, where a US appellate court stated that 'Austrian law clearly provides protection to OPEC as an international organization from all methods of service of process without its consent, and also requires that any service of process from abroad should be effected through Austrian authorities.'

118 *Mark Taitt v Caribbean Development Bank* (2019, High Court) CV No 1467 of 2017.

119 Vienna Convention of the Law of Treaties (opened for signature 23 May 1969, entered into force 27 January 1980) 1155 UNTS 331, 8 ILM 679 (Vienna Convention).

> start time running for subsequent procedural steps and may lead to a default if no action is taken. But so far as this is objectionable, it can only be because there is a relevant immunity from jurisdiction. It is not because the proceedings were brought to the diplomatic agent's attention by post. Otherwise the same objection would apply to any mode of service which starts time running, including service through diplomatic channels as proposed by the Secretary of State.[120]

In the end, if an IO does not accept service at its premises, substituted forms of notification ought to be permissible. This naturally includes service via post, with some PIL regimes even allowing service through social media where no other mode of service has proven effective.[121] Evidently, effective modes of legal cooperation between IO and national legal orders are absent. Normally, in cross-border civil proceedings, internationally accepted standards of PIL have created a network of state-based central authorities that facilitate the efficient cross-border service of documents, largely replacing the clunky diplomatic procedures historically used.[122] Such a system has not been so far extended to secure cooperation between IOs and states. Ideally, such cooperation should be achieved as a matter of priority. In the meantime, if needed, by allowing for substituted modes of service, national courts can ensure that their territorial jurisdiction is not undermined by a mere technicality, and at the same time, IOs are properly notified of the case put against them.

(C) STATE INTERESTS A national court may also take jurisdiction in a civil case if it involves the pursuit of an important state or governmental interest. This basis of jurisdiction has a positive and negative component. As has been explained:

> Positively . . . a state may base its jurisdiction on the desire to make sure that particularly important regulatory interests are enforced. But state interests can also have a negative impact: another state's strong regulatory interests may be a reason for a court to decline exercising its jurisdiction. In reality, it appears that courts are more willing to assert jurisdiction on the basis of their own state's regulatory interests than to decline its exercise in view of such regulatory interests elsewhere. Indeed, such foreign regulatory interests can frequently be accommodated through application of the foreign state's laws.[123]

120 *Reyes v Al-Malki & Anor* [2017] UKSC 61, paras 14–16.

121 See the discussion in E Davis, 'Social Media: A Good Alternative, for Alternative Service of Process' (2020) 52 Case Western Reserve Journal of International Law 1.

122 See the regime created by the HCCH Service Convention (n 114).

123 Michaels (n 4), 21.

In other words, the pursuit of a state or governmental interest also constitutes a distinct connecting factor in PIL. If jurisdiction is taken to pursue a state's regulatory interests, then the choice of law determination can readily accommodate an intrusion into another legal order's regulatory authority, assuming such an intrusion exists. For instance, there is evidence of national courts adjudicating claims against IOs even where the subject matter was squarely public in character, that is, tax law, but the rules applied to resolve the claim were the law of the IO.[124] In recent times, courts have also engaged in indirect forms of judicial review of administrative conduct by IOs. Impactful jurisprudence has emerged out of cases impugning IO decisions listing individuals on UN sanctions lists.[125] In such cases, states that are asked to implement IO decisions have been required to remedy the harm caused to private parties that are placed on a particular UN sanctions list arbitrarily, and where fair trial at the institutional level is denied.[126] Thus, administrative decisions that can ultimately be traced back to an IO are now increasingly being subjected to judicial review domestically.

The presence of national jurisdiction to adjudicate claims impugning institutional decisions harming private parties can be founded on a state's interest to

124 See *CECA c faillite des 'Acciaierie e Ferriere di Bogaro' SpA* (No 4621, 15 June 1968) (translation in excerpts in Journal des Tribunaux, Brussels), 403–5, where an Italian court took jurisdiction over the then European Coal and Steel Community against the bankrupt estate of an Italian steel company, applying Community law to the dispute; also see jurisprudence discussed in Seyersted (n 49), 535–7.

125 For a comprehensive discussion on the UN Security Council Sanctions regime and issues of due process in terms of access to justice for individuals impacted by UNSC sanctions, see generally, D Hovell, *The Power of Process: The Value of Due Process in Security Council Sanctions Decision-Making* (Oxford University Press 2016); for recent jurisprudence, including a potential 'arbitrariness' standard of judicial review in claims against IO decision-making, see *Al-Dulimi and Montana Management Inc v Switzerland* App no 5809/08 (ECtHR, 21 June 2016), paras 52 and 146–7; See further, *Nada v Switzerland judgment* App no 10593/08 (ECtHR, 12 September 2012); and the much discussed Joined Cases C 584/10 P, C 593/10 P and C 595/10 P *Commission and Others v Kadi* (18 July 2013, ECJ Grand Chamber) (Kadi litigation) and the case of Joined Cases C-402/05 P and C-415/05 P *Yassin Abdullah Kadi and Al Barakaat International Foundation v Council of the European Union and Commission of the European Communities* (3 September 2008, ECJ Grand Chamber) ECR 2008 I-06351. For a similar finding in a very different context (permissibility of judicial review of decisions of European Schools before German courts), see the English summary of the decision of the German Constitutional Court: 'Effective protection of fundamental rights must be guaranteed where sovereign powers are transferred to supranational' 2 BvR 1961/09 (Order of 24 July 2018, Press Release No 70/2018 of 29 August 2018) (Bundesverfassungsgericht, Germany) <www.bundesverfassungsgericht.de/SharedDocs/Pressemitteilungen/EN/2018/bvg18-070.html;jsessionid=DE5A5EF5D7B6193F832372CC08F0B859.1_cid393> accessed 30 April 2021. For a discussion about the judicial review of IO actions generally and the difficulties encountered, see generally, A Reinisch, *Challenging Acts of International Organizations Before National Courts* (Oxford University Press 2010).

126 Also see the discussion in Chapter 1.

ensure compliance with its own human rights obligations, namely, the provision of a fair trial for individuals who suffer the consequences of IO conduct in that particular state. Indeed, such a significant state interest could amount to the imposition of a jurisdictional duty to ensure access to justice for the victims of IO conduct.[127] Crucially, this basis of jurisdiction would allow national courts to even cautiously take jurisdiction in claims of an administrative law nature if doing so would realise access to justice.[128] Ultimately, whether a civil claim arises in tort, contract or for that matter as a result of the exercise of public or administrative power impacting on privately held rights, the question of adjudicative jurisdiction, especially in its prescriptive sense, remains unaffected per se. It is a completely different thing that a court may choose to defer the exercise of jurisdiction to the courts of the legal order where the administrative act impugned took place purely for reasons of comity.[129]

(D) EXORBITANT JURISDICTION The role that access to justice plays in establishing civil jurisdiction is becoming so central that some national courts are starting to take exorbitant forms of jurisdiction to ensure access to justice even where traditional kinds of connecting factors are absent. A final basis of civil jurisdiction in PIL is referred to as jurisdiction on extraordinary bases or exorbitant jurisdiction. Examples of such jurisdiction include jurisdiction based only on the claimant's nationality, jurisdiction based on the presence of assets belonging to the defendant and general jurisdiction based on a corporation 'doing business'.[130] Exorbitant jurisdiction is highly claimant friendly and may be motivated to ensure access to court for the plaintiff.[131] As has been pointed out:

> [E]xorbitant jurisdiction is closely related to so-called jurisdiction of necessity. Under this doctrine, a court may, exceptionally, assume jurisdiction even absent the normal connecting factors if this is necessary to provide the

[127] See Mills (n 19), 216 and 224.

[128] See the discussion in Chapter 1.

[129] Although in cases of an administrative law nature, where judicial review of a decision made by a public authority is sought, significant 'respect and restraint' is shown towards the legal order whose laws are impugned; and deference may be given to the jurisdiction of the courts located in the territory of the place whose administrative decision-making is challenged: see Fox and Webb (n 18), 85; and '[s]uch an attitude is dictated not by a rule of international law but by respect for the legislative jurisdiction of the other state because of its substantial connection with the subject matter': see A Lenhoff, 'International Law and Rules on International Jurisdiction' (1964) 50 Cornell Law Review <http://scholarship.law.cornell.edu/dr/vol50/iss172> accessed 30 April 2021, 5, 7.

[130] Michaels (n 4), 20–1.

[131] C Nwapi, 'Jurisdiction by Necessity and the Regulation of the Transnational Corporate Actor' (2014) 30 Utrecht Journal of International and European Law 24, 31.

> plaintiff with access to court. . . . Such necessity is thought to exist especially if no other competent court is available, either because other courts do not have or will not exercise jurisdiction, or because these other courts are incapable for other reasons of providing justice.[132]

Jurisdiction based on the ground of forum of necessity or *forum necessitatis* aims to prevent denials of justice at all costs.[133] Where a claimant does not have access to any court except the one seized, where the guarantees considered indispensable to the proper administration of justice can be realised or the plaintiff has received an unjust judgment elsewhere,[134] a national court may take jurisdiction regardless of the absence of traditional connecting factors. Such grounds of jurisdiction at the national level can equally be resorted to in claims against IOs. For instance, French courts took jurisdiction over an IO based on the nationality of the claimant where the organisation was not present in France.[135] In that case, a French national working for the AfDB sued the organisation for breach of his employment rights where the latter had not provided him with an alternative DRM.[136] Had French courts not taken jurisdiction, the claimant would have suffered a denial of justice. The need to take jurisdiction at the national level was compelling, and the court was ready to find the claimant's French nationality a sufficiently strong link that justified its competence.

Just because jurisdiction may be exorbitant, it does not follow that it is invariably contrary to the limits placed by public international law, and thus impermissible. For example, even though civil jurisdiction based on the claimant's nationality may be considered exorbitant, it roughly corresponds to the passive personality basis of jurisdiction in public international law.[137] The reason why exorbitant civil jurisdiction is problematic is not because it offends international law, but it can create significant unfairness for the defendant who may potentially be required to defend claims before any national court in the world.

Compared to consent, territoriality and even state interest-based jurisdiction, exorbitant jurisdiction does not provide for an overly strong basis of civil jurisdiction due to the absence of traditional connecting factors. However,

[132] Michaels (n 4), 20–1; see, for example, Federal Act on Private International Law Act (18 December 1987, in effect as from 1 January 2017) (1988 BBl I 5 as amended), art 3, para 28(1) Austrian JN; Civil Code of Quebec (SQ 1991, c 64), art 3136.

[133] See, generally for the development of this doctrine, Nwapi (n 131).

[134] Mills (n 19), 212.

[135] *African Development Bank v X* (25 January 2005) 04-41012, ILDC 778 (FR 2005), para 4.

[136] See, Chapter 4.

[137] Fox and Webb (n 18).

resort to exorbitant jurisdiction is not impermissible in international law, especially in its prescriptive sense. Indeed, the rationale behind jurisdiction of necessity has been acknowledged at the institutional level.[138] Reliance on this basis of jurisdiction is nevertheless to be avoided due to the unfairness it may cause to the defendant. Moreover, if jurisdiction of necessity is successfully invoked, there is always a risk that securing the cross-border enforcement of a judgment rendered pursuant to an exercise of exorbitant jurisdiction could prove difficult, making its use fraught. Jurisdiction of necessity should thus only be relied on where absolutely no other forum is available to a claimant to access justice.

5.4.1.3 A Jurisdictional Scheme in Claims against IOs

Based on the preceding discussion, three brief conclusions are drawn. First, the existence of civil jurisdiction should focus on PIL as opposed to public international law. This is because it is PIL that provides the detailed rules on establishing jurisdiction in civil cases. Second, whether a claim against an IO is in tort, contract, administrative law or concerns any other type of action that impacts privately held rights, PIL's connecting factors help decide issues of competent court. Put differently, a national court is capable of adjudicating all types of claims raised by private persons against IOs. Finally, the rules on civil jurisdiction should not only help realise justice for the claimant, but be fair to the IO too. If IOs are asked to defend claims before distant forums, it would undermine their functioning. Therefore, consent, general and subject matter jurisdiction based on territoriality, as well as the state interest ground of jurisdiction, can be said to constitute strong bases of jurisdiction. Where such grounds of jurisdiction are present, a national court should consider itself competent. Exorbitant jurisdiction should only be exercised reluctantly and as a matter of last resort. While all those bases of jurisdiction can establish jurisdiction at the national level, it does not mean that it should always be exercised.

5.4.2 *The Exercise of Jurisdiction: Locating the Proper Place*

It is one thing to possess adjudicative jurisdiction, and yet another to exercise it. I argue that a national court must exercise jurisdiction over an IO as a secondary intervention. This, of course, assumes that civil jurisdiction exists consistently with the principles stated in Section 5.4.1. The rules on IO

[138] See Chapter 3, Section 3.2.1.1(a).

immunities impact the precise circumstances in which jurisdiction should actually be exercised, and it is those circumstances that I clarify in the discussion that follows. First, it is important to point out that IO immunities do not remove jurisdiction, they just impact whether or not jurisdiction should be exercised in a given case (Section 5.4.2.1). Second, in any claim against an IO, national courts continue to possess civil jurisdiction assuming the relevant connecting factor can be established. As a result, both national and institutional DRMs possess concurrent jurisdiction to determine claims against IOs. As the national and institutional legal orders are co-equal for PIL's purposes, it is perfectly justified to use PIL techniques to allocate regulatory authority in terms of which court should exercise jurisdiction. The idea is that if multiple courts possess the competence to decide a case, only one of them should exercise jurisdiction to avoid the risk of parallel proceedings, inconsistent judgments and inefficiency in the administration of justice (Section 5.4.2.2). Finally, the chapter will discuss how access to justice can be used as a jurisdictional pivot to allocate regulatory authority between national and institutional DRMs (Section 5.4.2.3).

5.4.2.1 IO Immunities Do Not Impact the Presence or Absence of Adjudicative Jurisdiction

A significant degree of confusion still exists with regard to the impact IO immunities have on jurisdiction. The view that immunities remove or impact the very existence of jurisdiction is inaccurate. All that IO immunities do is to present a procedural bar to the exercise of jurisdiction that may otherwise validly exist. In other words, jurisdiction either exists or it does not, with immunities only impacting on its exercise. As the ICJ observed in the *Arrest Warrant* case,[139] without the existence of jurisdiction, the question of immunities will not even arise. The Court explained:

> [T]he rules governing the jurisdiction of national courts must be carefully distinguished from those governing jurisdictional immunities: jurisdiction does not imply absence of immunity, while absence of immunity does not imply jurisdiction.[140]

The fact that immunities do not impact the presence of jurisdiction has also been confirmed in cases involving IOs. In a claim against INTERPOL where

139 *Case Concerning the Arrest Warrant of 11 April 2000 (Democratic Republic of the Congo v Belgium)* [2002] ICJ Rep 24 (*Arrest Warrant Case*), para 46.

140 Ibid, para 59; also see *Jurisdictional Immunities of the State (Germany v Italy, Greece Intervening)* (2012) ICJ Rep 2012, p 99 (*Jurisdictional Immunities*), para 93.

the personal jurisdiction of US courts was contested, Circuit Judge Ginsburg (as she then was) commented:

> [W]ith regard to Interpol's arguments concerning sovereign immunity, the court found that its ruling was on the question of personal jurisdiction, of which immunity was not a facet. Where an appellate court simply rules on the question of personal jurisdiction, immunity is not a facet of that issue. Interpol also vigorously argues various issues of immunity. As my colleagues have noted, this action has yet to proceed on to the point where these may become relevant, and no question of official or sovereign immunity was tendered on appeal. We ruled simply on the question of personal jurisdiction, and it is generally accepted that immunity is not a facet of that issue.[141]

Similarly, in a contractual claim against certain NATO entities, where the respondent IO contended that its immunities meant that Dutch courts did not possess civil jurisdiction,[142] the CJEU said that reliance upon immunity 'does not affect the criteria for determining the international jurisdiction of a court'.[143] Equally, just because jurisdiction exists, it does not follow that immunities will not present a procedural bar to its exercise. Once jurisdiction is established, it is for the adjudicating court to determine whether immunities exist in a particular case.

5.4.2.2 National Courts Must Decide Questions of IO Immunity

Surely, the determination of whether IO immunities can be upheld cannot be abdicated to the IO itself.[144] It is absurd to ask a defendant whether a court should take jurisdiction over it for it is unlikely that the latter will ever agree. Similarly, while the views of the host state may be given weight,[145] it is ultimately up to the adjudicating court to decide whether it will exercise its

141 *Steinberg* (DC Cir 1981) 217 US App DC, 672 F2d 927. In the United Kingdom, the House of Lords have treated immunities as a substantive bar to jurisdiction: see *Holland v Lampen-Wolfe* [2002] 119 ILR 367, para 53 (per Lord Millett); however, that approach was not followed in *Jones v Ministry of the Interior of Saudi Arabia and Lieutenant Colonel Abdul Aziz* Case no A2 2003/2155 [2004] EWCA Civ 1394, para 81; the rule that immunities are only a procedural bar to the exercise of jurisdiction was also confirmed in the case of *Jones and Others v The United Kingdom* App nos 34356/06 and 40528/06 (ECtHR, 14 January 2014), para 164.

142 *Shape v Supreme* (n 53), para 21.

143 Ibid, para 77.

144 Although, the IO view should be properly taken into account, see *Difference Relating to Immunity from Legal Process of a Special Rapporteur of the Commission on Human Rights* (Advisory Opinion) [1999] ICJ Rep 62, ICGJ 204 (ICJ 1999), para 61.

145 See *Georges v United Nations* (US 2nd Cir, August 2018) No 15-455-cv, 12, where the court used the language of 'great weight'.

jurisdiction in a particular case.[146] The preferred approach to this question has been taken by the Supreme Court of the Philippines in *Liang v The People*,[147] which concerned a claim of defamation by an employee of the ADB against certain of its officials. The court disregarded the executive certificate put forward by the Department of Foreign Affairs of the Philippines on ADB's behalf, and held that no immunities existed on the facts of the case. It remarked:

> [C]ourts cannot blindly adhere and take on its face the communication from the DFA that petitioner is covered by any immunity. The DFAs determination that a certain person is covered by immunity is only preliminary which has no binding effect in courts. … The needed inquiry in what capacity petitioner was acting at the time of the alleged utterances requires for its resolution evidentiary basis that has yet to be presented at the proper time.[148]

While the aforementioned statement was made in the context of the scope of official immunity, the same logic ought to apply to the determination of the scope of IO immunities as well. When national courts adjudicate on whether immunities ought to be upheld, they must do this cost-effectively and efficiently. In general, a national court will have an 'obligation to deal with the question of immunity from legal process as a preliminary issue to be decided expeditiously *ex limine litis*'.[149] Access to justice is seriously undermined if excessive costs have to be incurred at this preliminary stage.[150] Lord Neuberger has aptly observed:

> [H]earings concerning the issue of appropriate forum should not involve masses of documents, long witness statements, detailed analysis of the issues, and long argument. It is self-defeating if, in order to determine whether an action should proceed to trial in this jurisdiction, the parties prepare for and conduct a hearing which approaches the putative trial itself, in terms of effort, time and cost. There is also a real danger that, if the hearing is an expensive and time-consuming exercise, it will be used by a richer party to wear down a poorer party, or by a party with a weak case to prevent, or at least to discourage, a party with a strong case from enforcing its rights. Quite apart

146 See Chukwuemeke Okeke (n 90), 292.

147 *Liang v People of the Philippines* (28 January 2000) GR No 125865 <http://sc.judiciary.gov.ph/jurisprudence/2000/jan2000/125865.html> accessed 30 April 2021.

148 Ibid.

149 *Difference Relating to Immunity from Legal Process of a Special Rapporteur of the Commission of Human Rights* (Advisory Opinion) (29 April 1999) ICJ Rep 1999, 62, para 67; *Jurisdictional Immunities* (n 140), para 82.

150 See especially the impact of costs on access to justice, Chapter 3, Section 3.3.2; also see the relevant discussion in Chapter 2.

from this, it is simply disproportionate for parties to incur costs, often running to hundreds of thousands of pounds each, and to spend many days in court, on such a hearing.[151]

When confronted with a claim against an IO, to ensure that the right to access justice is not undermined due to disproportionate cost implications, and that too on preliminary questions, the adjudicating DRM must thus make a considered but speedy determination whether immunities can be upheld. What is more, a claim to immunity should not be approached with a generous view as to its scope.[152] Often, cursory and trite statements referring to an IO's so-called functional independence are made to justify upholding broad IO immunities.[153] This is unfortunate. It was always the intention that IOs only possess an immunity that is strictly necessary for the performance of its functions.[154] The ILC Special Rapporteur on the relations between states and IOs has said 'functional requirements must be one of the main criteria, if not the only one, used in determining the extent and range of the privileges and immunities that are to be accorded to a given organization. The independence of the organization will thus be safeguarded to the extent necessary for it to perform its functions and accomplish its objectives'.[155]

If the taking of national jurisdiction is unlikely to impede the performance of the specific tasks assigned to an IO, immunities cannot apply.[156] Equally, if the defendant IO has engaged in conduct that is *ultra vires* or outside the scope of its functions, then no immunity may exist in respect of claims arising from such conduct.[157] As such, IOs with limited functions may not require broadly

151 See, *VTB Capital plc v Nutritek International Corp.* [2013] 2 AC 337, paras 82–3; also see *Vedanta Resources PLC v Lungowe* [2019] UKSC 20 (*Vedanta*), para 6.

152 Mills (n 19), 223.

153 See, for example, *Stichting Mothers of Srebrenica and Others v Netherlands and United Nations* (13 April 2012, Supreme Court of the Netherlands) LJN: BW1999; ILDC 1760, para 4.2; in one of the early cases regarding the General Convention, in *Manderlier v Organization of the United Nations and Belgium* (11 May 1966, Brussels Civil Tribunal) Journal des Tribunaux 1966, 721; (1972) 45 ILR 446, a Belgian court held that the General Convention grants a general immunity from jurisdiction and does not limit it to what necessity strictly demands for the fulfilment of the defendant's purposes.

154 KE Boon, 'The United Nations as Good Samaritan: Immunity and Responsibility' (2016) 16 Chicago Journal of International Law 2, 341, 382; see also PHF Bekker, *The Legal Position of Intergovernmental Organizations: A Functional Necessity Analysis of Their Legal Status and Immunities* (Brill 1994).

155 LD Gonzalez, Fourth Report on Relations between States and International Organizations (1989) UN Doc A/CN.4/424 and Corr.1, paras 26–7.

156 See Chapter 4.

157 For example, in *Siedler v Western European Union* (17 September 2003, Appeal Judgment) Journal des Tribunaux 2004; ILDC 53 (BE 2003), para 40, a Belgium court suggested that

framed immunities at all,[158] and where the immunities of IOs with broad mandates are at issue, a careful analysis of the functional scope of their immunities must be undertaken. As was discussed in Chapter 4, so far, courts have shied away from conducting such a nuanced analysis. However, it does not follow that whenever a national court finds that immunities are inapplicable, it has to exercise jurisdiction. Recall that in *Jam*, the US Supreme Court significantly slashed the scope of MDB immunities, limiting them to public acts.[159] Still, due to the alleged lack of a strong territorial connection between the core of the claim and the forum, a District Court in that country has held that:

> [E]ven accepting all of plaintiffs' allegations as true, plaintiffs have not established that this lawsuit is 'based upon' conduct 'carried on' in the United States. . . . Plaintiffs' suit is based upon IFC's failure to ensure that the plant was designed, constructed, and operated with due care so as not to harm plaintiffs' property, health, and way of life. That is the gravamen of the complaint. And plaintiffs have not established that such conduct was carried on in the United States; instead, it was focused in India, where the plant is and the harms occurred . . . the Court will dismiss the complaint for lack of subject matter jurisdiction.[160]

The court's finding may be questioned for, regardless of the connection between the core of the claim and the forum, the claimants sued the IO where it is headquartered, with the strongest basis of civil jurisdiction established.[161] Leaving to one side the correctness of that decision, for the moment, the point of note is that courts have started to closely consider whether the facts of a case warrant upholding immunities. This is a positive sign. In the end, the objective should be to strictly limit the application of IO immunities only to those situations where such immunities properly exist. Doing so will already considerably reduce instances of a denial of justice. When deciding on IO immunities, national courts ought to remind themselves that virtually all

under the functional necessity doctrine an international organisation's immunity could be lifted if the relevant acts of the international organisation were ultra vires.

158 Gonzalez (n 155), para 50, and at para 54 it was stated: 'it should not be forgotten that there are certain international organizations to which it may not be necessary to grant privileges and immunities, even if they have been established by an agreement between States. This would be true of intergovernmental international organizations established in such a form that they can function exclusively as legal entities under the domestic law of the host State'.

159 See the discussion in Chapter 4.

160 *Jam et al. v International Finance Corporation* (14 February 2020) No 15-612 (JDB) (*Jam v IFC*), 20.

161 The decision is probably impacted by the peculiarities of the legislative scheme in the United States: Ibid.

claimants invoke national jurisdiction with one overarching aim only: to access justice. The value now placed on access to justice requires that no more immunities are granted to an IO than are strictly necessary. Mills explains:

> [B]ecause the exercise of jurisdiction was understood to be a discretionary matter of state right, there was no reason why a state might not give more immunity than required under the rules of international law. The development of principles of access to justice, however, requires a state to exercise its jurisdictional powers, and perhaps to expand those jurisdictional powers as a matter of domestic law to encompass internationally permitted grounds for jurisdiction, or even to go beyond traditional territorial . . . based jurisdiction.[162]

The right to access justice is increasingly impacting the law of jurisdiction, affecting its existence as well as its exercise. Granting only those immunities that are strictly necessary under international law is not only desirable, but also a jurisdictional duty that ought to operate at the national level. This rationale applies to claims against IOs too. As has been argued, it is for the national court to decide whether IO immunities in a given situation exist. If the court decides immunities are inapplicable, then it is open for an otherwise competent national court to take jurisdiction. But the analysis cannot end here. Institutional DRMs may also possess jurisdiction to resolve claims against IOs. Which particular court should exercise jurisdiction where more than one competent court exists is a question of central importance.

5.4.2.3 The Concurrent Jurisdiction of National and Institutional Courts

Recall that in Chapter 3, we saw that institutional DRMs may be established by IOs as an attempt to comply with their access to justice obligation as a complement to IO immunities. Thus, there are two sets of courts or DRMs that may concurrently possess jurisdiction to resolve claims against IOs,[163] namely, institutional DRMs, and one or more national courts having civil jurisdiction. The basis on which national courts possess civil jurisdiction over IOs has already been discussed in Section 5.4.1.

DRMs established in the institutional order can also take jurisdiction in claims involving IOs. Usually, IOs do not possess their own territories,[164] so

162 Mills (n 19), 223–4.

163 The fact that national courts possess concurrent jurisdiction with the increasing number of international (and institutional courts) is now well understood: A Nollkaemper, *National Courts and the International Rule of Law* (Oxford University Press 2011), 27–8.

164 In exceptional situations, IOs can for temporary periods possess typically territorial jurisdiction when they become responsible for the administration of certain territories: see the discussion in Seyersted (n 49), 99 (citing the example of the League of Nations' role in the

they lack a territorial basis of jurisdiction. This does not mean that IOs lack the power to create courts within their own legal order. Indeed, IOs have their own independent legal orders that co-exist heterarchically with national legal orders, having the freedom to enact their own dispute resolution infrastructure within the sphere of their overall competence. For example, an IO possesses 'inherent jurisdiction' over its organs and officials.[165] Such inherent control over internal affairs is required to maintain IO independence. That is why IOs create IATs that are empowered to resolve employment claims raised against them.[166]

Moreover, an IO's power to create its own internal justice system is also founded in access to justice considerations. As was discussed in Chapter 1, IOs must create DRMs vested with the jurisdiction to resolve claims raised by third parties against them.[167] Such an obligation is often treaty based and requires IOs to provide for appropriate modes of dispute settlement whenever they impact privately held rights. Because the types of claims falling within the scope of this access to justice obligation are truly broad, institutional DRMs can possess wide-ranging personal and subject matter jurisdiction. Of course, once brought into existence, the specific jurisdictional scheme of each institutional DRM depends on the terms of its founding instrument. At its core, the adjudicative jurisdiction of DRMs located in the institutional order can be explained as being based on the ground of access to justice. Some institutional DRMs have referred to themselves as a 'jurisdiction of necessity' brought into existence given the difficulties private parties face in accessing a court at the national level due to IO immunities.[168] In the end, an IO has the regulatory freedom to create DRMs at the institutional level in virtually every type of claim by every type of claimant impugning its conduct.

The potential existence of adjudicative jurisdiction at an institutional DRM cannot and does not remove the competence of a national court to decide a claim against an IO.[169] Competent national and institutional courts possess adjudicative jurisdiction over claims against IOs simultaneously. When jurisdiction is possessed by multiple courts in distinct legal orders co-existing heterarchically, PIL helps to allocate regulatory authority in terms of which

Saar Basin until 1935, jurisdiction of International River Commissions on navigation and the administration of the UN in some former Italian colonies).

165 See Seyersted (n 49), 120–5.

166 See, Chapter 3.

167 Ibid. Whether such DRMs are created, or what the precise scope of their personal and subject matter jurisdiction is a different thing entirely.

168 Ibid, Section 3.2.1.1(a).

169 Although there is some confusion on the issue created by conflating issues of competent court and choice of law: see Seyersted (n 49), 123.

DRM should exercise its jurisdiction in a given case. Based on certain criteria captured by the doctrine of *forum non conveniens*, PIL helps determine which court should exercise its jurisdiction where more than one DRM possesses adjudicative jurisdiction. This doctrine now uses access to justice as a jurisdictional pivot and should be adopted to decide questions of competent court in claims involving IOs.

5.4.2.4 The General Rule on Allocating Jurisdiction

National and institutional courts may possess concurrent jurisdiction to resolve claims against IOs, so establishing a method that helps determine which court should exercise its jurisdiction is necessary. Without such a method, the risk of parallel proceedings, inconsistent judgments and inefficiencies in the administration of justice is high. When courts possess concurrent jurisdiction, PIL helps to allocate regulatory authority as to which court may take jurisdiction based on the *forum non conveniens* or proper place doctrine (a). I argue that subject to the presence of an institutional DRM, in general, national courts should not exercise jurisdiction over IOs whether or not IO immunities exist on the facts of a particular case (b). However, I will argue that a national court should take jurisdiction where the institutional DRM is unavailable or inadequate as a secondary intervention

(A) THE PROPER PLACE DOCTRINE As Brand and Jablonski explain, *forum non conveniens* is 'a doctrine applied in common law judicial systems allowing the court seized of a case the discretion to decline to exercise jurisdiction because the interests of justice are best served if the trial takes place in another court'.[170] In particular, the doctrine allows a court to refuse the exercise of its jurisdiction in favour of another court that it considers to be 'appropriate' in the circumstances.[171] The inquiry boils down to the consideration of whether

170 See RA Brand and SR Jablonski, *Common Law Forum Non Conveniens: Four Countries, Four Approaches* (Oxford University Press 2007), 1. For an excellent discussion of the history of the doctrine, see pages 1–6. While *forum non conveniens* is a common law doctrine, occasionally similar concepts have been used in civil law states (see pages 122–3). Generally, civil law states adopt the *lis alibi pendens* approach, which requires the court approached later in time to decline jurisdiction in favour of the court approached by the parties the first time around. This approach is criticised for triggering a race to the court. It is adopted within the EU: see Recast Brussels I Regulation (n 102), art 29.

171 See *Spiliada Maritime Corp v Cansulex Ltd* [1987] AC 460 (*Spiliada*), 476, 478; a similar approach has also been adopted in Canada: *Amchem Products Inc. v British Columbia (Workers' Compensation Board)* [1993] 1 S.C.R. 897, 921; for a slight variation, see the Australian approach set out in *Voth v Manildra Flour Mills Pty Ltd* (1990) 171 CLR 538 and

another forum is better suited to exercise jurisdiction due to its stronger links with the claim at hand. These linking factors include the location of the parties, the subject matter connections of the dispute, the law to be applied, as well as access to premises, evidence and witnesses, the enforceability of any judgment rendered and considerations around the efficient administration of justice.[172]

The proper place doctrine aims to defer the exercise of jurisdiction to the court having the closest links to a given dispute. However, if the alternative forum is unavailable or inadequate, then regardless of the strength of connections, it cannot constitute an 'appropriate' DRM. In such situations the alternative DRM is either completely non-existent or so deficient that it does not provide meaningful access to justice. Access to justice is ultimately the jurisdictional pivot in the operation of the proper place doctrine. For instance, US courts must exercise their jurisdiction if the alternative forum is absent, or is unable to render justice adequately. The availability and adequacy of an alternative forum, amongst other things, trigger considerations of the opportunity for the plaintiff to receive effective justice at that alternative forum. The notes to the Draft Fourth Restatement of US Foreign Relations Law provide:

> A federal court will not dismiss on grounds of forum non conveniens unless there exists an available and adequate alternative forum. An alternative forum is generally considered available if all parties are amenable to process and come within the foreign forum's jurisdiction. An alternative forum is [in] general considered adequate if the parties will not be deprived of all remedies or treated unfairly.[173]

Both 'availability' and 'adequacy' are disjunctive questions. On the one hand, if there is no alternative forum available, the court approached should exercise

Oceanic Sun Line Special Shipping Co Inc v Fay (1988) 165 CLR 197; the US approach to *forum non conveniens* has largely been developed in three cases; see *Piper Aircraft Co v Reyno* (1981) 454 US 235; *Gulf Oil Corp v Gilbert* (1947) 330 US 501; and *Koster v Lumbermens Mutual Casualty Co* (1947) 330 US 518. The rule is enshrined in section 304 of the American Law Institute, 'Restatement of the Law Fourth the Foreign Relations Law of the United States, Jurisdiction' (22 March 2016, Tentative Draft No 2) (Foreign Relations Law of the United States), 153; for a background to the American Law Institute's project on the Restatement Fourth, 'The Foreign Relations Law of the United States' (2018), see, <https://thealiadviser.org/us-foreign-relations-law/now-available-restatement-of-the-law-fourth-the-foreign-relations-law-of-the-united-states/> accessed 1 May 2021.

172 See the factors set out by Lord Goff in *Spiliada* (n 171), 476: where amongst other things, if the alternative forum is unavailable, jurisdiction is to be exercised, and the plaintiff's choice is generally not to be disturbed if the defendant is resident in the jurisdiction; see Brand and Jablonski (n 170), 34–5 for a detailed list of factors.

173 See Foreign Relations Law of the United States (n 171), 155.

jurisdiction.[174] Moreover, if the alternative forum lacks jurisdiction over the parties, including by virtue of any procedural bar, then the alternative forum is still considered unavailable.[175] Accordingly, where access to an alternative forum is absent, whatever the reason may be, there is in reality no jurisdictional competition and the court approached should readily exercise its jurisdiction, of course assuming it is otherwise competent. On the other hand, the question of adequacy looks at the quality of the forum in terms of whether a plaintiff will be treated 'fairly'.[176] 'Fairness' triggers the question as to whether or not a plaintiff can receive a fair trial in the alternative forum.

Where a claimant cannot access a fair trial at an alternative forum, the court approached should be willing to exercise its jurisdiction. Crucially, the analysis of whether a fair trial can be realised in a foreign jurisdiction must be precise and nuanced. This is increasingly the position taken by national courts.[177] Perhaps the best known case exemplifying this approach is the UK Supreme Court's decision in *Vedanta Resources PLC v Lungowe* ('*Vedanta*').[178] In *Vedanta*, more than 1,800 Zambian citizens belonging to poor rural communities commenced proceedings in English courts alleging that a Zambian subsidiary and its parent company based in England were responsible for toxic emissions from a copper mine located in the area where the claimants lived and worked. The plaintiffs alleged that the defendant companies were negligent, harming their health and farming activities, which suffered damage by repeated discharges of toxic matter from the Nchanga Copper Mine into watercourses regularly used by the claimants.[179]

Although the UK Supreme Court agreed that the natural forum of the claim was in Zambia as the discharge giving rise to the alleged harm occurred in that country,[180] it said that access to justice considerations formed the central issue determinative of whether jurisdiction in England should be exercised. The court explained:

> Even if the court concludes (as I would have in the present case) that a foreign jurisdiction is the proper place in which the case should be tried, the court

174 Ibid.
175 Ibid.
176 Ibid.
177 See especially P Webb, 'Forum Non Conveniens: A Comparative Perspective' in R Gulati et al. (eds), *The Elgar Companion to the Hague Conference on Private International Law* (Edward Elgar 2020), 390–404; discussing *Araya v Nevsun Resources Ltdi* [2016] BCSC 1856 (*Nevsun*) upheld on appeal in *Araya v Nevsun Resources Ltdi* [2017] BCCA 401.
178 *Vedanta* (n 151).
179 Ibid, para 5.
180 Ibid, para 87.

> may nonetheless permit (or refuse to set aside) service of English proceedings on the foreign defendant if satisfied, by cogent evidence, that there is a real risk that substantial justice will not be obtainable in that foreign jurisdiction. … The question whether there is a real risk that substantial justice will be unobtainable is generally treated as separate and distinct from the balancing of the connecting factors which lies at the heart of the issue as to proper place, but that is more because it calls for a separate and careful analysis of distinctly different evidence than because it is an inherently different question. *If there is a real risk of the denial of substantial justice in a particular jurisdiction, then it seems to me obvious that it is unlikely to be a forum in which the case can be tried most suitably for the interests of the parties and the ends of justice* (emphasis added).[181]

Ultimately, it was found that if English courts did not exercise jurisdiction, there was a real risk that the claimants would be denied 'substantial justice' in Zambia.[182] One of the most significant aspects of the judgment in *Vedanta* concerns the specificity of the access to justice analysis that was determinative of whether English courts were the proper place for the litigation. Concluding that the claimants faced a real risk of a denial of substantial justice in Zambia for lack of effective legal representation in that country, the court said:

> [T]he real risk … that substantial justice would be unavailable in Zambia had nothing to do with any lack of independence or competence in its judiciary or any lack of a fair civil procedure suitable for handling large group claims. Rather, it derived essentially from two factors: first, the practicable impossibility of funding such group claims where the claimants were all in extreme poverty; and secondly, the absence within Zambia of sufficiently substantial and suitably experienced legal teams to enable litigation of this size and complexity to be prosecuted effectively, in particular against a defendant (KCM) with a track record which suggested that it would prove an obdurate opponent … there was a real risk but a probability that the claimants would not obtain access to justice so that … and notwithstanding the need for caution and cogent evidence, this reason for preferring the English to the Zambian jurisdiction was established by a substantial margin beyond the real risk which the law requires.[183]

The preferred approach to the operation of the proper place doctrine is that where a court is required to decide whether an alternative forum can deliver substantial justice, it must closely scrutinise whether a fair trial can be practically realised at that alternative place. If there is cogent evidence demonstrating

181 Ibid, para 88.
182 Ibid, para 102.
183 Ibid, paras 88 and 102.

a real risk that the right to a fair trial is unrealisable at the alternative forum, then the court seized should usually exercise its jurisdiction. An assessment of the quality of justice provided at a foreign forum in the context of making jurisdictional determinations in no way undermines international comity. Endorsing the approach of the first instance judge in *Vedanta*, the UK Supreme Court observed:

> It is also evident that the judge was conscious of the need to exercise restraint on grounds of comity ... he said this: 'I am conscious that some of the foregoing paragraphs could be seen as a criticism of the Zambian legal system. I might even be accused of colonial condescension. But that is not the intention or purpose of this part of the judgment. I am not being asked to review the Zambian legal system. I simply have to reach a conclusion on a specific issue, based on the evidence before me. And it seems to me that, doing my best to assess that evidence, I am bound to conclude ... that the claimants would almost certainly not get access to justice if these claims were pursued in Zambia.'[184]

Therefore, a judicial determination on the prospects of a claimant being able to access a fair trial in a foreign forum does not impinge on the regulatory authority of the foreign forum or the legal order where that forum is based. Such determinations are regularly made by courts and are simply a manifestation of an adjudicating court fulfilling its jurisdictional duty to ensure access to justice for the claimant within its own legal order.[185] As commentators have pointed out, the discretionary rules on the proper place doctrine may translate into a jurisdictional obligation when access to justice is at stake. Mills has said:

> The ... effect of access to justice on private international law is in the context of jurisdictional discretion (in legal systems which accept such a discretion, such as those in the common law tradition) – the question of whether a court will in fact exercise adjudicatory authority. While this discretion is consistent with the traditional view of jurisdiction as a state right, the increasing influence of access to justice as an international requirement suggests a shift toward viewing jurisdiction as an obligation.[186]

For courts located in common law countries, using access to justice as a jurisdictional pivot to determine the proper place to adjudicate a claim

[184] Ibid, para 97; also see *Yukos Capital SARL v OJSC Rosneft Oil Company* [2012] EWCA Civ 855, paras 73, 86, 91 and 135 (per Lord Rix), where English courts have shown a willingness to evaluate a foreign judiciary where cogent evidence of fair trial deficits is present.

[185] JJ Fawcett, M Ni Shuilleabhain and S Shah, *Human Rights and Private International Law* (Oxford University Press 2016) (Human Rights and PIL), section 6.90.

[186] Mills (n 19), 222.

against an IO is therefore not a novel exercise.[187] Instead of considering whether an alternative national court can deliver a fair trial, all the adjudicating court needs to do is to substitute an alternative national court with an alternative institutional DRM for the purposes of the *forum non conveniens* or the proper place analysis. Even for courts based in countries following a civil law system, where discretion-based jurisdictional tests are usually avoided,[188] adopting a flexible approach to jurisdiction is not problematic.[189] Presently, the coordinative and allocative role of PIL hones in on mediating the relationship between the national and institutional legal order. Where two or more courts possess a valid basis of jurisdiction, common sense dictates that a method to determine which of those courts should exercise jurisdiction to avoid inefficiencies in the administration of justice is needed. What is more, courts in civil law states already take jurisdiction over IOs where institutional DRMs are absent or not 'reasonable'.[190] It is suggested that a discretionary test using access to justice as a jurisdictional pivot can best explain exercises of civil jurisdiction over IOs by courts located in civil law systems too.[191]

Finally, there is nothing preventing institutional DRMs to take a discretionary approach when deciding whether or not to exercise their jurisdiction in a particular case.[192] An institutional DRM, assuming it has also been approached, should be able to stay proceedings in favour of a competent national court if it considers doing so would be in the interests of justice.[193] However, I do not dwell on this possibility. In reality, the most difficult decisions to exercise or not to exercise jurisdiction over IOs are confronted by national courts. As was shown in Chapters 3 and 4, claimants end up approaching national courts only when they are unable to access

187 National courts already adopt the proper place test when deciding whether jurisdiction should be exercised although this is done to coordinate between national courts: see, for example, *Francisco S. v Aetna Life Insurance Co.* (D Utah 2020).

188 See the approach of the CJEU in *Owusu v NB Jackson and Others* [2005] Case C-281/02, ECR I-1445.

189 Discretionary tests on jurisdiction are not unknown in civil law jurisdictions either: see J Pauwelyn and LE Salles, 'Forum Shopping before International Tribunals: (Real) Concerns, (Im)Possible Solutions' (2009) 42 Cornell International Law Journal 1, 114. The author notes that 'it is important to note that many civil law countries have statutory provisions that operate much like forum non conveniens – namely rules on so-called "related actions"'.

190 See Chapter 4, Section 4.4.1.3(b).

191 See further Section 5.5.2.3(b).

192 Within the international system, authors have advocated adopting modified *forum non conveniens* approaches where there exist overlapping jurisdictions: see Pauwelyn and Salles (n 189), 113.

193 Although the statute of the court or tribunal may create issues where jurisdiction may be invoked as a matter of right.

justice at the institutional level. Therefore, it is the operation of the proper place doctrine at the national level that deserves close scrutiny. I argue that the doctrine should use access to justice as a jurisdictional pivot when coordinating regulatory authority between national and institutional DRMs, but it should be applied in a modified form.

(B) IO COURTS SHOULD DEFER TO INSTITUTIONAL DRMS AS A GENERAL RULE Assuming that a competent and adequate DRM exists at the institutional level, and the IO has not submitted to national jurisdiction, domestic courts should defer jurisdiction to institutional DRMs as a general rule. Legal policy considerations require that institutional courts get the first opportunity to adjudicate claims against IOs. In fact, the IO legal order could have stronger regulatory interests compared to the national legal order in certain subject matters. Institutional DRMs would be the natural forum in such circumstances in any event. As was said, IOs exercise a form of inherent jurisdiction over their staff, and as outlined in Section 5.5, it is IO law that governs employment disputes against IOs. Given the authority of an IO to regulate its internal employment arrangements, the appropriateness of IO courts to resolve employment disputes is readily apparent. To varying degrees, the same may be said of other disputes of an administrative law character.[194]

For other types of disputes, an IO court may not be the natural forum due to the applicable connecting factors, such as the place of the injury in a tort case, and place of performance in a contractual claim. An institutional DRM should still be generally deferred to.[195] Regardless of the degree to which a dispute may be connected to a national legal order, the suitability of IO-based DRMs is justified due to certain policy factors. Steinbruck Platise identifies the reasons why it is preferable that victims of IO conduct receive justice at the institutional level first. She argues that national courts may not be the preferred forum to resolve claims against IOs because: (1) IOs may become subject to unilateral control through the courts, especially that of the host state; (2) if national courts take jurisdiction, there is a real risk of fragmented jurisprudence, 'even with regard to the same organisation that could be sued with respect to the same subject matter in different states'; (3) it may prove difficult to enforce judgments against IOs; (4) national courts may lack relevant expertise, although this issue is overstated;[196] and (5) 'if each and

[194] See Chapter 1.

[195] Unless national courts possess exclusive jurisdiction. This can occur in cases involving property where the property is located in a particular jurisdiction.

[196] See especially Section 5.5.

every state were allowed to scrutinise the acts of international organisations and domestic acts that implement those international acts, the binding quality of international acts could be called into question'.[197]

The protection of a private person's rights 'against violations by international organisations at the domestic level can therefore be unsatisfactory'.[198] It is fair to conclude that national courts should generally defer to an institutional DRM when confronted with claims against IOs. The proper place analysis should commence with the presumption that despite the links of a dispute to the national legal order, unless an IO submits to jurisdiction, or a national court has exclusive competence, the appropriate courts to exercise adjudicative jurisdiction over IOs are the ones located within the IO legal order. But if the victims of IO conduct have access to reasonable alternative means of dispute resolution, the secondary intervention of national courts will not be required. As I demonstrated in Chapter 3, much too often, victims of IO conduct cannot access justice against IOs at all, and where institutional DRMs exist, they are deficient. Accordingly, the operation of the proper place doctrine would require that national courts use access to justice as a jurisdictional pivot in such circumstances.

5.4.2.5 Applying the Access to Justice Jurisdictional Pivot in Claims against IOs

Whether or not IO immunities are engaged in a particular case, a competent national court that has been approached should exercise its jurisdiction over an IO if an alternative forum is unavailable, or where that alternative forum is present, it is 'unreasonable', 'inappropriate', 'inadequate', or is incapable of providing 'substantial justice' to the claimant. All those terms that are now used interchangeably eventually refer back to whether a court can deliver justice consistently with fair trial standards found in IHRL. Those standards have already been set out in Chapter 2. Where immunities are inapplicable, the task for the national court is straightforward. If an institutional DRM is unavailable or inadequate, national jurisdiction ought to be readily exercised for it is the national forum that becomes the proper place to adjudicate the claim.

But even if immunities are engaged, if the alternative forum is unavailable or inadequate, a competent national court should still take jurisdiction over an IO and perform its jurisdictional duty to ensure access to justice. As has been

197 Steinbruck Platise (n 63), 93–4.
198 Ibid.

explained, the existence of immunities does not imply that a national court's civil jurisdiction suddenly disappears. All IO immunities do is to present a procedural bar to the exercise of jurisdiction. This procedural bar is not insuperable. As we saw in Chapter 4, many national courts can and do pierce IO immunities where doing so is necessary to realise a fair trial. Unintentionally perhaps, the proper place doctrine is already being applied at the national level. The real issue is not whether access to justice concerns can form a justification for breaching IO immunity, which they certainly can, but in what circumstances the former may trump the latter. To answer this question, we again must consider whether a competent DRM at the institutional forum exists, and if it does, whether it can deliver justice adequately?

Fundamentally, access to justice constitutes the jurisdictional pivot based on which a national court must decide whether or not to exercise jurisdiction over an IO. If an alternative forum is 'unavailable' or 'inadequate', deferring to an institutional court is clearly impermissible. This is the case whether or not IO immunities are at issue, although when immunities apply, they will need accommodation through other PIL techniques to ensure that the functional independence of an IO is not limited.[199] Where an alternative forum is completely unavailable, the presumption of jurisdictional deference in favour of an IO court is readily rebutted (a). Where an alternative forum exists but is deficient, a close scrutiny of its compliance with fair trial standards is needed (b).

(A) WHERE NO ALTERNATIVE MEANS ARE AVAILABLE Where institutional DRMs do not exist at all, or are otherwise inaccessible to a claimant due to jurisdictional limitations, a competent national court clearly becomes the proper place for the litigation. In such circumstances, the court approached ought to exercise its jurisdiction because the alternative forum is simply unavailable.[200] Such a stance is a straightforward application of the proper place doctrine. The application of the doctrine also ensures the realisation of the right to access to court, demonstrating the increased interaction between PIL and IHRL.[201] As occurred in the Haiti and Srebrenica cases,[202] in most

199 See, Sections 5.5–5.6.

200 Human Rights and PIL (n 185), section 6.84. Recently, some authors have in passing attempted to apply a similar *forum non conveniens* approach in the IO setting, however, without providing any detail on how the doctrine may apply in practice or how it relates to IO immunities: C Ferstman, *International Organizations and the Fight for Accountability: The Remedies and Reparations Gap* (Oxford University Press 2017), 131.

201 Human Rights and PIL (n 185), sections 4.62, 4.78, 4.88 and 5.93; also see, *Al Nashiri v Romania* App no 33234/12 (ECtHR, 31 May 2018), 242, para 597.

202 See Chapter 4.

instances, victims of IO conduct do not have access to DRMs at the institutional level as of now. As a result, the role that national courts should presently play in ensuring access to justice for the victims of IO conduct is considerable.

(B) WHERE THE ALTERNATIVE FORUM IS INADEQUATE Where an institutional DRM exists, a national court may be confronted with three possibilities. First, the claimant approaches a competent national court without ever approaching the institutional DRM, fearing that fair trial at the latter cannot be realised. In this situation, the proper place doctrine should be applied in its usual way, that is, just like it was applied in the *Vedanta* case discussed earlier. Based on the evidence presented,[203] it is for the national court to decide whether a real risk exists that the claimant will be denied a fair trial at the institutional DRM. To determine the adequacy of the alternative forum, the court must closely assess the justice machinery installed, and consider how that justice machinery is likely to be brought to bear in practice. That inquiry must be conducted by applying the standards of a fair trial found in IHRL. International law-based fair trial standards apply as much to states as they do to IOs.[204] Due to their universal nature and application, if national courts assess the foreign forum's access to justice credentials with international standards, an internationally consistent approach to the application of the proper place doctrine across the national and institutional orders can be better achieved.[205]

Second, a claimant may approach a national court after they have already filed a claim before an institutional DRM, with the case still pending a determination. In such a circumstance, a national court could very well be justified in refusing to exercise jurisdiction on the basis of *lis pendens*, that is, the court first seized should decide the dispute.[206] However, if a failure of justice is evident at the alternative forum, then a national court ought to exercise its jurisdiction. Recall that in the *Application for Review of Judgment No 158 of the United Nations Administrative Tribunal*,[207] the ICJ

[203] As has been pointed out, the evidence required to establish a real risk of a fair trial breach in the alternative forum should not be prohibitive, where general reports as to the prevailing situation in the foreign state should suffice to show that the individual in question would be affected by the prevailing deficiencies: Human Rights and PIL (n 185), sections 6.181–91; also see *Nevsun* (n 177), para 255: 'the plaintiffs must provide sufficient evidence such that the court can conclude that there is a real risk that they will not receive a fair trial in that forum'.

[204] See, especially Chapter 2.

[205] Human Rights and PIL (n 185), section 6.160–2 (advocating a combined PIL and human rights approach on the question of appropriate court).

[206] Pauwelyn and Salles (n 189), 106.

[207] *Application for Review of Judgment No 158 of the United Nations Administrative Tribunal* (Advisory Opinion) [1973] ICJ Rep 166 (*Review of Judgment No 158*).

had said that the fundamental rules of procedure that must be followed at a DRM include

> the right to an independent and impartial tribunal established by law; the right to have the case heard and determined within a reasonable time; the right to a reasonable opportunity to present the case to the tribunal and to comment upon the opponent's case; the right to equality in the proceedings, the opponent; and the right to a reasoned decision.[208]

Thus, where fundamental errors in procedure are established, such as where a DRM is not independent or impartial, or the claimant is being treated unfairly, a manifest breach of the right to a fair trial is evident. In such a situation, a national court must exercise its jurisdiction as the alternative forum is clearly proving inadequate. Finally, a claimant may approach a national court after the proceedings at the alternative DRM have concluded. Again, a national court should only exercise jurisdiction over such a claim where cogent evidence shows that a failure of justice has occurred at the institutional DRM. In this scenario, a failure of justice exists in a concrete case, and the alternative forum has proven inadequate. An application of the proper place doctrine would demand that the competent national court approached exercise its jurisdictional duty and ensure access to justice for the victim.

5.4.2.6 Summing Up When Adjudicative Jurisdiction Over IOs Must Be Exercised at the National Level

National and institutional DRMs possess concurrent jurisdiction over IOs. Where concurrent jurisdiction exists, through the proper place doctrine, PIL rules aim to ensure that the court having the stronger links with a claim adjudicates it. If a competent national court finds that an alternative DRM is unavailable to a claimant, or cannot provide 'substantial justice' consistently with internationally accepted fair trial standards, the doctrine would require that a national court perform its jurisdictional duty to ensure access to justice. This is the case whether or not IO immunities apply in a given case. Where a national court takes jurisdiction over an IO consistent with the scheme suggested, PIL techniques would have already gone a long way in performing their function by successfully mediating between the national and institutional order. Access to justice is realised, but an IO is only answerable before a national court having a valid basis of jurisdiction. This means that IOs do not

[208] Ibid, para 92.

have to defend claims before distant forums. Crucially, as national courts should generally defer to the institutional DRM, assuming it is available and adequate, IOs can readily avoid the exercise of national jurisdiction by creating fair trial compliant internal justice systems.

A PIL approach to civil jurisdiction can best coordinate the relationship between the national and institutional orders. Instead of answering the unresolvable question of when precisely IO immunities prevail over the right to access justice or vice versa, being the blunt debate carried out in the public international law realm, PIL mediates between the national and institutional orders by stating the precise conditions under which a national court may exercise its authority over an IO. Ultimately, PIL can help create a jurisdictional scheme that is capable of ensuring access to justice to the victims of IO conduct, but without compromising on the interests of an IO. Where a national court takes jurisdiction over an IO in this circumscribed way, the rules on applicable law (Section 5.5) and the recognition and enforcement of judgments (Section 5.6) can further be calibrated to coordinate between the national and IO legal orders in such a nuanced manner that the chance of intrusion into an IO's independence is eliminated.

5.5 CHOICE OF LAW

Where a national court takes jurisdiction over an IO, it is important that the prescriptive authority of the IO is respected. This can be achieved by applying IO law, where it is the applicable law, to resolve the substance of a dispute at the national level. Accordingly, the fear that the exercise of national jurisdiction may undermine an IO's functional independence by subjecting it to a varied set of municipal laws is addressed neatly (Section 5.5.1). Moreover, the perception that national courts should not adjudicate claims involving IOs as they lack judicial expertise is unwarranted. As I argue, national courts are perfectly capable of applying foreign law, including institutional law, if that is indeed the applicable law (Section 5.5.2). Finally, PIL allows for the disapplication of foreign law where it is contrary to public policy. This means that the law applicable can be tempered to ensure respect for the regulatory interests of a foreign legal order, including the institutional one (Section 5.5.3).

5.5.1 *Applying IO Law Can Safeguard Institutional Prescriptive Authority*

The justification often provided against the exercise of national jurisdiction over IOs is to avoid the application of national legal standards to their regulatory concerns. A good example is provided by employment cases where IOs have the regulatory freedom to legislate. In an employment dispute where the claimant argued that the World Bank's immunities were inapplicable due to the broadly framed waiver contained in its constituent arrangements,[209] limiting the operation of that waiver to the organisation's external activities only, a US court said:

> [T]his waiver would lay the Bank open to disruptive interference with its employment policies in each of the thirty-six countries in which it has resident missions, and the more than 140 nations in which it could be involved in its lending and financing activities. Revising and administering consistent employment policies for a large administrative staff which includes citizens from more than 100 countries is difficult enough. If the Bank were required to adopt the local employment policies of each of its member countries this task would become nearly impossible. The employment laws of member nations rarely coincide precisely, and frequently conflict with those of other member nations. National policies governing mandatory retirement at a certain age often directly contradict each other. So, too, do national laws governing discrimination in hiring. Thus, for example, the Bank would be hard pressed to establish and administer effective employment practices regarding Jewish employees in offices located in Middle Eastern countries, absent immunity for its employment related policies. Since a waiver of immunity from suits arising out of the Bank's internal relations would create such devastating administrative consequences without materially advancing its chartered objectives, Article VII section 3 should not be construed as abrogating the Bank's immunity to actions arising out of its internal affairs.[210]

The belief that exercising national jurisdiction over an IO necessarily leads to the application of national law to an IO is mistaken. Unfortunately, the court failed to appreciate that it could have taken jurisdiction over the case, and yet applied the employment law of the World Bank to it. Doing so would have meant that there was no risk of the organisation's prescriptive jurisdiction being undermined, and functional independence intruded into. Where a court takes jurisdiction over an IO, but nevertheless decides to apply the law of the IO to the merits of a case, assuming it is the correct applicable law, appropriate respect to the IO's regulatory authority is shown. This approach has already been taken by other national courts. Where a Belgian court took jurisdiction over an IO in an employment case because the organisation failed to provide any alternative means of dispute resolution to the claimant, the

[209] See, Chapter 4 where MDB immunities are discussed in detail.
[210] *Mendaro v World Bank* (D.C. Cir. 1983) 717 F.2d 610.

court required the application of the employment law of that IO to resolve the merits of the claim.[211] The court thus ensured that privately held rights were enforced, and at the same time deferred to the legislative jurisdiction of the IO in the sphere of employment relations. Similar divisions of regulatory authority can be readily adopted in respect of other types of disputes too.[212]

An appropriate choice of law determination at the national level is therefore capable of ensuring that access to justice is not denied to a claimant on the erroneous belief that the exercise of national jurisdiction would undermine the regulatory authority of an IO. By applying IO law to the merits of a case, assuming it is the proper law, the national order can show proper respect to the institutional order. But some commentators argued that national courts are not suited to take jurisdiction over IOs because they are unsuited to adjudicate the types of claims IOs face.

5.5.2 *National Courts Are Perfectly Equipped to Adjudicate Claims against IOs*

The contention that national courts are ill-suited to adjudicate claims against IOs is unwarranted.[213] PIL has developed a sophisticated method of determining what law applies to resolve the merits of a claim. Where foreign law is the applicable law, including non-state law, national courts regularly apply laws emanating from a different legal order when adjudicating transnational civil disputes. There is no reason why this method cannot be successfully employed to mediate the relationship between the national and institutional orders. Specifically, determining the applicable law involves three stages, namely, characterisation (Section 5.5.2.1), localisation (Section 5.5.2.2) and application (Section 5.5.2.3).[214] As is shown later in the chapter, a national court is perfectly able to methodically determine the law applicable in a particular case and then apply that law to the facts of the case before it.

5.5.2.1 Characterisation

The first step in a choice of law determination is referred to as 'characterisation' or 'qualification'. This step involves deciding which choice of law rule is

211 See *Western European Union v Siedler* (21 December 2009, Belgian Court of Cassation), discussed in C Ryngaert, 'Belgium' in A Reinisch (ed), *The Privileges and Immunities of International Organizations in Domestic Courts* (Oxford University Press 2013), 65–6.

212 See, for example, *CECA c faillite des 'Acciaierie e Ferriere di Bogaro' SpA* (n 124), 403–5.

213 Steinbruck Platise (n 63), 67–96, 93–4.

214 Symeonides (n 5), 64.

'principally applicable to the case at hand, by fitting the case into a legal category of tort, contract, and so forth, employed by the rule'.[215] While some cases can be readily fit into one category, others are susceptible to multiple characterisations. In claims involving IOs, the issue of characterisation can be significant. This is because the same set of facts can be qualified in multiple ways, with causes of action even emanating from different legal orders. The same factual matrix may give rise to a cause of action in domestic law, institutional law as well as the various branches of international law.[216]

Take, for example, the case of the Haitian cholera victims against the UN.[217] The facts give rise to claims in tort, but also amount to breaches of human rights, such as an infringement to the right to life and the right to health.[218] Similarly, the case advanced by the victims of the Srebrenica genocide against the UN can be characterised as claims arising in tort, infringements of the right to life and even contraventions of international humanitarian law given that this case arose during an armed conflict.[219] Also recall the *Jam* litigation discussed in Chapter 4, where the same set of facts can be characterised as claims in tort, as well as infringements of the right to health, right to livelihood and so on.[220] Even the facts giving rise to an employment claim can be susceptible to multiple qualifications. Such claims may be characterised as arising in contract, employment law, administrative law, tort law and also IHRL, with the right to work, non-discrimination, right to strike and other international labour law rights often at stake.

Where claims are susceptible to multiple characterisations, the qualification exercise is not an easy one. The present aim is not to solve this conundrum but to argue that the qualification process should not be used as a tool to avoid

215 Ibid.

216 See Human Rights and PIL (n 185), section 1.24.

217 See Chapter 4, where the Haiti cholera litigation is discussed.

218 See BAI/IJDH petition submitted to the UN on behalf of 5,000 clients, 3 November 2011, paras 80–1 <www.ijdh.org/cholera/cholera-litigation/> accessed 3 June 2016.

219 See especially, *Stichting Mothers of Srebrenica v The Netherlands* App no 65542/12 (ECtHR, 11 June 2013) (*Srebrenica case*), paras 40 (identifying breaches of international humanitarian law), 55 (breaches of tort and contract), 456 (breaches of public international law norms of state responsibility), 57 (identifying breaches of IHRL, especially the right to a remedy). See the discussion in C McLachlan, *Foreign Relations Law* (Cambridge University Press 2014), 290–3 (at sections 7.83–7). Liability in tort law can also arise during armed conflict, although the choice of law determination will be dependent on the circumstances that gave rise to the injury. As McLachlan has said, if the injury is caused outside of the context of the battle (a matter for the trial judge to determine on the facts of a case), tort law would apply in its normal course. However, where the injury occurs in the midst of battle, there may be triggered combat immunity from tort law. Here, IHL and IHRL could constitute the applicable law.

220 See the discussion in Chapter 4.

the exercise of national civil jurisdiction. Some national courts have refused to exercise jurisdiction over IOs on the basis of well-known avoidance techniques,[221] where the refusing court defers to a foreign jurisdiction saying that an alternative forum is better suited to adjudicate the claim as the law applicable to the substance of the dispute is not the forum's law. For example, if a national court chooses to qualify a claim as a breach of a rule of international law, as opposed to the commission of a domestic wrong, it may decide to defer the task of adjudication to a different forum altogether. In such a situation, a court may consider itself an inappropriate forum to resolve the claim due to alleged lack of manageable judicial standards or relevant expertise.[222] Such a perception is unjustified for at least four reasons.

First, in most types of private claims, a national judge is ideally suited to decide the substance of the dispute. For instance, if a claim is in tort or contract, where the governing law would be national law, a domestic court would routinely apply those bodies of law.[223] A national court is in fact better suited to decide the case compared to an institutional judge who may or may not be familiar with the applicable legal regime. Second, to the extent that foreign law is applied, including the internal law of the IO, national judges frequently make determinations on questions of foreign law based on expert opinion. Applying IO law as foreign law is no different.[224]

[221] For example, Reinisch refers to non-justiciability, a self-imposed restraint on the exercise of jurisdiction due to alleged interference in a state's foreign relations as one of the avoidance techniques adopted by national judges to refuse an exercise of jurisdiction over an IO. A Reinisch, *International Organizations Before National Courts* (Cambridge University Press 2000), 84–99. See *JH Rayner (Mincing Lane) Ltd v Department of Trade and Industry* [1989] 81 ILR 670, [1990] 29 ILM 670 (International Tin Council case), 695; also see the discussion of *Westland Helicopters Ltd v Arab Organisation for Industrialisation* [1995] 2 All ER 387 (QBD) in G Ossman, 'The Protection of International Organisations under the Rules of Conflict of Laws: Prevailing Subjectivity' ICCLR 1995; *International Association of Machinists (IAM) v OPEC* (9th Cir 1981) 6(11) 649 F2d 1354, 1361, 380–7; but see *Council v Amalgamet Inc* (25 January 1988) 138 Misc 2d 383, 524 NYS 2d 971, 3. Non-justiciability is unlikely to prevent a court from exercising jurisdiction nowadays; see *Belhaj and Another v Straw and Others* [2017] UKSC 3, [2017] 2 WLR 456 and *Rahmatullah (No 1) v Ministry of Defence and Another* [2017] UKSC 1, [2017] UKSC 3, para 41; also see McLachlan (n 219), 5 (at section 1.05), where the author states that 'foreign relations, despite their political dimension, are governed by law. They are not a zone of non-law within the municipal legal system'. And the method used to resolve such issues is to adopt a conflict of laws solution (pages 7–8, section 1.15).

[222] See, *Danikovic v State of the Netherlands* (6 July 2000, Court of Appeal of Amsterdam) Case No 759/99, SKG LJN: AO0070 (the Netherlands), [5.3.8], discussed in Nollkaemper (n 163), 8.

[223] K Wellens, *Remedies against International Organisations* (Cambridge University Press 2002), 117–18.

[224] See further 5.5.2.2.

Third, nowadays, national courts regularly adjudicate claims where the applicable law is international law.[225] Therefore, where the cause of action is based on a branch of public international law, such as IHRL, to say that a national court is incompetent because it lacks relevant judicial expertise is wrong. Finally, as was pointed out in Chapter 3, it is national judges who are often appointed to institutional DRMs, thus rendering the fear around the lack of judicial expertise at the national level hypocritical.

In the end, if jurisdiction is taken by a national court due to the unavailability or inadequacy of an institutional DRM, then the proper place analysis has already yielded the result that the national court is the appropriate court. In such a scenario, a national court must not abdicate its jurisdictional duty to ensure access to justice by then going on to refuse an exercise of its jurisdiction due to alleged lack of manageable judicial standards or expertise. National courts are perfectly able to apply different substantive law regimes when performing their judicial function. Therefore, where a plaintiff has a *bona fide* cause of action against an IO, there is no logical reason as to why an otherwise competent court should refuse to adjudicate the claims advanced by victims of IO conduct. As is argued next, the localisation and application stages can ensure that the prescriptive authority of the IO is respected, and a national court is able to access foreign law expertise where it is needed.

5.5.2.2 Localisation

The next step in the choice of law inquiry is known as 'localisation'. This step involves placing a dispute on the so-called map by determining where the tort occurred or the contract was made or was to be performed.[226] The localisation step obviously needs some adjustments when coordinating between the national and the institutional legal orders given that IOs do not possess their

[225] There is a vast literature on the role of national courts in the adjudication of international claims. Some argue this is a fragmentation of international adjudication, but the better view is a legal pluralist one. See W Burke-White, 'International Legal Pluralism' (2004) 25 Michigan Journal of International Law 963–79, 964–5; international law claims can also be pursued as domestic causes of action. For the various methods used by national courts to determine claims where inherently public international law disputes are determined by national courts, see Human Rights and PIL (n 185), section 1.22 (the US approach); and in other states, including the United Kingdom, an international law claim may be pursued through a domestic cause of action, such as the general law of tort, such as the tort of false imprisonment (relating to the right to liberty) and battery (relating to the right not to be tortured or subjected to ill-treatment). The applicable domestic substantive law can only be identified using private international law rules relating to the applicable law (section 1.24).

[226] Symeonides (n 5), 64, 68.

own territory. But the starting point is that some law would govern every cause of action. Just because the forum's own law may or may not apply to a particular legal issue, it does not follow that the rights and duties involved fall into a 'legal black hole'.[227] At its core, there are three main possibilities as to what law governs a dispute between a private actor and an IO, that is, the law applicable is IO law, national law or public international law. Of course, if a claimant pursues multiple causes of action emanating from different legal orders, all those bodies of law will have application in the resolution of the overall dispute.

First, where it is found that an IO properly possesses legislative jurisdiction over a subject matter, then regardless of where the dispute is adjudicated, the court must apply IO law. IOs 'exercise legislative ... powers over their organs and officials; and an IO's legal relations with its officials are governed by the internal law of the IO concerned'.[228] In an employment claim, the legal order that would thus usually supply the applicable law is that of the IO.[229] This body of law is known as international administrative or international civil service law.[230] By analogy, concerning any other dispute of a public or administrative law character,[231] assuming the law does not have any gaps, it should be the internal law of the IO that is applicable even if a dispute is being adjudicated at the national level. Doing so appropriately respects the regulatory authority of the IO concerning its internal affairs.

Second, in other types of private law claims, PIL rules would apply as they usually do, although appropriate adjustments may be required.[232] In respect of

227 Riles (n 14), 97.

228 Jenks (n 1), 36–7.

229 Although, there is significant confusion about the applicable law in disputes between IOs and consultants and contractors who are not in permanent or fixed-term employment of the employer IO. The law that probably applies is a combination of contract law, relevant principles of international commercial law, IO law, international labour law and IHRL. Note, concerning consultants and contractors, some IOs state that the general principles of international commercial law are said to apply. As to what that phrase means, this has not been clarified in the employment law sphere: see UN Secretariat, 'Administrative Instruction: Consultants and Individual Contractors' (19 December 2013) UN Doc ST/AI/2013/4, Annex 1 (General Conditions of Contracts for the Services of Consultants and Individual Contractors), clause 16.

230 There are some works identifying the substantive law that applies in international civil service disputes: see Jenks (n 1); CF Amerasinghe, *The Law of the International Civil Service: As Applied by International Administrative Tribunals*, vols 1 and 2 (Oxford University Press 1994); for a more recent work, see G Ullrich, *The Law of the International Civil Service: Institutional Law and Practice in International Organisations* (Duncker & Humblot 2018).

231 See Chapter 1.

232 See Seyersted (n 49), 450, 489 (noting that there are often no applicable law provisions in place; and PIL must take into account the unique nature of IOs in its application).

disputes concerning real or personal property, the applicable law will conventionally be the law of the place where the property is located.[233] In tortious claims, the applicable law may be determined by reference to the place where the damage occurred.[234] Admittedly, treaty provisions may modify the application of this rule where such provisions are included.[235] What is more, to protect IO independence, the extent of damages that a national court should be able to award may need to be restricted (see Section 5.5.2.3). In international commercial disputes of a contractual character, party autonomy should be upheld.[236] This means that if the IO and a private actor have made an express choice as to the applicable law, then the court must uphold that choice. A question that can create some difficulty relates to how a contractual arrangement intersects with IO law, which can happen from time to time.[237] In such situations, the contractual arrangements should form the core of the applicable law, with arbitral tribunals stating that it is unjustifiable to expect 'private parties to have an unreasonable level of familiarity regarding the intricacies of international organizations as subjects of private law'.[238]

Finally, certain disputes between IOs and private actors require the application of public international law, especially IHRL. If a cause of action is based on public international law, it is that body of law that a national court must apply to resolve the merits. However, its application may require a nuanced analysis on how the various branches of international law apply vis-à-vis IOs. Determining the applicable law in disputes involving IOs can be a challenging exercise, but this challenge exists regardless of the forum where

[233] It is a well-accepted PIL rule that the law of the situs applies to all questions of title to property.

[234] See, for example, Regulation (EC) No 864/2007 – the law applicable to non-contractual obligations (Rome II), which provides in part that the law applicable to a non-contractual obligation arising out of a tort/delict is the law of the country where the damage occurs; or the law of the country where both parties were primarily living or had their main place of business.

[235] There is much work to be done to clarify the precise way in which tort law is to apply to an IO as international instruments are ambiguous. See, for example, the Treaty Establishing the European Community (10 November 1997) Official Journal C 340; (31 August 1992) Official Journal C 224, art 288, which merely states: 'In the case on non-contractual liability, the Community shall, in accordance with the general principles common to the laws of the Member States, make good any damage caused by its institutions or by its servants in the performance of their duties'; see also the discussion in Seyersted (n 49), 488.

[236] Party autonomy is now the dominant view in this sphere: see the HCCH, 'Principles on Choice of Law in International Commercial Contracts' (2015) <www.hcch.net/en/instruments/conventions/full-text/?cid=135> accessed 1 May 2021.

[237] Seyersted (n 49), 473, where the author points out that MDB loan contracts also incorporate aspects of IO law, in addition to classical principles of contract law.

[238] See the award in *Polis Fondi Immobliari Di Banche Popolari S.G.R.p.A. (Italy) v International Fund For Agricultural Development* (17 December 2010) Case No 2010-08, para 175.

the dispute is being litigated and is best met at the application stage of the choice of law analysis.

5.5.2.3 Application

The final step in a choice of law determination is the 'application' stage. This involves several sub-steps. These include ascertaining the content of foreign law (a), considering whether any exceptions to the application of foreign law are operable (b), and applying the foreign law to the case at hand (c).[239] As the discussion next shows, national courts already possess the expertise, or can readily access it, when adjudicating claims against IOs. Thus, national courts must not abdicate jurisdiction simply because the law applicable to resolve the claim is not that of the forum.

(A) ASCERTAINING THE CONTENT OF THE FOREIGN LAW Once a court has qualified a claim and localised it in terms of what law is applicable, it must decide what is the content of the applicable law. If the forum's own law applies to the merits, then the question whether the court possesses the expertise to adjudicate the claim does not arise. In claims in tort, contract, property and so on, national law is likely to be the applicable law. Resolving such claims would constitute routine work for the relevant national court. The expertise that a national judge would possess over their own law would be naturally superior to that of a foreign judge, including a judge of an institutional DRM.

But where a national court decides that foreign law, including IO law governs the substance of the dispute, a court must find a way to establish the content of the applicable foreign law. In most common law systems, questions of foreign law are considered questions of fact. Expert evidence is used to prove its content.[240] In civil law jurisdictions, issues of foreign law are considered as questions of law.[241] On either approach, a court will be furnished with detailed

[239] Symeonides (n 5), 64.

[240] The general common law position on proof of foreign law has been well captured in Rule 18 of Lord Collins of Mapesbury (ed), *Dicey and Morris on the Conflict of Laws* (15th edn, Sweet and Maxwell 2012), 187, which states that foreign law is a fact, so that foreign law must be pleaded and proved; in general, foreign law must be proved by expert evidence. The United States takes a different approach, with foreign law being a question of law: see *Animal Science Products Inc v Hebei Welcome Pharmaceutical Co* (14 June 2018) No 16-1220, 1, referring to the Federal Rule of Civil Procedure 44.1, the US Supreme Court stated 'in determining foreign law, "the court may consider any relevant material or source . . . whether or not submitted by a party." As "[t]he court's determination must be treated as a ruling on a question of law"'.

[241] See, for example, G Dannemann, 'Establishing Foreign Law in a German Court' (1994) <https://germanlawarchive.iuscomp.org/?p=377> accessed 30 April 2021.

submissions on the content of foreign law. Thus, a national court can readily rely on expert submissions in determining the content of the applicable foreign law where such expertise is needed. Where IO law is the applicable law, a national court can rely on the same processes to elucidate its content that is used to prove foreign law in that forum in transnational civil proceedings.

Furthermore, a national court is perfectly able to apply IO law. For example, in employment disputes, IAL will usually be the applicable law. In *de Merode v The World Bank*,[242] the WBAT commented that a staff member's conditions of employment are to be determined with reference to the contract of employment, the enactments of the organisation (including its constituent instruments, staff regulations and staff rules), general principles of IAL and the practice of the organisation to the extent that it is 'limited to that of which there is evidence that it is followed by the organization in the conviction that it reflects a legal obligation'.[243] There is no reason why national judges cannot assess the aforementioned sources of law when determining the content of the applicable law in employment cases. Even in other types of claims of an administrative law character against IOs, the standards of review are not unknown to a national judge, with those standards more often than not deriving from domestic administrative law. As the significant evidence base gathered by the global administrative law movement has shown, in general, when IOs impact private rights through their public or administrative conduct, 'adequate standards of transparency, participation, reasoned decision, and legality' must be met.[244] Where these standards are breached, an administrative act may be annulled, although in administrative law cases, the submissions made by an IO on the scope of its regulatory authority should be given due respect.[245] Thus, national courts are perfectly able to conduct judicial review of the administrative acts of IOs, where such review becomes necessary.

242 *De Merode v World Bank (Decision No 1)* (5 June 1981) 1 WBAT Rep 734; see decision discussed in R Gulati, 'de Merode and ors v World Bank, 5th June 1981 (WBAT Decision No 1 (1981) 1 WBAT Rep 734), OXIO 229' (17 July 2017) <http://opil.ouplaw.com/oxlaw/entryview/viewoxlawoxchap/10.1093$002flaw-oxio$002fe229.013.1$002flaw-oxio-e229;jsessionid=7E1252 0A3922B299DC3FB1DDD274B051> accessed 6 June 2018.

243 See, *de Merode v World Bank* (n 242), paras 18–22; also see *Judgments of the Administrative Tribunal of the ILO* (Advisory Opinion) ICJ Rep 1956, 91, para 23; also see, Gulati (n 242).

244 See, B Kingsbury, N Krisch and RB Stewart, 'The Emergence of Global Administrative Law' (2005) 68 Law and Contemporary Problems 16–60, 17.

245 In *Animal Science Products Inc v Hebei Welcome Pharmaceutical Co* (n 240), 1, the US Supreme Court stated that a 'federal court should accord respectful consideration to a foreign government's submission, but is not bound to accord conclusive effect to the foreign government's statements'. The decision is available at <https://supreme.justia.com/cases/federal/us/585/16-1220/#tab-opinion-3915290>.

Finally, the fact that national courts can and regularly do apply public international law when adjudicating claims of an international character has already been mentioned. Therefore, applying legal principles based on public international law in claims against IOs, where international law is the applicable law, is nothing novel for a national court. Indeed, as was pointed out in Chapter 3, it is national judges that are usually appointed to DRMs at IOs.[246] Any suggestion that they lack the know-how to resolve claims against IOs is without basis. Therefore, irrespective of the nature of the cause of action pursued, a competent national court is well suited to adjudicate claims against IOs if it decides to exercise jurisdiction in a particular case.

(B) THE OPERATION OF THE ORDRE PUBLIC EXCEPTION A PIL framework on applying foreign law is not rigid, allowing for some flexibility for the forum court when applying foreign law through the operation of the doctrine of 'order public' or 'public policy' exception. Such a flexibility may prove important to ensure that the regulatory interests of the national and institutional orders are taken into account at the application stage of the choice of law analysis. This may become necessary where applying IO law is repugnant in the national legal order, but also where applying national standards to claims against IOs could unduly restrict an IO's functional independence.

In a narrow set of circumstances, courts located in one legal order can refuse to apply the applicable foreign law for reasons of public policy. The doctrine was expounded by Judge Cardozo in *Loucks v Standard Oil Co. of New York*.[247] It was held that the public policy exception applies if the foreign law 'offends our sense of justice or menaces the public welfare', 'shock[s] our sense of justice' or 'violate[s] some fundamental principle of justice, some prevalent conception of good morals, some deep-rooted tradition'.[248] Thus, a mere distinction between the laws of different legal orders is not enough to show that public policy forbids a court 'to enforce the foreign right'.[249] The exception may only be invoked in special cases. For the exception to apply, 'the application of foreign law must be "manifestly incompatible" with the forum's ordre public or with "fundamental principles" of the forum state'.[250]

In transnational civil cases, the public policy exception operates even more restrictively. The concept of '*ordre public* international' states that 'a forum should be more tolerant of certain results in multistate cases than in domestic

[246] See the relevant discussion in Chapter 3 on judicial appointments to IATs.

[247] *Loucks v Standard Oil Co. of New York* (NY 1918) 120 NE 198.

[248] Ibid, 202.

[249] Ibid.

[250] Symeonides (n 5), 78–9.

cases'.[251] Accordingly, the *public* policy exception does not undermine the prescriptive authority of a foreign legal order as it is applied in very exceptional circumstances. Assuming it can even apply, the doctrine only disapplies foreign law in a particular case, as opposed to invalidating the foreign law as such.[252] Claims against IOs, which fundamentally are a type of transnational civil claim, may thus attract the operation of the public policy exception or the *ordre public* doctrine, howsoever it may be labelled.

The public policy exception can indeed form a powerful tool to balance competing regulatory interests whenever the accommodation of the interests of the national and institutional order is required. For example, while national courts should usually apply international civil service law applicable at an IO when adjudicating an employment claim involving an international institution, 'however, if the substantive internal law of the organization were manifestly deficient, by, for instance, providing for a ridiculously low indemnity allowance, domestic courts should be allowed not to give effect to such internal law, possibly citing ordre public considerations drawn from private international law, and apply domestic law'.[253] Where the law of the IO is manifestly deficient, or perhaps even absent, the *ordre public* doctrine could allow national laws to play a gap-filling role to the limited extent necessary. In doing so, the regulatory interests of the forum state are not undermined. At the same time, the independence of the IO is maintained because the *ordre public* doctrine operates only when the most compelling circumstances exist.

Such compelling reasons were said to exist where the AfDB did not provide any alternative means of dispute resolution to an aggrieved official, with French courts setting aside the immunities of the organisation for doing so would have offended the *ordre public* of the forum state, of which the right to a fair trial was an aspect.[254] A French expert explained the application of the doctrine in that case as follows:

> It has been argued that the French *ordre public* international aims at setting aside a foreign rule. This might be true for matters concerning the substance of a case. But in the special case of the principle prohibiting the denial of

[251] Ibid.

[252] Ibid, 80.

[253] See the discussion of *Western European Union v Siedler* (n 211) in Ryngaert (n 211), 65–6.

[254] In *African Development Bank v X* (n 135), para 3, the Court of Cassation said: 'The jurisdictional immunity of an international organization could not be relied upon in relation to proceedings brought by an employee when no international administrative tribunal had been instituted by that organization with jurisdiction to hear complaints brought by its employees. It would otherwise be a denial of justice, in violation of the right to a court which, in France, was part of the "international public order".'

> justice, it is applied if the forum state is not competent according to its regular (national) rules of competence and if no other court has jurisdiction, in order to avoid denial of justice. So, this particular rule may actually 'set aside' the rule of the forum state denying a national court's competence.[255]

As was said earlier, the taking of French jurisdiction in the aforementioned case is better explained by the application of the proper place doctrine as opposed to the *ordre public* doctrine. This is because *ordre public* works to disapply a repugnant foreign law, as opposed to dealing with an unjust foreign practice.[256] The rules on immunities on their own do not violate public policy, but it is the absence of a reasonable alternative means of dispute resolution that ultimately caused the denial of justice to the claimant. Still, whether one resorts to the proper place or the *ordre public* doctrine, the end result is the correct one, that is, the exercise of national jurisdiction where an institutional DRM is unavailable or inadequate. The noteworthy point is that the *ordre public* doctrine can be invoked where doing so is necessary to alleviate the harm that may flow to a person from the application of manifestly unjust IO laws.

Equally, there are exceptional circumstances where certain aspects of national law should not be applied in claims against IOs. One of these exceptional situations concerns the general rule in PIL that the penal laws of one legal order do not extend to a foreign legal order.[257] A penal statute is one which 'punish[es] an offense against the public justice of the state ... [as opposed to affording] a private remedy to a person injured by the wrongful act'.[258] Exemplary or punitive damages in civil cases (which are seen as penal in nature) may not be awarded or enforced based on the *ordre public* doctrine.[259] Therefore, where foreign law governs a tort, some states have enacted laws stating that the amount of damages may not exceed the amount available under the *lex fori*, that is, the law of the forum in which the claim is being decided.[260]

According to the approach suggested by this author, a national court is to take jurisdiction over an IO as a secondary intervention, where it is necessary to ensure access to justice for the victims of institutional conduct. The

255 See AM Thevenot-Werner, 'The Right of Staff Members to a Tribunal as a Limit to the Jurisdictional Immunity of International Organisations in Europe' (2014) <https://rm.coe.int/the-right-of-staff-members-to-a-tribunal-as-a-limit-to-the-jurisdictio/16808b3ac9> accessed 30 April 2021, 126–7.

256 For a leading view on the issue, see R Garnett, *Substance and Procedure in Private International Law* (Oxford University Press 2012).

257 See, *The Antelope* (1825) 23 US (10 Wheat), 66.

258 See, *Huntington v Attrill* (1892) 146 US 657, 673–4.

259 Symeonides (n 5), 84.

260 Ibid, giving the example of Germany and South Korea.

objective is to realise a fair trial and effective remedy for the claimant, as opposed to imposing a penalty on the respondent IO. Ultimately, national courts play a critical but subordinate role to institutional DRMs in adjudicating claims against IOs. Regardless of the law that applies, it is unlikely that an institutional DRM would be willing to grant punitive damages against an IO. In extreme cases, granting punitive damages could even render an IO bankrupt.[261] Applying exemplary or punitive damages could thus impact the functioning of an IO due to the potential of significant financial costs on it. In general, the *ordre public* doctrine would demand that where a national court takes jurisdiction over an IO, it does not apply the aspects of national law that can undermine the IO's financial viability, even where the applicable law is national law.

(C) APPLYING THE APPLICABLE LAW The final step in a choice of law analysis is to apply the applicable law to the case at hand. This would mean that where the applicable law is the forum's national law, a court would apply it to the facts of the case before it. Where the applicable law is foreign law, including IO law, a national court could rely on expert evidence to determine its content, and then decide the merits based on the applicable foreign law. If the law to be applied is derived from public international law, such as IHRL, then a national court should apply international law to resolve the merits. Based on the public policy exception, only in extreme situations a court may refuse to apply foreign law, or an aspect of that law. This may be done where the foreign law is repugnant and manifestly unjust. Equally, to avoid intrusions into the functioning of an IO, a national court must not award punitive damages against an IO even where the applicable law is national law, and it allows for the imposition of such damages. In many situations, determining the applicable law is unlikely to present much difficulty. However, there could be scenarios where the applicable law could become difficult to determine due to how national, institutional and international laws interact, potentially creating a special type of hybrid law. The discussion about whether such a hybrid law exists, or is in the process of developing, is an important aspect that is left for another day. For the moment, the conclusion to be drawn is that if a national court exercises jurisdiction over an IO, the prescriptive authority

261 A good example is provided by the Haiti cholera litigation already discussed in Chapter 4. Note that in the Haiti cholera litigation, the victims' lawyers claimed a total of approximately USD36.5 billion. The annual budget of the UN at the time was approximately USD20 billion. The cap for damages at the UN for third-party loss is USD50,000. Clearly, had the damages claimed been awarded, the functioning of the UN would have been significantly adversely effected: see the discussion in Boon (n 154), 348 and 370.

of the institutional legal order can be maintained through carefully crafted choice of law rules. Thus, regulatory authority between the national and institutional orders can be coordinated and allocated in a way that secures access to justice without compromising on institutional independence.[262]

5.6 RECOGNITION AND ENFORCEMENT

If a claimant succeeds in obtaining a judgment in their favour but is unable to enforce it, that judgment is of little value. For the right to a fair trial to be practically realised, and an effective remedy to be delivered, a judgment must be enforceable.[263] The 'execution of a judgment given by any court must . . . be regarded as an integral part' of the right to a fair trial.[264] And as De Brabandere states, '[t]here is no reason to presuppose that such would not be the case in the event of measures of constraint taken against international organisations'.[265] Therefore, PIL and IHRL closely interact at the enforcement stage.[266] Both these spheres of law work hand in hand to create a jurisdictional duty on national courts to ensure access to justice in a civil case at the enforcement stage too.

The final substantive section of this book briefly sets out how PIL should mediate between the national and institutional legal orders concerning the recognition and enforcement of judgments that require an IO to compensate a claimant. Concerning recognition and enforcement, three possibilities exist. First, an institutional DRM delivers a judgment in a claimant's favour, but it requires enforcement at the national level (Section 5.6.1). Second, a national court's judgment against an IO is subject to enforcement in the forum of that same court (Section 5.6.2). Finally, a claimant seeks to enforce a judgment against an IO by one national court in another state (Section 5.6.3).

5.6.1 *Seeking Enforcement of Decisions of Institutional DRMs*

On the rare occasions where an IO refuses to comply with the binding decisions of institutional DRMs, save for diplomatic intervention, the only realistic way in

262 A proper choice of law determination 'separates the question of applicable substantive law from the procedural question of a claimant's access to a remedy – [doing] justice to both the interests of the individual claimant and the autonomy of the international organization': Ryngaert (n 211), 69.

263 See Chapter 2.

264 See *Hornsby v Greece* App No 18357/91 (ECtHR, 19 March 1997), para 40.

265 E De Brabandere, 'Measures of Constraint and the Immunity of International Organisations' in T Ruys, N Angelet and L Ferro (eds), *The Cambridge Handbook of Immunities and International Law* (Cambridge University Press 2019), 327–49, 338.

266 See Human Rights and PIL (n 185), 41.

which a claimant may access justice is through domestic courts.[267] One possibility is that a national court adjudicates the merits of the claim again for the institutional DRM has proven inadequate. In this situation, a competent court could exercise its jurisdiction over the IO based on the proper place doctrine. A more efficient solution that would avoid the claimant having to re-litigate the entire case would be to seek enforcement of judgments by institutional DRMs using conventional PIL techniques before national courts. In such a scenario, PIL treats an institutional DRM and a national court co-equally, with the free circulation of civil judgments across the national and institutional orders desirable and necessary to avoid inefficiencies in the administration of justice.

The real question concerns under what circumstances should a national court recognise and enforce a judgment of an institutional DRM? Fundamentally, if the institutional DRM was competent to adjudicate the claim at hand, a national court should enforce such a judgment. Normally, recognition and enforcement engage two jurisdictional inquiries: the jurisdiction of the court originally asked to determine a claim (direct jurisdiction), and the jurisdiction of the court asked to enforce the judgment (indirect jurisdiction).[268] Where a court is asked to recognise and enforce a foreign judgment, it needs to consider whether the court rendering the original decision did in fact possess civil jurisdiction in the first place. If not, recognition and enforcement should be refused.

Obviously, unlike national courts whose civil jurisdiction is primarily based on the connecting factor of territoriality, an institutional DRM's competence is enshrined in its founding statute. If the institutional court has validly exercised jurisdiction, with deference given to their jurisdictional pronouncements, then a national court must assume that jurisdiction at the IO level was properly exercised. It should proceed to give the same wait to an institutional judgment that the recognising court would give to the judgment of any other national court.[269] In general, a judgment validly rendered by an institutional court should thus be recognised and enforced at the national level.[270] If this approach is

267 Where the alternative DRM is arbitration, the international framework on the enforcement of arbitral awards could prove advantageous: see the relevant discussion in Chapters 3–4.

268 Michaels (n 4), 8.

269 See further Section 5.6.3. See especially the decision of the South African Constitutional Court in *Government of Zimbabwe v Louis Karel Fick and Others* [2013] ZACC 22, para 69, where the common law on recognition and enforcement was developed to ensure the right of access to courts by facilitating enforcement of the decisions of relevant international courts in South Africa. In this particular case, a judgment of the Southern African Development Community Tribunal was treated similar to the judgment of a foreign domestic court for the purposes of recognition and enforcement in PIL.

270 Seyersted (n 49), 121.

adopted, the free flow of judgments across the institutional and national orders is achieved. This removes the potential of the re-litigation of claims, which seriously undermines access to justice as it exponentially increases party costs, leads to undue delays in the administration of justice and creates significant uncertainty.

What is more, IO immunities from execution, assuming they are engaged,[271] must not be applied where the judgment subject to the enforcement proceedings is that of an institutional court. Logically, as the judgment sought to be enforced emanates from the institutional legal order, immunities from enforcement should not apply as the national court is simply implementing what the IO's own court has decided. As such, exercising enforcement jurisdiction at the national level in no way intrudes into the independence of an IO. In other words, the functional independence of an organisation cannot possibly be compromised where its own decisions are being implemented. Because the very basis of IO immunities is functional in nature (see Chapter 4), IO immunities cannot apply so as to prevent the execution of a decision where there is no prospect of intrusion into an IO's functional independence.[272]

5.6.2 *Seeking Enforcement of a National Court's Judgment in the Forum's Legal Order*

The most likely scenario where the enforcement of decisions involving IOs is likely to be at issue is when a national court exercises jurisdiction over an IO and a claimant seeks to enforce the resulting judgment. One possibility is that the IO to whom the decision is directed accords with the judgment of its own accord. IOs already seem to treat national judgments as having an effect within the IO legal order. This is especially where national courts pronounce on the rights of IO staff members, with such judgments generally recognised by IOs. For example, where a UNHCR employee failed to comply with certain family law orders made by a national court, upholding the IO's decision to impose a sanction on the staff member for failing to comply with his private obligations consistently with a national court judgment, the UNAT noted:

[271] Recall MDB immunities are subject to express waiver provisions in their constituent arrangements: see the discussion in Chapter 4.

[272] Note that immunities from enforcement have been mostly treated differently from immunities from adjudication as such: for an excellent analysis, see De Brabandere (n 265), 327–49. IO immunities from enforcement or execution should not exist where they are not necessary to uphold an IO's functional independence. As the CJEU said in *Tertir-Terminais de Portugal SA v Commission* (14 December 2004) Case C-1/04 SA, ECR I-11931, para 11: 'a measure of constraint such as a garnishee order may be authorized if it is not liable to interfere with the Communities' functioning'.

> First, the fact of referring the matter to the national courts indicates that Mr. Benamar had in fact relied on the national justice system to solve the unfortunate private issue he was facing with his former partner, despite his freedom to disagree with and appeal against the decision. Second, while we understand Mr. Benamar's despair in not having what he considers to be a sufficient response to his official complaints before the national courts, we must consider that Mr. Benamar does have other legal means at his disposal for criticising and appealing against the decision he does not agree with – as he did before the Supreme Court of Burkina Faso or could possibly have done before the African Commission on Human and Peoples' Rights, assuming with the possible consequences therefor. Third, although a decision of a national court may be subject to criticism by both parties (and also by a third party), it must be obeyed if and to the extent that it is enforceable. Consequently, the parties should generally comply with an executable judicial decision; otherwise they would be taking justice into their own hands, which is not acceptable according to general principles based on the rule of law.[273]

More recently, some institutional DRMs have attempted to diminish the impact of national court judgments within the institutional legal order where it would lead to unfairness to the addressee of the decision.[274] This amounts to a refusal to recognise the effect of a national judgment within an IO where the person subject of the decision did not receive due process before a national court, or on the grounds of what are essentially public policy reasons. As I explain in Section 5.6.3, these are valid bases to resist recognition and enforcement.[275] For the moment, the important point is that IOs give significant deference to national judgments as a matter of comity. Accordingly, where a judgment is directly addressed at an IO, there is no rational reason why such decisions should also not be respected and recognised. If a national court validly exercises jurisdiction over an IO because the latter has failed to ensure access to justice for the claimant within its own legal order, an IO must comply with the resulting judgment. Where it fails to do so, the court should perform its jurisdictional duty to ensure access to justice and use measures of execution to guarantee that a fair trial and an effective remedy for the claimant is realised. In such a scenario, taking enforcement action against an IO would not overstep the limits of public international law.

First, it is the territorial court taking enforcement action. Therefore, there is no question that the court possesses the jurisdiction to enforce as such.[276] Second,

[273] *Benamar v Secretary-General of the United Nations* (27 October 2017) 2017-UNAT-797, paras 42–4.

[274] See *Ozturk v Secretary-General of the United Nations* (26 October 2018) 2018-UNAT-892, para 33; *Ozturk v Secretary-General of the United Nations* (1 May 2018) Judgment No 2018/055, para 67.

[275] See Section 5.6.3.

[276] See Section 5.4.

any immunity from enforcement cannot operate where national jurisdiction is exercised due to the lack of an adequate means of dispute resolution at the IO level. If a national court agrees to adjudicate a claim against an IO as a last resort, with PIL techniques already accommodating IO independence, then immunities from enforcement ought not to be operable. Indeed, territorial courts have started to take enforcement action against IOs to ensure that the right to access to court is real and effective, and not illusory.[277] In the end, any enforcement action at the national level will only be in respect of the actual damage suffered by the claimant (see Section 5.5). Thus, when asked to take enforcement action, a court is able to perform its jurisdictional duty to ensure meaningful access to justice, but without unduly intruding into an IO's financial viability or functioning.

5.6.3 *Seeking Enforcement through Another National Court*

If a claimant is unable to satisfy the judgment in the forum of the court that delivered it, they may seek enforcement before another national court located in a jurisdiction where the respondent IO may have assets. In this final scenario, the traditional rules of judgment recognition are triggered, that is, a national court judgment becomes subject to recognition and enforcement proceedings before the courts of a foreign state. The recognition and enforcement regime adopted by each country is somewhat different. It is beyond the scope of this work to consider the regime of each state for that is a vast undertaking on which others have embarked. Presently, the aim is to briefly outline the broad approach a national court should take to enforce a foreign judgment issued against an IO.

There will be circumstances where the mutual trust between jurisdictions is very high. This is the case amongst the twenty-seven member states of the EU whose recognition and enforcement regime is enshrined in the Recast Brussels I Regulation.[278] At its core, if a civil judgment is issued by a court of an EU member state, the judgment is then enforceable within all EU member states as if it was delivered by the national court of the place where enforcement is

[277] See, for example, in *Lutchmaya v General Secretariat of the ACP Group* (4 March 2003, Brussels Court of Appeal, 9th Chamber) Journal des Tribunaux 2003, 684; ILDC 1363 (BE 2003) (Belgium); and in *General Secretariat of the ACP Group v Lutchmaya* (21 December 2009, Court of Cassation of Belgium, 3rd Chamber) Cass Nr C 03 0328 F; ILDC 1573 (BE 2009) (Belgium), Belgian courts permitted execution measures in a case where the claimant had no reasonable alternative means of enforcement. For a discussion of case law in this area, which is diverging, see De Brabandere (n 265), 338–9.

[278] Recast Brussels I Regulation (n 102).

sought.[279] Accordingly, where the court of an EU member state renders a decision against an IO, in principle, that decision should be readily enforced by the courts of all other EU member states. An EU member state court must not second guess whether the court rendering the original decision properly took jurisdiction over the IO concerned. Moreover, for the reasons already mentioned, immunities from enforcement should not be applied where jurisdiction at the national level is exercised due to the unavailability or inadequacy of the institutional forum.

In fact, an enforcement-friendly approach to judgment recognition is justified more broadly for it enhances access to justice. Any recognition and enforcement scheme should work on the assumption that where a court exercises its jurisdiction validly, the resulting judgment should have broad circulation. After decades of effort, a global convention on the recognition and enforcement of civil and commercial judgments has now been negotiated. The Convention of 2 July 2019 on the Recognition and Enforcement of Foreign Judgments in Civil or Commercial Matters (HCCH Judgments Convention), although not yet in force, prescribes the situations in which foreign judgments should be enforced. While that treaty has some gaps, it will also apply to civil and commercial judgments involving IOs, of course subject to the convention being ratified by the forum state.[280]

Article 5 of the HCCH Judgments Convention provides a good indication of the circumstances in which an exercise of civil jurisdiction should be internationally recognised. Applying some of those permissible circumstances to judgments involving IOs, it can be said that such decisions should be internationally enforceable if the organisation was 'habitually resident' or had an office in the forum of the court that rendered the original decision at the time it became party to the proceeding, the IO submitted to jurisdiction, the judgment subject to enforcement ruled 'on a contractual obligation and it was given by a court of the State in which performance of that obligation took place, or should have taken place', the judgment was given by a court of the state in which the property is situated, 'the judgment ruled on a non-contractual obligation

279 See Chapter 3 of the Recast Brussels I Regulation (n 102), especially arts 36, 39, 40 and 41. Enforcement can be resisted on very narrow grounds, for example, where a judgment is 'manifestly contrary to public policy' (Article 45).

280 See HCCH, 'Convention on the Recognition and Enforcement of Foreign Judgments in Civil or Commercial Matters' (concluded 2 July 2019) <https://assets.hcch.net/docs/806e290e-bbd8-413d-b15e-8e3e1bf1496d.pdf> accessed 30 April 2021 (HCCH Judgments Convention), arts 1 and 2(4). However, the HCCH Judgments Convention does not deal with state or IO immunity, which is a real gap: see Article 2(5). Other gaps in the treaty relate to certain exclusions, including claims of an administrative law character, and judgments relating to the activities of armed forces: see Articles 1 and 2(1)(n).

arising from death, physical injury, damage to or loss of tangible property, and the act or omission directly causing such harm occurred in the State of origin, irrespective of where that harm occurred', or the judgment was given by a court designated in an agreement between the parties.[281] Each of those grounds that may independently justify recognition and enforcement constitutes a well-established basis of civil jurisdiction.[282]

Moreover, recognition and enforcement of foreign judgments should be refused in very limited circumstances. Article 7 of the HCCH Judgments Convention indicates the situations in which a defendant could resist enforcement. This could allow an IO to resist enforcement where, for instance, it can show that it was denied due process or procedural fairness before the original court or the judgment was obtained by fraud, 'recognition or enforcement would be manifestly incompatible with the public policy of the requested state' or the proceedings in the court of origin were contrary to a choice of court agreement between the parties. Crucially, at the recognition and enforcement stage too, a court can ensure that the functioning of an IO is not undermined where punitive damages have been imposed. While national courts should not award exemplary damages against IOs based on considerations of *ordre public*, if such damages are still awarded, internationally accepted PIL standards would allow an IO to resist enforcement 'if, and to the extent that, the judgment awards damages, including exemplary or punitive damages, that do not compensate a party for actual loss or harm suffered'.[283] Finally, where the recognition and enforcement of foreign judgments against IOs is sought, immunities from enforcement should not be applicable as long as the original court validly exercised jurisdiction over an IO. If adjudicative jurisdiction at the national level is exercised because institutional DRMs are unavailable or inadequate, a valid basis of civil jurisdiction will generally be present. Where such jurisdiction is exercised, any resulting judgment should be recognised and enforced internationally without the need to re-litigate the entire claim. Ultimately, enforcing a judgment against an IO to the extent that it awards compensation for actual loss suffered practically realises access to justice for the victims of IO conduct, but without undermining an IO's functional independence.

281 Note that exclusive choice of court agreements are regulated by the HCCH Choice of Court Convention (n 85), which creates a robust jurisdiction and recognition and enforcement regime where a judgment is rendered in accordance with an exclusive choice of court agreement.

282 See the discussion in Section 5.4, stating the permissible grounds of direct jurisdiction.

283 HCCH Judgments Convention (n 280), art 10.

5.7 CONCLUSION

The chapter addressed one of the most difficult conundrums in international law today, namely, if a national court is asked to adjudicate a claim against an IO, how can the right to a fair trial be ensured without compromising on IO independence. Both of these values are equally important. Clearly, public international law has not been able to balance them. Without abandoning the limits placed by public international law, we must look for new solutions. This solution must allow access to justice for the victims of IO conduct to be realised, but without adversely impacting on an IO's functional autonomy. PIL techniques can achieve this objective by coordinating regulatory authority between the national and institutional legal orders in a nuanced manner. In particular, by tailoring the rules of jurisdiction, choice of law and recognition and enforcement, this chapter demonstrated how access to justice can be guaranteed without impinging on an IO's overall functioning. Not only did the discussion clarify the very basis of civil jurisdiction, it also considered the specific circumstances in which jurisdiction over IOs should be exercised.

It is submitted that national courts should exercise jurisdiction over an IO only as a secondary intervention. Just because national intervention is secondary, it does not mean that the role of domestic courts in ensuring access to justice for the victims of IO conduct is unimportant. Where an IO fails to comply with its obligation to provide a fair trial compliant DRM to a victim of institutional conduct, a competent national court must exercise its jurisdiction over an IO. Doing so ought to constitute a jurisdictional duty incumbent on national courts, with access to justice being the jurisdictional pivot on which the decision to exercise adjudicative jurisdiction ultimately turns. To ensure consistency on how this jurisdictional pivot operates, courts must refer to fair trial standards found in IHRL.

Where a national court takes jurisdiction over an IO because an institutional DRM is absent or inadequate, it must fully respect the prescriptive authority of the defendant IO by applying carefully calibrated choice of law and recognition and enforcement rules. This means that if the applicable law is IO law, it is applied proficiently. It is also necessary to ensure that the overall functioning of an IO is not undermined. Punitive damages should thus not be imposed on IOs. If they are still granted, such damages should not be enforced internationally. In the final analysis, PIL is ideally suited to mediate the relationship between the national and institutional order so as to ensure access to justice for the victims of IO conduct, but without undermining IO independence.

Conclusion

If IOs comply with their international legal obligation to provide an appropriate mode of dispute resolution to private persons they impact, there will be little need for national courts to take jurisdiction in claims against IOs. An appropriate DRM must deliver justice independently, impartially and fairly. What precisely these key component fair trial guarantees require was set out in Chapter 2. That discussion can prove of much benefit to IOs wishing to establish fair trial compliant internal justice systems, as well as to all those who may be required to assess the quality of justice delivered at an institutional DRM. In the end, whether a dispute is resolved at an institutional DRM, through an arbitral process or through another mode of dispute resolution, justice must be delivered consistently with the right to a fair trial as developed in IHRL. This book does not state a preference for what type of DRM IOs should establish.[1] All that is asserted here is that if a DRM is to be considered appropriate, it must provide meaningful access to justice.

But as was demonstrated in Chapter 3, for the victims of IO conduct, the situation is precarious. In the limited instances where judicial mechanisms are present, they are deficient. Neither the UN tribunals nor the ILOAT is providing justice to IO staff members consistently with modern fair trial standards. The UN tribunals only started operation around ten years ago. They were created to address the grave due process shortcomings of the pre-2009 internal justice system prevalent at the UN. It is thus even more concerning that the structural independence of the UN is already facing serious challenges. What is more, the ILOAT's shortcomings have been well

[1] When creating DRMs, it is important to learn from past experience. It is especially challenging to create DRMs for mass claims. For a very good discussion on the issue, see HM Holtzmann and E Kristjánsdóttir (eds), *International Mass Claims Processes: Legal and Practical Perspectives* (Oxford University Press 2007).

traversed. The modest reforms pursued to the ILOAT are unlikely to address the systemic due process deficits that were identified.[2] Of most concern is the limited jurisdiction that IATs possess. Even in employment cases, a vast proportion of international civil servants, that is, contractors and consultants retained by IOs, are unable to generally access an IAT's protection. For such claimants, the predicament is most serious.

With IATs under ever-increasing budgetary pressures and already struggling to provide fair trial compliant justice, unless significant structural reforms are made, it will be unwise to substantially expand their jurisdiction. Other solutions must be found to ensure that victims of IO conduct can access justice at the institutional level. As Chapter 3 also pointed out, while arbitral mechanisms can in principle provide for an appropriate DRM, including in employment claims, as currently used, they do not do so in practice. If arbitration as a mode of dispute resolution is to succeed in providing an adequate alternative to national courts to resolve claims against IOs, a specialised arbitral framework that can provide independent, impartial, fair, transparent and affordable justice needs to be created. Such a framework does not presently exist.

Finally, Chapter 3 highlighted that non-judicialised mechanisms, such as ombudsman processes, are becoming a feature of dispute resolution at IOs. This should be welcomed for informal DRMs can play an important role to resolve disputes in a cost-effective way. Such mechanisms cannot and do not replace a judicialised DRM that is capable of rendering binding decisions after a fair process has been followed. Accordingly, an IO will not discharge its access to justice obligation by pointing to the non-judicialised DRMs that it has created, or may establish in the future. Alarmingly, as was evident in the various cases discussed throughout this book, too many victims of IO conduct are provided no mode of dispute resolution at all. This is why the victims of the Haiti cholera epidemic, the Srebrenica genocide, MDB project affected communities and many more ended up approaching national courts as a last resort.

In Chapter 4, it was shown how IO immunities are misunderstood, misapplied and result in denials of justice at the national level too. This occurs at most courts, in most countries and in most types of claims. Whereas IOs only ought to enjoy functional immunities, they tend to be granted de facto absolute immunities. Unable to limit the scope of IO immunities through the concept of functionalism, claimants have argued that immunities must be

[2] Proposed Amendments to the Statute of the Tribunal' (19 February 2021) GB.341/PFA/15/1.

made contingent on an IO's compliance with its access to justice obligation. As the discussion demonstrated, the principle that IOs must provide reasonable alternative means of dispute resolution if immunity is to be retained is gaining acceptance. But most national courts still deny claims against IOs without the merits ever being ventilated. Some courts refuse to make immunities contingent on the existence of an alternative mode of dispute resolution at all. Where a court is willing to do so, instead of checking whether the alternative forum is actually 'reasonable' and delivers justice consistently with fair trial standards,[3] close scrutiny on the quality of justice provided is absent. If such a level of scrutiny was undertaken in individual cases, surely, immunities would have been pierced much more often than is currently the case. Ultimately, real or perceived concerns about IO independence, which justifies the grant of jurisdictional immunities to international institutions, tend to trump the right to a fair trial. Both these values are equally important. They must be reflected in any solution to the conundrum of ensuring that a fair trial for the victims of IO conduct can be practically realised, but without compromising on institutional independence.

Chapter 5 solved the conundrum posed. Fundamentally, public international law has been unable to appropriately balance access to justice with IO immunities, with immunities generally prevailing over the right to a fair trial. We need a new framework to coordinate between the national and institutional legal orders that helps allocate regulatory authority in a nuanced way. A PIL framework can achieve this objective. By separating issues of jurisdiction, applicable law and the recognition and enforcement of judgments across legal orders, PIL is able to allocate regulatory authority in such a way that access to justice can be realised without compromising on IO independence. In particular, the chapter clarified that we must not conflate the concept of jurisdiction and immunities. Just because immunities might be engaged, it does not mean that jurisdiction is absent.

The existence of civil jurisdiction at the national level is best determined with reference to PIL rules on adjudicative jurisdiction. Where adjudicative jurisdiction exists due to the presence of connecting factors, such as territoriality, a national court possesses the competence to adjudicate a claim regardless of the identity of a defendant. Accordingly, national courts can in principle adjudicate claims against IOs. The real question is whether such regulatory authority should actually be exercised. It was suggested that the first chance to deliver justice to the victims of IO conduct must be given to an institutional DRM. This is the case whether or not IO immunities are

3 Such a scrutiny was conducted in Chapter 3.

engaged. Doing so serves important legal policy interests, including the consistent resolution of claims against IOs internationally. But if an IO fails to provide an appropriate DRM, then an otherwise competent court must exercise its jurisdiction. In such circumstances, a national court becomes the proper place for the claim to be adjudicated as there is no other DRM that is available to deliver justice adequately.

Crucially, to determine whether an alternative DRM has delivered, or can deliver justice adequately, regard must be had for the standards contained in IHRL. If internationally accepted fair trial standards form the basis on which the jurisdictional pivot of access to justice operates, then a consistent approach to the exercise of national adjudicative jurisdiction over IOs can be readily achieved. Where the exercise of jurisdiction at the national level becomes necessary to ensure access to justice for the victims of IO conduct, the applicable law determination, as well as the rules on recognition and enforcement, can be calibrated to ensure that the prescriptive authority of an IO is not undermined. In the final analysis, PIL is able to slice regulatory authority in a way that does not sacrifice a fair trial in the pursuit of an IO's functional independence. This has indeed been the central objective of this work.

How the proposed framework can be implemented is an important question. When asked to adjudicate claims against IOs, national courts could simply apply PIL techniques which they regularly adopt when resolving transnational civil and commercial disputes. A real advantage of this approach is that it does not require multilateral action at the international level, which is time-consuming and often unachievable. However, it of course would be beneficial for a globally coherent coordination of regulatory authority between the national and institutional orders, if this authority was allocated through an international agreement. A global treaty enshrining carefully calibrated PIL rules on jurisdiction, applicable law and the recognition and enforcement of judgments, specifically aimed at mediating between the national and institutional orders, could go a long way in ensuring that far-reaching coordination between the IO and national legal orders can be achieved.